Praise for *Miriam*

"Davidson's journalistic eye captures the legacy of squalor misery that greed and irresponsibility have created along the borderlands. . . . Davidson shares these lessons well."

—*National Catholic Reporter*

"Timely and compelling."

—*Booklist*

"Davidson's stories that stand out the most are her vivid portraits of those who have been left behind by economic progress."

—*New York Times Book Review*

"American journalist Davidson writes a vivid portrait . . ."

—*Choice*

"Davidson's impassioned writing and acute investigative talents reveal the human faces often lost to the attention focused on increasing political rhetoric and now-commonplace headlines of tragedy."

—*Bloomsbury Review*

"Davidson recounts the suffering that drives them to flee and to risk dangers in crossing our border and persecution by American authorities."

—*Publisher's Weekly*

"Davidson details one of the most notable grassroots movements of this decade."

—*Library Journal*

"Davidson relates this tale [of the Sanctuary Movement] with all the skill of a John McPhee."

—*Kirkus Reviews*

"Davidson's book is a thoughtful and interesting log."

—*California Lawyer*

The Beloved Border

The Beloved Border

HUMANITY AND HOPE IN A CONTESTED LAND

MIRIAM DAVIDSON

THE UNIVERSITY OF
ARIZONA PRESS
TUCSON

The University of Arizona Press
www.uapress.arizona.edu

ISBN-13: 978-0-8165-4216-1 (paperback)

Cover design by Leigh McDonald
Cover art: *Picnic at the Border* by JR, Tecate, 2017

Chapter 2 includes quotations from PLANE WRECK AT LOS GATOS (Deportee). Words by Woody
Guthrie; Music by Martin Hoffman. WGP/TRO-© Copyright 1961 (Renewed), 1963 (Renewed) Woody
Guthrie Publications, Inc., & Ludlow Music, Inc., New York, NY, administered by Ludlow Music, Inc.
International Copyright Secured. Made in U.S.A. All Rights Reserved Including Public Performance
for Profit. Used by Permission.

Library of Congress Cataloging-in-Publication Data
Names: Davidson, Miriam, author.
Title: The beloved border : humanity and hope in a contested land / Miriam Davidson.
Description: Tucson : University of Arizona Press, 2021. | Includes bibliographical references and
    index.
Identifiers: LCCN 2021012099 | ISBN 9780816542161 (paperback)
Subjects: LCSH: Mexican-American Border Region—Social conditions—21st century.
Classification: LCC F787 .D37 2021 | DDC 972/.1—dc23
LC record available at https://lccn.loc.gov/2021012099

Printed in the United States of America
♾ This paper meets the requirements of ANSI/NISO Z39.48-1992 (Permanence of Paper).

This book is dedicated to my friend Yolanda, and to all the good people of the U.S.-Mexico borderlands, especially those who've suffered and died there, with gratitude for leading the way toward a new international reality of peaceful coexistence.

———

A true border, a true place of encounter, is by nature permeable. It is not like medieval armor, but rather like skin. Our skin does set a limit to where our body begins and where it ends. But if we ever close up our skin, we die.

—CUBAN AMERICAN THEOLOGIAN JUSTO GONZÁLEZ

We have to repeat continuously, although it is a voice crying in the desert: No to violence, yes to peace.

—SALVADORAN ARCHBISHOP ÓSCAR ROMERO, ASSASSINATED WHILE SAYING MASS, MARCH 24, 1980, AFTER CALLING FOR SOLDIERS TO LAY DOWN THEIR WEAPONS

Contents

The Beloved Border

Prologue

A Fable for Tomorrow

O nce upon a time, and far, far away, there was a special place. It was one of the most biodiverse places on Earth. It had majestic mountains, fast-flowing rivers, dense forests, and vast deserts. Many strange and colorful animals lived there, from the tiniest iridescent birds and butterflies to rattlesnakes with diamonds on their backs and orange-and-black beaded lizards and even the great spotted jaguar. This place also had many marvelous plants that appeared nowhere else, such as the giant saguaro cactus, which lived for hundreds of years, stood more than fifty feet tall, and had arms that sheltered generations of birds and insects. Native people, who shared in the feast of red fruits provided by the saguaros, believed they embodied the spirits of their ancestors.

Although the special place could be harsh and unforgiving, native people lived in harmony with the plants and animals. They were far away from the rest of the world. Then, one day, strangers came to conquer and colonize them and their land. The strangers killed and drove out many native people and fought for centuries over the special place, until they finally made it the dividing line between them. On one side, the special place became part of a rich and powerful empire. On the other, it became part of the empire's poorer and less powerful neighbor.

The special place was now a borderland, a place where people came to buy, sell, trade, and barter. Merchants and businessmen arrived from all over. They supplied the citizens of the empire with the things they needed, like minerals, food, drugs, and workers.

More strangers came, hoping to seek their fortune in the empire. They, too, were accepted, since border people were pragmatic and knew that, except for the natives, they themselves were once strangers in the special place. The borderland became a multicultural locale where people of all races, ethnicities, faiths, and nationalities lived peacefully with one another. And since they were still far away from everything, border people developed their own language, food, music, and art.

But the citizens of the empire, seeing the border people happy, grew jealous. They began to blame the border for their problems. They were led by their leaders to believe the border people had brought crime and violence to the empire, when in fact it was the other way around. The empire had made it against the law to supply drugs and workers and had sent policemen and guns and built walls to enforce these laws. Yet the empire could not repeal the laws of supply and demand, so crime and violence had come to the border.

Border people, especially on the poor side, had fallen to fighting and killing each other over the trade in drugs, workers, or other commodities, and sometimes over nothing at all. Thousands had perished in the deserts or drowned in the rivers or were chased to their deaths for trying to get a job on the rich side. Police on both sides were empowered to arrest and even kill people for no reason. To discourage poor families from seeking safety in the empire, babies were taken from their parents and locked in secret dungeons far away.

The border people tried to tell the citizens of the empire that what they were doing was wrong. But the citizens of the empire didn't listen. They cheered when the emperor said he was going to build a wall across the borderland. And they closed their eyes when he sent bulldozers and excavators to rip up the ancient saguaros and drain the desert springs and kill the amazing animals so he could erect a giant ugly fence that ran for hundreds of miles through the middle of the special place. Native people wept at the destruction wrought by the emperor's new wall.

Then the empire entered a dark time. A plague swept the land, sickening millions and killing hundreds of thousands. Economic collapse followed, destroying the jobs of tens of millions and causing much pain. The citizens were scared. The emperor tried to blame the border people and insisted his wall would stop the plague. But few believed him, and no one but the border people cared about the wall anymore.

The border people were not spared by the plague. Trade was down, and many lost their lives. Native people especially suffered. But border people were used to suffering and knew what to do. They pulled together to protect and care for their elders and to keep looking out for those who were even less fortunate. They kept fighting for clean water, fresh food, and the health and welfare of people on both sides. They fought for an end not only to the plague but to the violence and destruction they and their land had been enduring for so long.

When the citizens of the empire saw what the border people were doing, their eyes were opened at last. They realized they had been misled about the border. They came to value the lives and work of border people, however humble, and to respect the native people's reverence for the plants and animals of the special place. They saw the suffering they were inflicting on the border was hurting them as well. They decided they did not want to go back to the way it was before.

With the border people leading the way, the citizens of the empire embarked on a new era. They voted the emperor out and tore down his wall. They voted to legalize and regularize the trade in drugs and workers, control the gun trade, and end police abuse. They made and enforced laws to protect the lives and human rights of everyone on both sides, regardless of where they were from. They tried, as best they could, to restore the special place, and they promised to preserve it from then on. They transformed the border into a land where the people were able to get back to business, enjoy their unique culture, and serve as a worldwide example of international peace and prosperity. And they all lived happily ever after.

This could still happen. It's not too late. It's up to us.

I
Gangland

One

Mexico's Torment

My Mexican friend Yolanda, who I've known for more than twenty years, called from her home in Nogales, Sonora, just before Christmas 2017. In a trembling voice, she said her younger brother Filiberto, who was in his early sixties, had been beaten nearly to death by his stepson and members of the stepson's gang.

Filiberto owned a house in Puerto Peñasco (Rocky Point, a seacoast town at the top of the Gulf of California) that the gang had been using to stash and sell drugs. Yoli said the gang had left the house when Filiberto showed up, and even though he hadn't thrown them out and there was no fight, they came back later that night and attacked him. They broke all his ribs and damaged his internal organs. She said he lay in the house for a week until another family member—a niece, I think—went to check on him and found him there. She took him to a hospital, but after a day or two, saying there was nothing it could do, the hospital discharged him. When Yoli called me, Filiberto was at their sister's house in Mexicali.

She called back three days later to say he was dead. I sent a couple hundred dollars to contribute to the cost of having his body prepared and returned for burial to Bacobampo, the farming village in southern Sonora where he and Yoli were born and raised.

I wrote about Yoli in *Lives on the Line*, my book about border issues as seen through the microcosm of Nogales, Arizona, and Nogales, Sonora. She was my example of a woman who had moved to the border to make a new life for herself and her children by working in the *maquiladoras* (U.S.-owned factories). I went with her once to Bacobampo in the late 1990s. It's a town of a few thousand people, with dusty, tree-lined streets centered around a small square and church, near the Sinaloa state line, about an eight-hour drive south of the border. It's on the same road as Álamos—a Spanish colonial silver-mining mecca up in the Sierra Madre that's now a wealthy tourist destination—but in the opposite direction. The road crosses the highway just after you pass through the closest city, Navojoa, whose residents, I am told, frequently serve as the butt of Mexican country-bumpkin jokes.

Coincidentally, not long after Filiberto's funeral, Bacobampo made U.S. news as the site of the capture of three suspects in the slaying of a prominent journalist the previous spring. Miroslava Breach Velducea, correspondent for the national newspaper *La Jornada*, had been shot eight times by assailants on motorcycles near her home in the capital city of Chihuahua, Chihuahua, around 7 a.m. on March 23. She was driving her car to take her teenage son, who was left unhurt, to school. Yoli said the cops had helicopters and chased the suspects into an arroyo on Christmas Day, killing two of them— details not reported in the story I read.

It was difficult to imagine this sleepy village the site of drug shootouts, but all of Mexico had fallen under the grip of this demonic terror. Filiberto's murder was just one more in the record year of 2017, when, among other cases, a location scout for Netflix's *Narcos* was found shot to death in his car in a remote region in Mexico State in September, and a vacationing California city official was shot and killed in a hotel parking lot in the Pacific resort town of Ixtapa, Guerrero, on December 28. The official murder count at year-end topped thirty-one thousand, some four thousand more than in 2011, which had previously been the worst year since the military-led crackdown on drug traffickers began in 2006. But Filiberto's murder, like so many others, wouldn't even be counted among the total. He didn't want anyone to say anything, even after his death, Yoli said, because "if you report it, they come and kill your family."

"Oh, Yoli," I said. "It must be hard for people to stay brave."

"It's not worth it to be brave anymore," she said. *No vale la pena.*

"The cemeteries are full of brave ones."

Yolanda's words inspired me to write this book and dedicate it to her. It's a collection of twenty-seven interconnected essays about border issues, based mostly on reporting I did between 2017 and 2020. These were pivotal years for the border and border concerns nationally, as Donald Trump made cracking down on immigrants and building the wall the centerpiece of his presidency. In 2018 and 2019, drug war violence, and other man-made and natural disasters, drove tens of thousands of Mexican and Central American families to attempt to cross the border and seek asylum in the United States. This book describes what occurred, including the spike in violence in Mexico, family separations at the border, migrant deaths in the deserts and river, children dying in border patrol custody, and devastating destruction of the border environment.

While all these tragic events occurred under Trump, they were hardly unprecedented. By putting them in historical and other contexts, I wanted to show how Trump's policies, as well as the appalling slaughter in Mexico, were in fact the culmination of decades of crackdowns, wall building, and

The border wall in Arizona, around the time Trump was elected on a promise to "build the wall." (©iStock.com/razyph)

prohibition on the border. I also wanted to demonstrate that these problems did not represent the sum total of border life. By including positive stories of people celebrating on special days and striving for a better future, I wanted to show Yoli that all hope was not lost—even though she couldn't read what I wrote, since it's in English.

Yolanda was actually the one who taught me not to give up. We met in 1996, after I'd already lived on the border many years but still felt like an outsider. I'd written a book about the 1980s sanctuary movement and trial and wanted to write another book about women workers in maquiladoras. After studying the subject in graduate school in L.A. and Mexico City, I returned to Tucson and got a part-time job as a reporter writing about, among other things, labor struggles in Nogales *maquilas*. I joined a binational project to organize maquila workers in Agua Prieta, Sonora. Yet until I met Yolanda, I couldn't figure out how to enter their world. One night, she hosted me through BorderLinks, a Tucson-based experiential education nonprofit that takes student and church groups on border tours and homestays. She served a simple, delicious dinner, using bottled water and produce purchased across the line (though it probably originated in Mexico), so her gringo guests wouldn't get sick. She talked about her life in Spanish I could understand and made a bed for me in her *casa de cartón* (cardboard house). I felt welcomed and cared for and went on to interview her and her family many times for *Lives on the Line*.

Yolanda and I had been friends several years when, in short order, I got married and had two children. My husband and I were older first-time parents, and Yoli, by then a grandmother, was invaluable help. She taught Spanish, Mexican folk remedies, and resilience to our son and daughter. In a laborious process I would never attempt, she handmade for us incredibly light flour tortillas that puffed like pillows as they cooked. The kids went to Davis Bilingual Elementary, a Tucson public school where students learn to play and sing mariachi, and when she could, Yolanda attended their performances, beaming like the *nana* (grandma) she was.

Through Yolanda, and other friends I've made over thirty-five years, I've met many people working for peace, social justice, migrant rights, the environment, and other worthy causes on the border. These friends also inspired me to write this book, and it's dedicated to them as well. I wanted to show

how, while the problems of the border existed long before Trump and continue now that he's gone, border people are working on solutions. These stories are about their battles with powerful enemies—not only external ones like entrenched, systemic corruption and violence, but internal ones like rage, fear, shame, and silence. This book is about the efforts of many border people to bring a better world into being, starting with themselves and where they live.

The body of the book contains three parts, each portraying a different aspect of border life. The first, "Gangland," looks at the impact and origins of the drug war in Mexico. It begins by examining the endemic violence against the press. It then gives a brief history of the land and peoples of the border; the formation of the international line; Prohibition; drug and migrant smuggling; and, starting in the 1990s, increased law enforcement and wall building. The final chapter in this part looks at the Fast and Furious case and other examples of crimes and atrocities connected to the legal and illegal transfer of guns, ammo, and surveillance equipment to Mexico. It concludes with a look at how big banks have profited from cartel money laundering.

The second part, "Slavery," looks at issues related to the crackdown on undocumented migrants over the past thirty years. It describes Operation Streamline court proceedings, a Southwest Key facility for unaccompanied minors, and shelters for deportees and asylum seekers in Mexico. This part of the book also addresses the deaths of an estimated ten thousand migrants on the border since the mid-1990s. It describes efforts to care for the dead and missing, as well as controversy over the provision of humanitarian aid in the desert. The last chapter in this section looks at crimes, abuses of authority, mismanagement and other issues related to the influx of border patrol agents to the region, especially after 9/11.

The final third of the book, "The Peaceable Kingdom," focuses on the natural beauty of the border and all the good that's happening here. It begins with a history of the sanctuary movement, from its beginning in the 1980s to widespread national and international acceptance today. The second chapter tells how jaguars and other endangered animals are coming up from Mexico, and how their presence has had a major impact on legal battles over border walls and a planned copper mine near Tucson. The last chapter describes some joyful events in the lives of border people, including a mariachi Mass for the Virgin of Guadalupe and a visit from civil rights leader Bernard Lafayette Jr. to talk about "Kingian Nonviolence and the Border." It also describes a few visionary projects border people are working on to promote the health and well-being of those around them.

The epilogue, "A Positive Vision for the U.S.-Mexico Region," updates the reader on many of the issues and controversies presented earlier, and further addresses the pandemic's severe impact on border communities. It also looks to a better future, examining five ways to lessen the death and suffering: by ending drug prohibition, ending the flow of arms to Mexico, regularizing farm labor, reforming immigration laws to treat migrants humanely, and repurposing harmful and wasteful wall funding to needed projects on the border and in Central America. The book concludes with a few examples of these needed projects, which show how the people of El Norte are building the beloved community, right here on the border between the United States and Mexico.

As this first chapter makes clear, there's work to be done. A U.S.-funded and U.S.-armed war on drugs has caused violence and impunity to spiral out of control in Mexico. The situation for reporters is especially dire.

From Paradise to Gangland

The video opens with Frank Sinatra singing about heading down Acapulco way, his immortal voice providing jaunty accompaniment to 1950s glamour shots. Fancy hotels line pristine beaches, celebrities frolic in the surf, smiling señoritas serve margaritas, and the famed cliff divers make their dangerous leaps. Then the music turns ominous, and the photos change to contemporary Acapulco street scenes. There are buildings, cars, palm trees, Corona beer signs, and it takes a few seconds before I register what I'm looking at: picture after picture after picture of people shot dead in the street, on sidewalks, in homes, in restaurants, in cars, in doorways, in courtyards, in front of small stores, almost all young men and teenage boys but women and children and babies and old people too, body after body after body, bullet-ridden bodies, dismembered bodies, headless bodies, bodiless heads, body parts amid blood-soaked clothes and floors, bodies sprawled in shorts and flip flops, bodies being loaded into meat wagons, until I had to look away but felt obligated not to.

"Acapulco: Former jet set paradise turned into Al Capone's Chicago," the screen read.

These grim photos, to which the audience reacted in stunned silence, were part of a February 13, 2018, presentation on the work of Mexican photojournalist Bernandino Hernández at the University of Arizona library in Tucson. Hernández sat to one side of the stage, a small, quiet figure who still bore the scars of an attack by members of the Guerrero state police a month before. With him and a translator were Associated Press photo editor Enric Martí and University of Arizona journalism professor Mort Rosenblum.

A handsome, dark-skinned man with flowing hair, Hernández displayed a new camera. It was a present, Martí said, from the governor of Guerrero, whose state police had smashed his previous one during the attack.

Guerrero is a poor, mountainous southern state with Acapulco at its seacoast base. A drug-producing and smuggling region with a history of organized crime, it also has a history of armed insurrection against various forms of injustice and oppression. This particular protest erupted not over drugs but over the long-planned construction of a hydroelectric dam that was going to wipe out all or part of two dozen small towns. Since 2003 environmental activists led by brothers Vicente and Marco Antonio Suástegui had successfully blocked construction of La Parota Dam by showing in court how local governments had been bribed and manipulated into supporting the project. But their self-defense force had also come under criticism for abusive behavior.

In the late morning of January 7, the defense force assembled in the Sierra Madre del Sur town of La Concepción, and there was a confrontation with other locals who supported the dam. Gunfire erupted, and eight people were killed, two from the self-defense force and six from the pro-dam contingent. Afterwards, the state police conducted a raid that led to the arrest of the Suástegui brothers and the death of three more members of the self-defense force.

Shortly after the first shootout, Hernández, forty-eight, a stringer for a Mexican news agency and the Associated Press, was in the street taking pictures of state police beating up some of the anti-dam protestors, when the cops saw him and told him to stop.

"I'm with the press," he said. The cops said they didn't care and "would make him disappear" if he kept taking pictures. They beat and kicked him, smashed his camera, and took his money and digital memory cards.

Unconscious, Hernández was dragged away by several colleagues. They put him in a car and drove him to the Guerrero state capital of Chilpancingo, where he reported the attack to the authorities. The other journalists then took him to a hospital in Acapulco.

Hernández suffered a concussion and bruises on his legs, torso, and head. A federal police officer was posted outside his hospital room and, after he was released, for a time at his home.

Although placed under a Mexican federal protection plan called *el mechanismo*, Hernández still felt threatened, and left the country. The evening I saw him in Tucson, he did not know when he would return. Of the mechanism, he said, "In reality, it doesn't exist." Martí, who was born in Spain and worked as the Associated Press photo editor in Mexico City, agreed it was "more of a show off than something that really works."

At Hernández's talk the hundred or so attendees, who looked to be primarily journalism and Latin American studies students, seemed overwhelmed by the horror depicted in his photos. They asked few questions and kept returning to the same basic one: how could Hernández keep doing what he's doing, knowing each day could be his last?

"Because I am an orphan," he said, seemingly incongruously. It took a second for me to understand what he meant: he had no family to lose. The video had explained that, when he was a boy, his father and all the other men in his family were killed by their "landlord" because they'd protested mistreatment. Hernández had to flee his village or be killed himself.

As an eleven-year-old street kid in Acapulco, Hernández started selling coconut oil to tourists on the beach. He got into photography as a teen, taking wedding and party photos to supplement his paltry income as a photojournalist. It was through his work as a news photographer that he began to document the mounting piles of bodies amid the gang violence and the Mexican government's war on drugs. By this time he was married, but "I had to leave my family because I did not want to expose them to what would happen."

I knew from experience that being a stringer for a large news organization was barely above not being employed at all, because you're still a freelancer, the pay is peanuts, and they're in no way responsible for you. Local stringers in war zones and violent countries get killed all the time. To say being a stringer for Associated Press is not worth your life would be a vast understatement. So, someone asked again, why does he do it?

He spoke quietly, in Spanish, into the mic. "You have to bear witness," he said. "You have to do your part."

"It's something that I have inside me," he had said earlier. "One person alone cannot change the world, but we can all do it together."

One question from an older white woman drew a sharp response from the stage. It was premised on the frequently repeated idea that, since the time of the Conquest and the Aztecs and probably long before, Mexico was simply an irredeemably corrupt and violent place. What was the point of giving your life trying to save it?

Mexico is not beyond saving, Hernández said. Too many honest and honorable people have died for that to be true. Mexico, he said, is a beautiful and beloved country that will, by the grace of God, be delivered from this hell.

The last photo in the slideshow was of Hernández and a fellow Mexican journalist standing side by side and smiling. The other journalist was wearing a dark red T-shirt promoting the AMC series *The Walking Dead*. I admired the irony but felt weird chuckling in the face of such sadness, and wondered how long it would be before Hernández and his compadre were themselves literally what the shirt was proclaiming them to be.

No Excuse

Javier Valdez Cárdenas, fifty, was the editor of the weekly newspaper *Ríodoce* in Culiacán, Sinaloa. A bearded bear of a man known for his sense of humor, tan Panama hat, and love for his wife and children, Valdez cofounded *Ríodoce* in the Sinaloan capital in 2003. As one of the few local news outlets not dependent on government advertising, *Ríodoce* covered organized crime, corruption, regional politics, and the narcoculture. Valdez wrote a column about the intersection of poverty and crime called "Malayerba" (Bad Weed). He also worked as a correspondent for the national newspaper *La Jornada* and had authored a series of books about the Mexican drug wars. In 2011 the New York City–based Committee to Protect Journalists gave Valdez an international press freedom award. During his acceptance speech he said,

> In my books *Miss Narco* and *The Kids of the Drug Trade*, I have told of the tragedy Mexico is living, a tragedy that should shame us. The youth will remember this as a time of war. Their DNA is tattooed with bullets and guns and blood, and this is a form of killing tomorrow. We are murderers of our own future.
>
> This is a war, yes, but one for control by the *narcos*, but we the citizens are providing the deaths, and the governments of Mexico and the United States, the guns. And they, the eminent, invisible and hidden ones, within and outside of the governments, they take the profits.

Ríodoce was under constant threat. In 2009 someone threw a grenade at the office, and in 2011 a cyberattack forced it offline for several days. Then, in late February 2017, Valdez reported to the Mexican press freedom group Article 19 that armed people had bought up almost every copy of the paper's latest issue, though it was unclear which story they were trying to bury.

On March 23, after Miroslava Breach was shot dead in her car in front of her son, he tweeted, "Let them kill us all, if that is the death penalty for reporting this hell. No to silence."

Around midday on Monday, May 15, Valdez left the *Ríodoce* office after editing an article about a protest over teachers being attacked while traveling in remote areas of Sinaloa. At least six had been killed in the state so far that year. He had just driven away in his red Toyota Corolla when he was stopped by several assailants. They forced him out of the car and shot him twelve times. (*Ríodoce* means "twelfth river.") They then fled in the Corolla, which was found abandoned nearby, laptop and cell phone missing.

With his signature Panama hat nearby, Valdez lay face down in the middle of the sunny street, a block from his office between a kindergarten and a restaurant, for forty minutes. His friends and colleagues saw the delay in retrieving his corpse as an additional warning—as if any were needed.

A week and a half before Valdez was killed, on World Press Freedom Day, May 3, the Committee to Protect Journalists (CPJ) had issued a report titled *No Excuse: Mexico Must Break Cycle of Impunity in Journalists' Murders*. The report was an indictment of Mexico's utter failure to stop attacks on the press and on the underlying police and judicial corruption that allowed impunity to flourish. The next day, a CPJ delegation presented the report to Mexican president Enrique Peña Nieto during a ninety-minute press conference at Los Piños, the presidential mansion in Mexico City. Peña Nieto pledged to combat impunity. He and other officials vowed that the safety and protection of the press would be their top priority.

Despite their pledge to do more, 2017 turned out to be another record year for murders of Mexican journalists. Statistics vary, due to the uncertain circumstances surrounding these attacks—there is a lot of random street crime in Mexico, you know—as well as for a lot of other reasons, but the Mexican attorney general's office counted more than one hundred reporters killed or disappeared for reasons related to their work between 2006 and 2016. The CPJ, which was founded in 1981 to document attacks and protect journalists under threat worldwide, only counted definite cases, and in 2017 it rated Mexico the most dangerous country in the world for the press, more so even than war-torn Syria and Afghanistan. This truth hardly made the news in the States.

Historically, Mexico lacked an independent press. Journalists were practically an arm of the state and were known for being paid for favorable coverage with money in an envelope called the *bolsa*. Those who tried to be independent faced a brutal choice: *plata o plomo*, silver (corruption) or lead (bullets).

Murders of independent journalists have occurred with regularity since at least 1988, when Héctor "El Gato" Félix Miranda, cofounder of the Tijuana weekly magazine *Zeta*, was killed by security guards employed by Jorge Hank Rhon, a wealthy businessman and scion of a powerful political family. (The son of a former mayor of Mexico City, Rhon owned Mexico's biggest sports betting company, Grupo Caliente, and served as mayor of Tijuana from December 2004 to February 2007.) *Zeta*, founded in 1980, covered local and federal government corruption as well as organized crime. Another cofounder, Jesús Blancornelas, was nearly killed in 1997, and one of his bodyguards died in the attack. The third cofounder, Francisco Javier Ortíz Franco, was murdered in June 2004, evidently for his reporting on the Tijuana cartel.

In a foreword to the *No Excuse* report, *Zeta* editorial director Adela Navarro Bello wrote:

> At *Zeta*, we have experienced firsthand both the dangers of impunity and corruption and the frustration of not being able to secure justice for our slain colleagues. In the 29 years since journalist Héctor Félix Miranda was murdered, the Baja California State Attorney General's Office hasn't pinpointed the mastermind. [As of 2018, *Zeta* was still running a full page ad with white letters reading: "Jorge Hank, why did your bodyguards assassinate me?"] And in the 20 years since the attempted murder of Jesús Blancornelas, the federal attorney general's office hasn't been able to prosecute and sentence a single one of the 10 perpetrators. Thirteen years have passed since the murder of our editor, Francisco Javier Ortíz Franco, with none of his murderers—be it the perpetrators or the mastermind—identified, let alone prosecuted.

Although initially unresponsive, after an attack on the Nuevo Laredo–based *El Mañana* newspaper in February 2006, the Mexican government began taking steps to protect journalists. President Vicente Fox created an office that later became the special prosecutor for crimes against freedom of expression (abbreviated in Spanish as FEADLE). Expanded in 2010 and given constitutional authority in 2013, this office operated under the auspices of the sub-prosecutor for human rights. It had authority to conduct independent investigations of crimes against journalists and news outlets. Hundreds of cases were opened and investigated in its first ten years of existence, but with only three convictions, ineffectuality was its hallmark.

The Federal Protection Mechanism of Human Rights Defenders (*el mechanismo*) was set up around the same time as the FEADLE. Intended to provide some measure of security for journalists, it was charged with assessing threats against reporters and activists and providing them with a panic button, police protection, and evacuation for them and their families to safe houses if necessary. In cases of immediate danger, the mechanism was supposed to act within three hours. It opened 388 cases between 2012 and 2017, 220 of them journalists. By 2017 it had a staff of 37 and an annual budget of approximately $10 million and provided some form of protection to about 500 people, including 174 journalists.

But as Bernandino Hernández and Enric Martí said, most of these journalists found that protection distinctly lacking. *No Excuse* mentions the case of Veracruz-based editor Miguel Ángel Díaz, who asked for the mechanism's help in 2015, after a photographer from Veracruz, Rubén Espinosa Becerril, was murdered in Mexico City. Díaz, cofounder of an independent news website in the Veracruz state capitol of Xalapa called *Plumas Libres*, said police cars were circling his office and monitoring him from street corners. But all the mechanism did was provide him with a panic button, which did not make him feel any safer, and he was contacted only a handful of times during the year he was under its protection.

Faced with this situation, Mexican journalists have taken steps to protect themselves. After Javier Valdez's death, the staff at *Ríodoce* gathered to make a list of their friends and enemies. The enemies list was long and included *narcos*, politicians, suspect journalists, and spies. The friends list consisted of other trustworthy journalists, activists, and national and international supporters. From this list, a core emergency response and mutual support network was formed. It had to be primarily local to be effective, but outside support was also important.

International organizations helped organize these rapid response networks, and found ways to help threatened reporters escape the country, if only for a while. CPJ arranged for Miguel Díaz to go to Argentina, for example, though he missed his old life and eventually went home. American academics were also trying to do their part by providing positions for visiting Mexican journalists, as well as documenting and teaching about the ongoing crisis.

In November 2014 the University of Arizona Special Collections Library opened an all-access digital archive called the Documented Border. It contained, among many other materials, interviews with some sixty journalists about the risks of reporting in Mexico. University of Arizona journalism professors Celeste González de Bustamante and Jeannine Relly and their students conducted most of the interviews, which revealed the terror felt by so many and the self-censorship that resulted.

"They say, 'Not only do I not know what's going on, I don't want to know. Because no one cares.' No story is worth your life," said Alfredo Corchado, Mexico City bureau chief for the *Dallas Morning News*, who spoke at the archive's opening. Author of *Midnight in Mexico*, Corchado was at the time a visiting professor at Arizona State University in Tempe. "We are dying because of American drug consumption, but we also need institutions that work," he said.

The timing of the Javier Valdez murder, just twelve days after the *No Excuse* report was released with fanfare at Los Piños, raised the question of whether international attention was making the problem worse. CPJ North American Program Coordinator Alexandra Ellerbeck said she didn't think so. Fear of reprisal prevented local journalists from inquiring too much into the murders of their colleagues, so outsiders could help make sure investigations got done.

"It's a long game," Ellerbeck added. "Calling attention to it has helped keep the pressure on the government, although it hasn't translated into convictions in the vast majority of cases."

International organizations were also helping threatened journalists apply for political asylum in the States. One such case was that of freelance photographer Miguel Ángel López, who went to his parents' home in the early hours of June 20, 2011, to find his father, mother, and brother lying slaughtered in pools of blood. López's father had been a senior editor and his brother a photographer at *Notiver*, a major newspaper in the port city of Veracruz, Veracruz. With its long coast and extensive highways, Veracruz was a transportation hub for both oil and drugs and one of the most dangerous places in Mexico. López's father and brother were among at least fourteen journalists killed there during the term of Governor Javier Duarte de Ochoa (2010–2016). Three others disappeared, and the CPJ was investigating attacks on eleven more.

López, a stringer for *Notiver* and *La Jornada*, fled to Mexico City and hid out with friends for seven months. He and his wife were eventually able to escape to the United States on tourist visas, and in 2013, with the help of CPJ and other organizations, they received political asylum. Their El Paso–based lawyer, Carlos Spector, also represented other Mexican reporters who got asylum, including cameraman Alejandro Hernández in 2012 and Ciudad Juárez website owner Jorge Luis Aguirre in 2010. About fifteen Mexican journalists received asylum in the United States between 2006 and 2016—many, like López, after enduring great suffering.

Many others, however, were denied asylum. (Mexico had one of the lowest acceptance rates of any country, with fewer than 2 percent of applicants receiving asylum.) In 2005 Emilio Gutiérrez Soto, a reporter for a small newspaper in Chihuahua, started receiving death threats after writing about Mexican soldiers stealing from migrants. He was threatened and his home ransacked and surveilled. In 2008, after receiving a friend's warning that he'd better leave town right away, Gutiérrez fled with his fifteen-year-old son, Oscar. He went to the U.S. border and asked for asylum, telling an agent, "We're not afraid; we're terrified."

Father and son were detained several months, then released as their case wound through the system. They settled in Las Cruces, New Mexico, and operated a taco truck. Gutiérrez was assured he would not be detained or deported as long as he kept checking in with authorities.

On December 7, 2017, two months after receiving the National Press Club's Aubuchon Freedom of the Press Award on behalf of Mexican journalists, Gutiérrez was arrested again. He had come in for a routine check-in with Immigration and Customs Enforcement (ICE), only to learn his asylum claim had been denied and he was being deported. His supporters at the Press Club and other organizations jumped in and were able to stop the deportation. But authorities considered Gutiérrez to be a flight risk and sent him and his son to a detention center to await the decision on his appeal.

As denials and detentions of asylum seekers increased under Trump, some gave up. In May 2018 Mexican reporter Martín Mendez dropped his claim for asylum and agreed to be deported after being held for four months.

A Litany of Impunity

The following is a partial list of murders, beatings, arrests, and other events related to attacks on Mexican journalists in 2017 and 2018:

- On January 5, 2017, reporters and photographers covering a protest over the new year's steep rise in gas prices were beaten by state police and Special Forces in Monclova, Coahuila. At least five were injured. Two other reporters were seriously injured and another twelve beaten, threatened, or detained covering a similar protest in Rosarito, Baja California, on January 7.
- On January 8 Bernandino Hernández and several other reporters were attacked by state police in La Concepción, Guerrero.
- On March 2 Cecilio Pineda Birto, thirty-eight, a local crime reporter and founder of *La Voz de Tierra Caliente*, was slain by ten shots from two gunmen on a motorcycle while waiting in a hammock at a car wash around 7 p.m., in Ciudad Altamirano, Guerrero. Pineda, who had survived a previous assassination attempt, left behind two young daughters.
- On March 19 Ricardo Monlui Cabrera, fifty-seven, editorial director and columnist for the Córdoba, Veracruz–based *El Político*, was shot and killed by assailants on a motorcycle as he left a restaurant with his wife and son around 10 a.m. in Yanga, Veracruz. Monlui was also spokesman for the National Union of Sugar Cane Producers.
- On March 23 Miroslava Breach Velducea, fifty-four, was slain in front of her son in Chihuahua, Chihuahua. A sign left at the scene said, "tattletale."
- On March 28 a bodyguard protecting former independent news website director Julio Omar Gomez was killed while repelling an attack at Gomez's home in San José del Cabo, Baja California Sur. Gomez, who survived unhurt, had received protection after two previous attempts on his life.
- On March 29 Armando Arrieta Granados, fifty-one, editorial director of Veracruz daily *La Opinión*, was shot four times as he returned to his home in Poza Rica, Veracruz. He was hospitalized with gunshot wounds to the chest and a punctured lung but survived.

- On April 2, in response to the Breach murder, a newspaper with a thirty-year history in the border town of Ciudad Juárez, Chihuahua, went out of business. "Adiós!" read the headline in *Norte*. "Everything in life has a beginning and an end, a price to pay," wrote publisher Óscar Cantú Murguía. "And if this is life, I am not prepared for any more of my collaborators to pay for it, nor with my own person."

- On April 14 police reporter Maximino Rodríguez was shot and killed while sitting in his car around noon in La Paz, Baja California Sur. His wife, who was with him, was unhurt.

- On May 15 Javier Valdez Cárdenas was murdered near his office in Culiacán, Sinaloa.

- On May 18 Salvador Adame Pardo, director of the television station 6TV, was abducted off the street by armed men in a black SUV around 8 p.m. in Nueva Italia, Michoacán. Adame had covered news and politics in the Múgica region for two decades. In 2016, local police had detained him and his wife after they filmed the police forcibly removing protestors from city hall. Although Adame had reported this and other threatening incidents, on May 30 the Michoacán attorney general said his kidnapping may have been related to debts or personal problems. On June 14 his charred remains were found in the town of Gabriel Zamora.

- On May 29 Carlos Barrios, a reporter for the news website *Aspectos* in Playa del Carmen, Quintana Roo, had part of his ear cut off and was threatened with death by a knife-wielding assailant.

- On October 6 photographer Edgar Daniel Esqueda Castro was found dead near the airport in San Luis Potosí, capital of the state of San Luis Potosí. Esqueda had been shot three times and his body showed signs of torture. A freelance photographer for local news websites *Metropoli San Luis* and *Vox Populi*, Esqueda had recently reported two incidents to state authorities and human rights commission: on July 4 several policemen beat him while he was photographing the scene of a shootout, and on July 13 other officers took pictures of his ID card and told him he was under surveillance. He was offered protection from the mechanism but refused. On the night of October 5, armed men dressed in civilian clothes claiming to be members of the state investigative police abducted him from his home. His body was found the next day.

- On November 19 Adolfo Lagos Espinosa, a producer for the TV network Grupo Televisa, was shot to death by his own bodyguards while bicycling near Teotihuacán, the pre-Aztec pyramids about twenty-five miles northeast of Mexico City. The bodyguards were following Lagos in a car and claimed they accidentally shot him "in the crossfire" after robbers intending to steal his nine-thousand-dollar bike approached on foot. They said the robbers fired several shots before disappearing, without the bike, into a stand of *nopal* (prickly pear) cactus. But only the bodyguards' casings and bullets were found in Lagos and at the scene. A few hours later, the state attorney general was quoted saying, "We are certain that the bodyguard tried to defend his boss. We have no evidence to establish that there was any intent." (The CPJ did not include Lagos on its annual list of journalists killed in connection with their work.)

- On November 28 an ice chest containing two severed heads was left outside the Televisa network offices in Guadalajara, Jalisco. The chest also contained a death threat against a local judge. It was signed CJNG, the Spanish acronym for the Jalisco New Generation Cartel. The identity of the severed heads was unknown.

- On December 19 Gumaro Pérez Aguilando, thirty-four, was shot to death by unknown assailants in front of dozens of children and parents at his child's elementary school Christmas party in Xalapa, Veracruz. Pérez, founder of the online news outlet *La Voz del Sur*, had been under protection of the Veracruz State Commission for Attention to and Protection of Journalists. The governor of Veracruz ordered an investigation and sent police to guard Pérez's family.

- On Christmas Day three suspects were arrested in Bacobampo, Sonora, for the March 23 murder of *La Jornada* correspondent Miroslava Breach Velducea.

- On January 13, 2018, seventy-seven-year-old opinion columnist Carlos Domínguez Rodríguez was stabbed to death in front of his son, daughter-in-law, and grandchildren while stopped at a light in Nuevo Laredo, Tamaulipas. Two assailants, both of whom got away, approached his car midafternoon on a Saturday, opened the driver's door, and stabbed Domínguez twenty-one times. The day before, he had published a column on the news website *Horizonte de Matamoros* decrying political violence in Mexico. Officials said they were investigating whether the attack was connected with his work.

- On February 5 blogger and satirist Pamika Montenegro was shot and killed in the restaurant she and her husband owned in Acapulco. A friend of Bernandino Hernández, Montenegro was editor of the online magazine *El Sillón* and performed as the character La Nana Pelucas (The Grandma in Wigs) on her YouTube channel El Sillón TV. She often mocked local politicians and had reportedly been threatened. The Guerrero state attorney general claimed she was killed at the behest of an Acapulco drug lord, Javi Daniel Cervantes Magno, but no arrests were made.

- On March 21 veteran news reporter Leobardo Vázquez Atzin was murdered in the restaurant he owned in Gutiérrez Zamora, Veracruz. Vásquez had recently been posting articles on the Facebook page Enlace Informativo Regional that were critical of the mayor of the nearby town of Tecolutla. On March 9 he'd reported being threatened and offered bribes, but he was not under federal protection.

- On March 23 two policemen were convicted and sentenced to twenty-five years for their involvement in the January 2015 abduction and murder of reporter Moisés Sánchez Cerezo in Medellín del Bravo, Veracruz. Sánchez, forty-nine, had railed against local government corruption in his newspaper *La Unión*. The two convicted cops were said to be part of a group of five ordered to kill Sánchez by deputy police chief Martín López Meneses, who also served as the bodyguard and driver for Medellín del Bravo mayor Omar Reyes. Another one of the five, policeman-turned-drug-trafficker Clemente Noé Rodríguez, led authorities to Sánchez's decapitated and dismembered body three weeks after his abduction. López Meneses and Reyes were charged with murder, but remained at large in 2020. The other suspects were also still at large, and it was unclear if Noé Rodríguez would stand trial.

- On March 28 Tamaulipas state prosecutors announced they'd arrested six suspects in the January 13 stabbing death of Carlos Domínguez Rodríguez in Nuevo Laredo. Although the motive remained unclear, Breitbart News reported that three of the six were reporters, two were hitmen, and one, Rodolfo "El Rorro" Cantú García, was related to former Nuevo Laredo mayor Carlos Canturosas.

- On April 23 Mexico's interior secretary announced the arrest of twenty-six-year-old Heriberto N., alias "El Koala," as an accomplice in the killing of Javier Valdez Cárdenas. (In early 2020, a federal court in Culiacán sentenced El Koala to fourteen years and eight months. Another suspect, Juan Francisco N., "El Quillo," was under arrest and awaiting trial, and CPJ was calling for prosecution of a third, the alleged mastermind Dámaso López Serrano. "El Mini Lic," as he was known, was leader of an offshoot of the Sinaloa cartel, and had been in U.S. custody since surrendering to authorities in July 2017.)

- On May 15, the one-year anniversary of Valdez's death, radio journalist Juan Carlos Huerta was assassinated in a hail of bullets while leaving his subdivision on the outskirts of Villahermosa, Tabasco. The killers blocked his path and shattered the windshield of his silver BMW, leaving him slumped over the wheel. Huerta had hosted the radio show *Without Reservations* and was a well-known media figure. The state governor said it was unclear if his murder was related to his work, and no suspects were identified.

- On May 29 Héctor González Antonio, thirty-nine, a reporter for the national newspaper *Excelsior* and broadcaster Imagen, was found dead in Ciudad Victoria, Tamaulipas. His face showed signs of having been beaten by rocks. His last articles in *Excelsior* had been about gang battles in Reynosa and the arrest of four police officers in connection with a kidnapping on May 26. He had reported no threats and was not under protection of the mechanism. FEADLE officials said they were opening an investigation.

- On June 29 José Guadalupe Chan Dzib, forty-three, was shot and killed by an unidentified assailant in La Baticueva bar in Sabán, Quintana Roo. One of Chan Dzib's last stories for the *Semanario Playa News*, an online outlet based in the nearby resort town of Playa del Carmen, had been about the assassination of a Sabán political leader. (Scores of political candidates were killed across Mexico in the lead-up to the July 1 election.) Chan Dzib was not known to have been threatened. His boss, however, had been: Rubén Pat Cauich, cofounder of *Semanario Playa*

News, was under protection of the mechanism after being detained and beaten by Playa del Carmen police the previous year. On July 4 Pat spoke to the CPJ about Chan Dzib's murder and the danger he was in. "I think I need to leave Playa del Carmen for a while," he said. "No one guarantees my safety."

- On July 8 a Mexico City police commander was suspended after two journalists were beaten by cops while reporting on street-level drug arrests in the city's tough Doctores district. Photos of the swollen and bloody face of *Reforma* photographer Alejandro Mendoza appeared online. A TV Azteca reporter was also injured.

- On July 24 Rubén Pat, forty-one, was shot and killed in Playa del Carmen. He was exiting a bar called the Arre with an unidentified woman around 6 a.m. when a man in a cap, who got away, approached and shot him six times. The FEADLE announced it would help local authorities investigate whether Pat's death was related to his work and why the mechanism had failed to protect him.

- On July 26 Emilio Gutiérrez Soto, the journalist from Chihuahua being held with his teenage son in a U.S. immigration prison, was released after seven months' detainment. ICE had jailed Gutiérrez pending a rehearing of the denial of his asylum claim, but the appeals board ordered him and his son freed. Awarded a Knight-Wallace Reporting Fellowship, Gutiérrez began residency at the University of Michigan that fall. But the following spring, his asylum claim was denied again, and he and his son were ordered deported.

- On August 29 Javier Enrique Rodríguez Valladares, a cameraman with the local TV station Canal 10, was shot and killed along with another man around 6 p.m. in a residential neighborhood of Cancún. It was the third deadly attack on journalists in Quintana Roo in two months. Canal 10 had also been attacked on October 24, 2017, when assailants fired bullets at the building, wounding an employee. But the state attorney general wasn't sure if Rodríguez's death was connected to his work. He was apparently in the process of selling a car to the other victim when both were slain.

- On September 20 Mario Gómez, a reporter for *El Heraldo de Chiapas*, was killed in his home in Yajalón, Chiapas, by two gunmen on motorcycles. A surveillance camera captured the crime, and three days later, authorities arrested one suspect, whom they said acted as lookout. A Chiapas homicide prosecutor also named three more suspects—head of a local drug gang, his wife, and right-hand man—who remained at large.

- On December 4 a spokesman for newly elected president Andrés Manuel López Obrador confirmed that Jesús Márquez Jiménez, a reporter for the Orion Informativo website, had been found slain in the Pacific coast state of Nayarit. The press freedom group Reporters Without Borders said Marquez was evidently killed for criticizing local politicians' connections to cartels. He was, the group said, the tenth journalist killed in Mexico in 2018.

The CPJ agreed that ten journalists had been murdered in 2018 but could only confirm four were related to their work. Whatever the total, it was enough for Mexico to earn the dubious distinction of being named the most dangerous country for the press in the Western Hemisphere in 2018.

The murders and assaults continued in 2019. On January 22 a radio reporter under protection of the mechanism, Rafael Murúa Manríquez, was found dead near Santa Rosalía, Baja California Sur. On January 29 another reporter from the same state, news website founder Martín Valtierra García, was attacked by men with baseball bats outside his home in Comondú, Baja California Sur. On February 9 radio journalist Jesús Ramos was gunned down while eating breakfast at a restaurant in the Gulf Coast state of Tabasco. And on Friday night, March 15, Santiago Barroso, a columnist for *Semanario Contrasena* and radio host in San Luis Río Colorado, Sonora—a border town twenty-five miles south of Yuma—was shot and killed after answering a knock at the door.

Investigators got right on the case, and by March 26, they arrested a man from Guasave, Sinaloa, as the killer. They said the suspect had forced a woman to drive to Barroso's house at gunpoint, where he felled the reporter with two bullets from a .38 Special. Concluding the murder was not related to Barroso's work, the prosecutor said, "We know now the strongest line of investigation was related to the personal arena and his romantic relationships."

I was skeptical, but my friend Yolanda said she believed the prosecutor. She said she seemed honest and honorable. I was glad to hear her say that, even if it wasn't true. The head of the Sonoran Journalists Network said the group was neither accepting nor rejecting the finding but wanted to see more evidence.

Another murder occurred on March 24, a sports reporter from Sinaloa named Omar Iván Camacho Mascareño. He left home in the morning to cover a baseball game and was found dead later that night in the town of Salvador Alvarado, Sinaloa. His wife said he had not been threatened and was not under protection of the mechanism. Authorities were investigating whether the attack had anything to do with his work.

Amid the ongoing attacks, new president López Obrador, or AMLO for short, sent some discouraging signals for press freedom. After first saying he would reform the practice of government advertising in media outlets, which many believed led to cronyism and corruption, he left it intact. And on April 15, he told a roomful of journalists, "If you go too far, you know what will happen." A lot of listeners heard the remark as a thinly veiled threat, though AMLO later said he was not condoning violence.

On May 2—the day before World Press Freedom Day and the two-year anniversary of the release of the *No Excuse* report—AMLO was confronted during his daily press briefing by the son of slain journalist Carlos Domínguez, the seventy-seven-year-old columnist who had been stabbed twenty-one times while stopped with his family at a traffic light in Nuevo Laredo on January 13, 2018. His son believed the mastermind was former Nuevo Laredo mayor Carlos Canturosas, whom the elder Domínguez had been investigating for corruption and links to organized crime. One of the six suspects arrested in March 2018 was Canturosas's uncle. But more than a year had passed since then, and little progress had been made. AMLO said he would ask the federal attorney general's office to meet with Domínguez's son and take over the case if necessary. He vowed to do more to stop journalist murders.

Yet that very same day, another journalist was found dead. The bullet-ridden body of Telésforo Santiago Enríquez, director of a community radio station and teachers' union leader, was discovered in the late afternoon in his car in San Agustín Loxicha, Oaxaca. Santiago's station, El Cafetal, focused on the regionally dominant Zapotec culture and language. He also had run unsuccessfully for mayor of San Agustín and reportedly told colleagues that the brother of the incumbent mayor had threatened his life. A FEADLE spokesperson, who asked to remain anonymous when interviewed by the CPJ, said Santiago had not reported any threats and was not under its protection.

Over the summer, two attacks occurred within three days. In late July a newspaper in the northern city of Parral, Chihuahua, ceased publication after assailants threw gasoline bombs at its offices. And in early August journalist Jorge Celestino Ruíz Vásquez, who'd been set to testify about threats against him, was shot dead at his home in Actopan, Veracruz.

By the end of the year, the number of Mexican reporters murdered again numbered at least ten, though CPJ only counted five whose murders were definitely related to their work. Whatever the total, it was enough for Mexico, along with Syria, to be named the deadliest country in the world for journalists in 2019. Those two countries alone made up nearly half the worldwide total of twenty-five.

The year also saw an increase in cyberattacks. An anti-corruption group called MCCI (Mexicanos Contra la Corrupción y la Impunidad) had its website hacked and homepage replaced by an image of a helicopter in flames and the likenesses of two Mexican politicians killed in a copter crash the previous December. According to the University of Toronto–based watchdog group Citizen Lab, MCCI was among more than two dozen organizations and individuals targeted for cyberspying by the Mexican government under the Peña Nieto administration. The report said Pegasus spyware was used to monitor cell phones of journalists, lawyers, and activists, one of whom was Griselda Triana, widow of slain *Ríodoce* editor and founder Javier Valdez.

In late May and early June 2020, the problem of police corruption and brutality toward journalists came to the fore north of the border as well, when scores of reporters covering the George Floyd protests were attacked by police forces across the United States. The CPJ counted more than three hundred such instances in the first two weeks of protest after release of a video in which a white Minneapolis cop killed a Black man, George Floyd, by pressing his knee into his neck for some nine minutes. Reporters recorded themselves being shot with rubber bullets, tear-gassed, pepper-sprayed, beaten, having guns pointed at them, knocked to the ground, and arrested on false charges. Photojournalist Linda Tirado was blinded in one eye after being shot by a foam bullet while covering protests in Minneapolis. Reporters also were attacked by people angry about being photographed, which was triply ironic, given that Floyd's murder would've hardly been known of had it not been filmed, everyone else was taking and posting pictures and videos, and protestors were *supposed* to be wearing masks because of the pandemic! Strange times indeed. Attackers may have been additionally incited by the climate of media distrust fomented by Trump, as well as by the commonly held opinion that reporters are vultures who feed off the misery of others.

While these attacks scarcely compared to what journalists in Mexico endured every day, they were a reminder of the vulnerabilities of reporters everywhere, as well as of the dangers faced by all who dare to expose wrongdoing, or even just record what's going on.

Two

Prohibition Then and Now

With its steep hills, deep arroyos, and temperate, rocky caves, the land around Nogales has always been good country for smugglers. During Prohibition (from 1920 to 1933), bootleggers operated stills throughout the mountains both north and south of the line. Strings of donkeys trod narrow paths carrying tequila, whiskey, and other spirits to places where men waited in trucks to drive the booze to Tucson, Phoenix, and points beyond.

One story is told about a rancher who got into the act with four pack mules he kept stabled on the east side of the Tumacácori Mountains, about eighteen miles north of the border. When darkness fell, he put empty saddles on the mules and led them on his horse into Peck Canyon. The trail went west across a couple neighboring ranches, across the north slopes of the Atascosa Mountains, past Yanks Spring and then down through Sycamore Canyon into Mexico. The journey took all night. The next day, the mules rested and ate a bunch of hay, and at dusk, they were loaded with hooch and turned loose. They made a beeline back to Tumacácori, while the rancher went home by another route. The self-directing mules consistently arrived at the ranch well before daylight, ready to be unloaded.

Customs agents were alerted and staked out a narrow part of Peck Canyon. Several days later, the liquor-laden mules came by, and the agents caught them, confiscated the booze, and put the mules in government corrals in Nogales. The rancher showed up, claimed the mules were stolen, and since there was no proof he was involved, he got them back. This went on for two years. Finally, the revenuers set him up. They followed the loaded mules to the ranch and, alarmed by barking dogs, the rancher ran right into more agents approaching from the other side. He was arrested and fined, and the mules were sold off to a miner who used them to haul ore.

It sounds quaint, compared to the deadly cat-and-mouse that played out between drug smugglers and government agents after the 1990s border crackdown. Yet Prohibition was a time of serious violence on the border (and in Chicago, for that matter). Cross-border networks of organized crime families, the predecessors of modern cartels, were becoming established, and as they jockeyed for routes and networks, there was bloodshed. In 1926, just two years after the U.S. Border Patrol was formed, two Tucson agents were killed by liquor smugglers within the span of three months. On April 23, 1926, Inspector William McKee was shot while chasing suspected bootleggers near Tucson. On July 25 Inspector Lon Parker got in a gunfight with two smugglers in the Huachuca Mountains and killed one before being shot and killed himself.

In a sign of how quiet things became, seventy-two years passed before another Nogales border patrol agent was killed by smugglers. Around one in the morning on June 3, 1998, Agent Alexander Kirpnick was fatally shot while trying to arrest a group of marijuana smugglers in Potrero Canyon west of town. A multilingual Jewish immigrant from Ukraine, the twenty-seven-year-old Kirpnick had been on the force only a year and a half. His killer was a twenty-five-year-old Nogales, Sonora, man with a long rap sheet. Kirpnick's death signaled the beginning of a new wave of smuggling-related violence, this time over drugs and, as the century went on, migrants.

The Border Then

The U.S.-Mexico border has always been a remote, forbidding, and danger-ous place. Other than the densely settled Rio Grande Valley, its cities, towns, and villages are spread out like jewels along a nearly two-thousand-mile strip, far from each other and from everywhere else. In between settlements are tens of thousands of square miles of empty, desolate territory, mostly mountain ranges rising from deserts that make perfect hideouts for bandits, cattle rustlers, horse thieves, and other assorted criminals. Before the 1500s the region was sparsely populated by Indigenous peoples, who developed trade and travel routes from what is now central Mexico to the southwestern United States that were later followed by Spanish explorers and missionaries.

Some of those paths were trod by Padre Eusebio Francisco Kino, the Spanish Jesuit priest who founded a string of missions and ranches in the late 1600s along rivers that run through what is now northern Sonora and southern Arizona. Kino is said to have conducted the first-ever Palm Sunday Mass in Arizona at Quitobaquito Springs, a Sonoran Desert oasis near the present-day border town of Lukeville, in 1698 or 1699.

For millennia Quitobaquito Springs served as a life-giving way station on the Camino del Diablo (Devil's Road), one of several paths that crossed the no-man's-land between northern Sonora and the promised land of Cal-ifornia. This path traversed nearly one hundred miles of desert along what is now the Arizona-Sonora border, from Lukeville to Tinajas Altas, as well as another seventy miles northwest through the desert up to the Colorado River at Yuma.

Author and adventurer John Annerino walked the Camino del Diablo with migrants and catalogued the historic death toll in his 1999 book *Dead in Their Tracks*. The first person recorded to have died, he wrote, was Spanish explorer Melchior Díaz, who passed away on January 18, 1541, near Sonoyta, Sonora: "Twenty days earlier, Díaz had thrown his lance at a dog that was bothering some sheep; the lance stuck in the ground, and when Díaz went to retrieve it, his horse ran over the lance which pierced Díaz's abdomen."

Following the conquistadores and missionaries, Spanish settlers moved into parts of what is now California, southern Arizona, New Mexico, as far north as Colorado, and south Texas. Some of these settlers received land grants that came into play nearly three hundred years later, when the federal government started taking land for the border wall. Due to the harsh environment and vast distance from power centers, these settlers were extremely independent, wrote journalist and historian Colin Woodard in his 2011 bestseller *American Nations*. Woodard distinguished different parts of North America by the histories and cultural characteristics of the people who settled there, and he calls the border region—which includes large swaths of both the southwestern United States and northern Mexico—El Norte, "a land apart." The settlers of this region, he wrote, were known across New Spain for being "adaptable, self-sufficient, hard-working, aggressive, and intolerant of tyranny." The region was a "hotbed of democratic reform and revolutionary sentiment." Woodard noted the ongoing presence of Native peoples and their desire for self-determination also had a profound influence on border culture.

Mexico won independence from Spain in the 1820s, but too underpopulated to repel a subsequent invasion from the north, it lost more than half its territory to the United States in the 1840s. The Americans conquered all of what is now California, Nevada, and Utah, most of Arizona, and parts of Colorado, Wyoming, and New Mexico. Texas's history is more complicated; in addition to belonging to Spain, France, and Mexico, it was its own country for nine years before joining the United States in 1845. During the Civil War it was also part of the Confederacy, though they're downplaying that nowadays, for a total of six flags over Texas.

Other than the addition of the Gadsden Purchase (29,670 square miles of southern Arizona and New Mexico, bought for $10 million in 1854), the current border was essentially set with the signing of the Treaty of Guadalupe Hidalgo on February 2, 1848. The estimated three million Mexican citizens living in what then became the United States were automatically bestowed U.S. citizenship. For a while, most continued to live their lives as before, conducting business and keeping public records in Spanish.

The arrival of Northern European immigrants led to much conflict with these prior residents of El Norte. But the two groups also joined forces to contain rebellious Natives on both sides of the line. On April 30, 1871, forty-seven Mexican American and seven white men, including several founding fathers of Tucson, conducted a massacre of about 125 Pinal and Aravaipa

Apaches who had surrendered to the U.S. Army at Camp Grant, about sixty miles northeast of town. All but eight of the victims were women and children. A different band of Apaches, the Chiricahuas, led by Cochise and then by Geronimo, went on to fight fiercely on both sides of the border for another fifteen years. Geronimo had a particular antipathy for Mexicans after a company of soldiers from Sonora massacred his mother, wife, and three children in 1858. During the last five months before his capture in 1886, the governor of Sonora claimed, Geronimo's sixteen warriors slaughtered between five hundred and six hundred Mexicans.

Even after Geronimo's band was relocated to Oklahoma, New Mexico, and other places far from their ancestral lands in the Chiricahua Mountains, a few border tribes battled on. Inspired by Santa Teresa Urrea, a rancher's daughter from Cabora, Sonora, who became a spiritual leader of the poor and persecuted on the border, about seventy Yaquis and other Native peoples attacked the Nogales, Arizona, customs house on August 12, 1896. Several city officials were killed. (Urrea had already been exiled from Mexico for her revolutionary activities and vilified as a crazy witch and troublemaker by both the Mexican and American press. In January 1897 newspapers in El Paso, where she was living, reported the Mexican government tried to kill her. She ended up moving to California and died of tuberculosis in 1906, at age thirty-two.)

Like Urrea, many Yaquis died from communicable diseases. Others were captured and deported to slavery on sisal plantations in the Yucatán. But a few still live in Sonora, where they maintain their traditions despite being plagued by poverty and oppression. I saw Yaqui dancers perform with wooden deer-head masks, drums, and rattles when I visited Yolanda's village during Holy Week before Easter. The final three-day ceremony reenacts Christ's crucifixion, death, and resurrection. Among other rituals, on Holy Saturday, when the Gospels say darkness covered the Earth at midday, masked dancers wielding sticks and branches ran three choreographed assaults on the church. The dancers, representing demons, were ultimately defeated and their masks and branches burned in a bonfire. The entire town came out to watch and then attend a nearby festival with carnival rides and rodeo events. Yoli also took me to visit some Mayo friends of hers, who appeared to be living peaceful lives in open-air houses beside giant cottonwood trees on the banks of the Río Mayo.

By the early 1900s, a community of Yaquis who'd fled persecution in Mexico had established themselves in Tucson; the group later became the Pasqua Yaqui Tribe. Numbering about eleven thousand in 2020, the tribe owns about 1,100 acres southwest of the city, where it operates a casino, outdoor concert venue, hotel, and golf course called the Casino del Sol Resort. For years the mariachi conference was held there each spring. The Pasqua Yaquis also have settlements in Guadalupe, near Phoenix, and a village in central Tucson, where they perform deer dance ceremonies during Holy Week and at other times. One is held each year to commemorate a massacre of four hundred Yaquis in the mountains of Sonora in January 1900. Yaquis from Mexico have been hassled crossing the border to attend these events because some of their sacred objects are made from animal skins, bones, feathers, and other prohibited items.

The Tohono O'odham, the Indigenous people of the Sonoran Desert formerly called the Pápago, managed a different fate. They were able to hang on to not only their mission church, the San Xavier del Bac, founded by Padre Kino, and the land around it just south of Tucson, but a big chunk of southwestern Arizona as well. In 1917 this tribe—which had helped massacre their historic enemies the Apaches at Camp Grant—was allotted an enormous reservation that encompasses almost 4,400 square miles. The second-largest reservation in the nation (after the Navajo reservation, which encompasses more than 25,000 square miles), it's almost as big as the state of Connecticut and includes about 63 miles of border. However, the O'odham also saw their traditional lands and people divided forever by the international line, and as on most reservations, the ills of poverty are widespread.

Meanwhile, the first, and for a long time only, people to be officially banned from America were the Chinese. After Chinese immigrants started arriving in large numbers to work on the railroads in the mid-nineteenth century, both whites and Mexican Americans objected vehemently to their presence. On October 24, 1871, inflamed by an incident in which a policeman was wounded and a rancher killed, some five hundred Mexican Americans and whites joined in a riot in Los Angeles in which scores of Chinese people were attacked and robbed and their homes and businesses ransacked and burned. About twenty Chinese men were tortured, shot, mutilated, and hanged around downtown. This is still the largest mass lynching in U.S.

history. In 1882, in response to continued complaints about competition from Chinese workers in California after the Gold Rush, Congress passed the Chinese Exclusion Act. A clandestine trade in Chinese laborers sprung up along the border, and, just like today, human smuggling led to abuses and unsolved killings in Nogales and many other places.

It's one of the many paradoxes of the border that a place of exclusion can also be a place of tolerance. Barred from America until the Exclusion Act was repealed in 1943, Chinese immigrants joined other dispossessed groups on the border. Chinese, Blacks, Arabs, and Jews settled on both sides of the line. Lieutenant Henry O. Flipper, the first African American graduate of West Point, lived in Nogales, Arizona, from 1891 to 1906, surveying and settling land claims. This small town of outsiders is also the birthplace of the great jazz bassist, composer, and bandleader Charles Mingus. Although the family soon moved to Watts, his army sergeant dad was posted with an all-Black unit at Camp Little in Nogales when Mingus was born on April 22, 1922.

The United States Border Patrol was established in 1924 primarily to enforce the Chinese Exclusion Act, and Prohibition. It was also meant to supplant the many state, local, and private militias that had been policing the border since before the Civil War, when "slave patrols" had gone out to catch runaways before they reached Mexico. These groups were implicated in numerous atrocities, most notably the Texas Rangers' massacre of fifteen Mexican American men and boys in Porvenir (near present-day Marfa), Texas, on January 28, 1918. While this well-documented event resulted in investigations and reforms, no one was ever convicted of anything, and many former Texas Rangers later joined the newly formed border patrol.

The law that created the border patrol was also the first to set immigration quotas, after a huge influx of Europeans through Ellis Island in the late nineteenth and early twentieth centuries. Mexicans were not among the restricted groups. The border remained essentially open to them. Over the next few decades, circular migration grew between communities in Mexico and farms and ranches in the United States. People went north to harvest crops and then returned home for holidays, weddings, birthdays, baptisms, and the off-season. There were sending and receiving communities, like sister cities. Growers would go into Mexico and recruit people, and government programs were set up to provide visas to farmworkers when the need was great. A few employers made sure their workers were legal, but many did not. Family and friend networks made it easy for those without documents or with false documents to get work. Undocumented people got married, had families, and put down roots in the States.

It wasn't always good times. Working conditions were bad, migrants were exploited, and there were periodic deportations during economic down-turns, such as the Depression. In the late 1940s and 1950s, under Operation Wetback, some three hundred thousand people were separated from their families, treated abusively, and thrown back across the border. An accident during one of these deportation events, a plane crash in Los Gatos Canyon, California, on January 28, 1948, killed thirty-two and inspired the Woody Guthrie song "Deportee." Here is one of the verses and the chorus:

We died in your hills, we died in your deserts
We died in your valleys and died on your plains
We died 'neath your trees and we died in your bushes
Both sides of the river, we died just the same.

Goodbye to my Juan, goodbye Rosalita
Adiós mis amigos Jesús y María
You won't have your names when you ride the big airplane
All they will call you will be "deportees."

The McCarran-Walter Act in 1952 made undocumented entry and reentry an offense, though it was rarely enforced before 1986. The 1950s also saw the Bracero program, a guest-worker scheme that resulted in some people getting their papers and others being sent back to Mexico with worthless promises of compensation. Another regularization took place in 1972, but again, many never bothered to sign up because it still wasn't that big a deal to be caught crossing the border without documentation. People could take "voluntary departure" and be back at work in the States the next day.

Throughout the middle of the twentieth century, with Prohibition over and migration routes forming closer to jobs and highways in Texas and California, Nogales's usefulness as a smuggling corridor faded. Small-town life resumed. Locals went back and forth through holes in the fence to go shopping or visiting, and no one cared. Border agents, who often knew people by name, would give free rides back to the port of entry. A children's parade on Oct. 4, the feast day of Saint Francis, wound back and forth across the international line. Triple Crown–winning horse trainer Bob Baffert grew up on a ranch in Nogales during this time. "We'd cross the border like you'd cross the street," his brother told a TV reporter in 2018. Lawmen were still getting killed chasing criminals into Mexico and such, and legal prostitution in places like Boys Town in Nuevo Laredo continued a seedy reputation begun during Prohibition. But for the most part, this was a golden age on the border.

The world began to turn in the late 1960s and early 1970s. With Nixon declaring a War on Drugs at the same time as demand for cannabis was rising, the hills around Nogales regained their role as prime smuggling country. In April 1974 two customs agents were shot and killed while trying to stop marijuana smugglers driving a truck in Nogales, Arizona. The 1970s also saw the rise of the Somoza brothers, a notorious family of marijuana smugglers who terrorized the Arizona-Sonora border region for years.

Called "Los Quemados" due to mysterious scars on the neck and face of the older brother, José Luis Somoza Frasquillo and younger sibling Jesús Antonio were known for their flashy lifestyle and brazen intimidation of rivals. Jesús, "El Quemadito" (the Little Burned One), was said to have slain two men in a hail of bullets from an AK-47 in front of numerous witnesses in a Nogales, Sonora, brothel, before escaping one hundred miles southwest to kill a rival in Caborca, Sonora, eluding capture for a week, and then returning to Nogales to finish off another, "El Kaliman." He also was said to have killed a seventy-one-year-old convicted drug smuggler named José Means López by shooting him through the door of Means López's home in Nogales, Arizona, then escaping through a hole in the border fence.

José Luis Somoza, the older brother, had several run-ins with U.S. law enforcement, including convictions for marijuana smuggling. He served a year and a half in prison in Florence. During one episode, he led Nogales, Arizona, police on a high-speed chase, rammed a police car repeatedly, and crashed into a pole before being arrested at gunpoint. Five hundred pounds of pot were found in his vehicle. The Somozas were said to be untouchable because of their connections to high-ranking Nogales, Sonora, officials.

But the law finally caught up with them, more or less. In 1986 Mexican soldiers raided the family compound on the outskirts of Nogales, Sonora, and remained there for months. Many expensive cars and at least twenty-five tons of marijuana were seized, though the pot later went missing and the Somozas themselves escaped.

In addition to the increase in drug smuggling in the 1960s and 1970s, an end to the Bracero program, economic stagnation, and population growth in Mexico prompted more people, mostly young men, to cross the border to work. Refugees from bloody Central American civil wars also started arriving on the border in the late 1970s, leading to the establishment of the sanctuary movement in Tucson in 1982 (discussed in chapter 7). Although would-be migrants were still relatively few, public fears of a "tide" flooding the border began to rise.

The first fences intended to prevent people from crossing were built in the late 1970s. Called the Tortilla Curtain, these chain-link barriers were erected to coincide with a general crackdown on undocumented immigrants around the popular crossing spots of El Paso, Texas, and San Ysidro, California. Amid rumors they would be topped with razor wire, the fences generated widespread opposition in Mexico, as did the border patrol's heavy-handed tactics during the crackdown. In his book *Troublesome Border*, historian Oscar Martínez quoted René Mascareñas, the ex-mayor of El Paso's sister city Ciudad Juárez, who spoke for many when he said,

> I don't like the idea of fences. We don't live between East and West Germany. The communist wall that is there is a slap in the face to any nation that boasts of being democratic. We want greater fluidity and communication between us. We don't want barriers; we don't want barbed wire fence. We brag we are two neighborly countries, two friendly nations, and that this is the longest border in the world where one does not see a single soldier, a single rifle, a single bayonet, or a single affronting or discriminatory sign. Besides, if a fence is put up, it won't last, because Mexicans have much ability to tear it down.

Martínez went on to report that, as of the late 1980s, Mascareñas's prediction had come true. The fence had been built but was full of holes: "El Paso's

'Tortilla Curtain,' with its abundant person-sized holes," Martínez wrote, "is now practically useless as a deterrent to illegal immigration."

Yet change was coming, and it was coming fast. At the same time as Martínez was writing about the failure of the Tortilla Curtain, anti-immigrant sentiment was building in California. Upset about reports of dozens of people running across the border in waves and overwhelming the border patrol, members of a group called Light Up the Border began lining their cars up at dusk, with their headlights on, facing the Tijuana hills south of San Ysidro. An ex-mayor of San Diego named Roger Hedgecock had a radio talk show in which he railed against the undocumented. Vigilante and militia groups formed, and attacks on migrants, some deadly, occurred. The stage was set for the election of Republican governor Pete Wilson and the passage of an anti-immigrant statewide ballot initiative called Prop. 187 in the early 1990s.

The real turning point in terms of the border, however, was the U.S. government's enactment of the Immigration Reform and Control Act, or IRCA, in 1986. Although this Reagan-era law did ultimately legalize about 2.7 million long-term and law-abiding undocumented, it also created a Faustian bargain linking their amnesty to the fantasy that no more amnesties, and no more undocumented immigrants, would be allowed. IRCA moved immigration enforcement primarily from work sites to the border and vastly increased funding for border security. It established the goal of net-zero illegal immigration at the border as a prerequisite for immigration reform, which, even after it was achieved at tremendous economic, environmental, and human cost, resulted in no real reform, other than more border security, and more criminalization of the undocumented, for the next thirty years.

The Border Transformed

The post-IRCA border control strategy, called "Prevention through Deterrence," began in earnest in 1993 at the two busiest crossing spots, El Paso, Texas, and San Ysidro, California. In El Paso, Operation Blockade (later renamed Hold the Line) entailed stationing agents at close intervals along the levees and banks of the Rio Grande. Within months, apprehensions

Migrants under arrest in the Rio Grande Valley. (©iStock.com/vichinterlang)

dropped from several thousand a day to five hundred. Similar results were achieved in San Ysidro with Operation Gatekeeper. Apprehensions dropped precipitously after a massive wall was built that stretched several miles inland from the ocean, arroyos where people had hidden to cross each night were flattened, stadium lights erected, and one thousand agents added.

With those places essentially sealed off, migrant traffic quickly shifted to Arizona and the Rio Grande Valley. In 1994 the border patrol's Tucson Sector, which covers 281 linear miles from New Mexico to Yuma, became the busiest crossing spot on the border. "We were catching ten thousand a month here, more," a Nogales border agent told me. "You could never get enough [agents]." Operation Safeguard, the Arizona portion of the crackdown, began that year. Miles of fences standing nearly twenty feet tall were erected through downtown Nogales, Douglas, Naco, and other border towns, and the number of agents in the sector tripled to more than a thousand.

Some scholars perceived a connection between the timing of the border crackdown and passage of the North American Free Trade Agreement, which also occurred in 1994. NAFTA placed small-scale Mexican farmers in direct competition with large Mexican and U.S. agribusinesses, driving thousands from their land. Combined with a devastating peso devaluation the following year, the agreement led to a big jump in people coming to the border to find work. Many, like Yolanda ten years before, got jobs in the booming maquiladora sector. Others attempted to seek their fortunes in the United States, where they were met by an increasingly elaborate system designed to detect, detain, and deport them. NAFTA ensured goods and money could flow easily across the border, while the crackdown ensured workers couldn't, not without risking their lives and living in fear. The value of their labor was therefore strictly controlled on both sides of the line.

The mid-1990s also saw a wave of anti-immigrant laws and sentiment sweep the land in the wake of California's Prop. 187. The wave crested with passage of the Illegal Immigration Reform and Immigrant Responsibility Act in 1996. Supported by a bipartisan group of lawmakers, including then-senator Joe Biden, it was promptly signed into law by President Bill Clinton. Among other provisions, the act ordered the extension of the San Ysidro fence fourteen miles inland, added five thousand more border patrol agents, expanded the list of crimes that made a person deportable, and increased sanctions against the undocumented. Fatefully, it also created the 287(g) program, which allowed local police to act as immigration agents, an idea that would later prove highly controversial.

Another fateful border security idea was that of sending troops to stop drug smugglers. The plan resulted in disaster on May 20, 1997, when a teenager pasturing his goats by the Rio Grande was killed by a single shot from the M-16 of a young Marine who'd been camped out for three days on anti-drug maneuvers. Although the Marine was cleared of wrongdoing, the heartbroken parents of Esequiel Hernández Jr., eighteen, of Redford, Texas, later received a $1.9 million settlement from the U.S. government. Hernández was, after all, an innocent, small-town American boy, not an undocumented immigrant or drug smuggler. His librarian mother had been named one of President George H. W. Bush's "Thousand Points of Light," in recognition of her volunteerism. Bush had been the first president to send drug-fighting troops to the border, in 1989.

Esequiel Hernández's death, the first killing of a civilian by the military on U.S. soil since Kent State, ended any further attempts to put troops in direct law-enforcement roles on the border. But it was not the end of military involvement in border security by any means. The National Guard was deployed in a backup role for the border patrol many times thereafter, placing sensors in the ground, monitoring video screens, operating drones, even hauling hay for horses—a task some felt was not a good use of their skills or training.

As the border buildup proceeded, the question of how to measure its effectiveness arose. Measuring the success of interdiction efforts on the border had always been a problem, since there was no real way to know how many migrants or how much contraband crossed undetected, either currently or historically. There was no agreement on the accuracy of the available data, let alone what it meant. Even the apprehension numbers were questionable. Before the mid-2000s, people could take "voluntary departure" without being processed, so the border patrol had no idea how many apprehensions were the same person caught multiple times. Apart from that basic confusion, in terms of deterrent effect, it was impossible to separate out the walls from other factors influencing capture rates, or from other factors influencing a person's decision to migrate. One survey of migrants found that, despite the crackdown, 86 percent were ultimately able to enter the United States, often after repeated tries. It also found that conditions at home and the availability of jobs in the States were far greater factors than walls or other border enforcement in their decision to, in the words of a mariachi song, "cruzar la cara de la luna" (cross the face of the moon).

If the crackdown's effect on migration was hard to measure, quantifying its effect on drug smuggling was even harder. Walls and fences in urban areas had funneled more pot smugglers into the countryside, and for a while marijuana seizures went up. But who knew what impact these developments were having, if any, on the total amount of marijuana coming across. The crackdown's impact on hard-drug smuggling was also unquantifiable. Walls apparently made little difference, since most seizures of heroin, coke, meth, and, increasingly, fentanyl took place at ports of entry, as they always had. Less bulky and more valuable than pot, these drugs were easier to hide and maintain control over inside cars, trucks, semis, suitcases, mouths, and other places as they passed through the ports, sometimes under the watchful eye of corrupt officials. Similar things happened during Prohibition, when cars with false roofs and floorboards and other hidden compartments were found to be packed with expensive booze, while cheaper stuff came in over the hills and through the desert.

Underground traffic was an additional unknown variable. Honeycombed with drainage tunnels, Nogales also boasted two cavernous, stone passageways, built by the Works Progress Administration in the 1930s to control flooding in the Nogales Wash. For a while in the 1990s, these underground tunnels housed a gang of homeless children who would use them to come over to the U.S. side, commit crimes, and then run back to Mexico. The border patrol and the Mexican border police force Grupo Beta eventually ran the "tunnel kids" out and took control over the official entrances and exits. But illicit offshoots and connections to these tunnels, as well as illicit tunnels under other parts of Nogales and under other border cities, continued to be found with regularity. A Drug Enforcement Administration survey done in 2016 counted 185 original tunnels found under the U.S.-Mexico border since 1990.

The notorious Joaquín "El Chapo" Guzmán Loera and the Sinaloa cartel were said to have built the border's first "supertunnel," under the wall between Agua Prieta, Sonora, and Douglas, Arizona, in the 1980s. Discovered in 1990, it featured lights, air conditioning, and rail tracks. A pool table on hydraulic lifts concealed the entrance inside a house on the Mexican side. A 2015 *New Yorker* article on this and other supertunnels said some were thousands of feet long, as deep as seventy feet underground, and tall enough for a man to stand up in. They featured elevators and water pumps and cost well over $1 million each to build. The article also said the men who built the Douglas–Agua Prieta tunnel ended up in a mass grave when the work was done.

While the crackdown's overall impact on smuggling patterns remained obscure, some impacts were clear. The main effect was to funnel migrants into remote areas, increasing the cost of coyotes (human smugglers), from four thousand to seven thousand dollars or more for the journey from Central America, as well as exposing migrants to far more danger from criminals and the elements. When the Arizona portion of the crackdown took hold, the number of border deaths—as indicated by the number of bodies found on the Camino del Diablo and elsewhere in the desert—began to increase rapidly. In 1995, 8 sets of remains were classified as undocumented border crossers by the Pima County medical examiner. By 2000, the figure grew to 70. It leaped to 143 in 2002 and continued to average more than 150 a year from then on, even as the number of apprehensions declined.

Although none of the nineteen hijackers who perpetrated the September 11, 2001, attacks entered through Mexico, 9/11 led to further reinforcement of the southern border. The Immigration and Naturalization Service, blamed for failing to stop the terrorists, was split up, and its functions were moved from the Justice Department to the newly created Department of Homeland Security (DHS). The law creating the DHS also gave the INS's successor agencies, U.S. Immigration and Customs Enforcement (ICE) and U.S. Customs and Border Protection (CBP), increased budgets and enforcement powers. The Secure Fence Act, signed by President George W. Bush in 2006, provided some $90 billion over ten years to these and other agencies to build hundreds more miles of fencing, hire ten thousand more border agents, and purchase military-style equipment including weapons, helicopters, drones, and surveillance systems specifically for use in border enforcement.

During debate, some lawmakers proposed the fence be electrified. Rep. Steve King (R-Iowa) demonstrated on the House floor a model of a fence he designed "with the kind of current that would not kill somebody." King noted, "We do this with livestock all the time."

That didn't happen, but one post-9/11 action did have a huge impact on wall construction. A provision of the 2005 Real ID Act waived compliance with the Endangered Species Act, the National Environmental Policy Act, the Clean Water Act, and dozens of other laws and regulations protecting Native American graveyards, sacred sites, riparian areas, and other priceless resources, if their enforcement interfered with wall construction, security installations or border patrol operations.

This provision cleared the way for rapid fence construction across Arizona's protected deserts. Vehicle fences—four-foot-tall bollards cemented in the ground in some places, and less expensive Normandy (named for the World War II beach landing) cross-rail fences in others—went up along Organ Pipe Cactus National Monument, where park ranger Kris Eggle had been killed in a gun battle with smugglers in 2002. Vehicle fences were also erected along the Cabeza Prieta National Wildlife Refuge, and the Barry M. Goldwater Range, which was used as a bombing and live-fire practice range by fighter jets flying out of airfields near Yuma and Phoenix. Park rangers had reported the increased traffic was damaging the sensitive environment, resulting in the ironic headline "Migrants Called Threat to Bombing Range."

The Tohono O'odham, for their part, strongly opposed exempting border security measures from environmental and cultural protection laws. However, with their land overrun by migrants and smugglers since at least the mid-nineties, they had no choice but to agree to more walls and agents. This included pedestrian fencing at the San Miguel Gate, vehicle fencing elsewhere, and more checkpoints and forward bases. But the nation insisted the border patrol respect its rights and not damage its land any more than absolutely necessary.

If fence building in remote and delicate deserts was difficult, fence building along a constantly-shifting riverbank was even more so. Wall construction in the Rio Grande Valley proceeded slowly, not only because of the complex environmental and engineering challenges, but because most of the land was privately owned. Unlike Arizona, where most of the walls and fences were built on public and tribal lands, the land in south Texas had to be taken through eminent domain. The government sued more than four hundred landowners, which resulted in years of legal fights, mostly over the valuations but also over environmental issues and property rights. As previously mentioned, some riverfront property owners had Spanish land grants dating back to the 1700s. The wall went up in piecemeal fashion. Portions of it were built a mile or more inland, and as a result many people found themselves living on the "Mexican side" of the barriers. Several families had keys to gates in walls bisecting their land. (The battle was still very much on in 2018, when a Catholic church in Mission, Texas, backed by the local diocese and lawyers from Georgetown Law School, sued to prevent the government from building a section of wall that would leave the chapel in "no-man's-land.")

In addition to physical walls and fences, the 2006 law supplied the border patrol with sophisticated, military-style surveillance equipment, including truck-mounted systems, tower-mounted cameras with day and night capability, packable radar, night-vision goggles, drones mounted with radar, ground sensors, aircraft, and other supplies. Technology was developed at the Military Intelligence Training Center at Fort Huachuca near Sierra Vista, Arizona, at the University of Arizona in Tucson, and at many other national and international agencies, institutions, and corporations.

The border was proving ground for a lot of super-secret technology, including "virtual fence" systems that failed to work. The Government

Accountability Office, Congress's investigative arm, found CBP spent about $429 million between 1998 and 2005 on surveillance systems that could be set off by trains, animals, and wind. Starting in 2009, a virtual fence called SBInet (for Secure Border Initiative network), developed by Boeing, went up along the border near Sasabe, Arizona. It was made up of fifteen nearly hundred-foot-tall surveillance towers equipped with radar, cameras, and other sensors said to be capable of covering fifty-three miles of territory.

On August 6, Hiroshima Day, 2009, a Franciscan priest and a Quaker activist were arrested for praying at the base of one of the newly installed towers. Jerry Zawada, seventy-two, and John Heid, fifty-four, were charged with trespassing after they knelt in response to a security guard's order to leave the site. (Zawada was also arrested for protesting military intelligence interrogation training at Fort Huachuca in 2005, a crime for which he served two months in federal prison.) They said they were protesting the virtual fence because it was part of a border militarization policy driving people to their deaths. Residents of Arivaca, Arizona, a small town twelve miles northeast of Sasabe, also objected, saying the towers were unsightly, compromised their privacy and freedom, and would have no impact on undocumented immigration.

Nogales Wall and surveillance tower viewed from U.S. side. (©iStock.com/ Rex_Wholster)

Although the protestors didn't stop it, SBInet was plagued by cost over-runs and performance issues and ultimately canceled. Homeland Security Secretary Janet Napolitano ended the program in January 2011, after nearly $1 billion had been spent and only the initial fifteen towers made operational.

Surveillance systems did work well in urban areas, however, and many stretches of wall, including in downtown Nogales, were outfitted with them. On the night of October 10, 2012, video cameras positioned along the fence just west of the Deconcini Port of Entry recorded images of border patrol agent Lonnie Swartz shooting sixteen times between the fence poles into Mexico, killing Nogales, Sonora, teenager José Antonio Elena Rodríguez. The video would be shown many times at Swartz's murder trial in 2018.

The Border Now

Fourth-generation Cochise County rancher Robert Krentz was a large man with a white handlebar mustache. He owned a thirty-five-thousand-acre cattle ranch northeast of the border town of Douglas, Arizona, and was considered a pillar of the community. Interviewed several times about the impact on local ranches after migrants began crossing there in large numbers, he told PBS in 1999, "If they come and ask for water, I'll still give them water. You know, that's just my nature." But by 2005 he told a Tucson TV station that migrants and smugglers had caused more than $8 million in damage to his ranch over the previous five years.

On March 26, 2010, federal agents were called to the Krentz ranch, where they arrested eight smugglers and seized 250 pounds of pot. The following morning, a Saturday, Krentz went out to patrol the property on his ATV, armed as usual. Around 10:30, he radioed his brother to say he'd seen a migrant in distress and to call the border patrol. He was never heard from again. He and his dog Blue were found dead of gunshot wounds in a remote section of the ranch several hours later. He had apparently tried to escape on his ATV after being shot. He had not been robbed, and his gun was still in its holster. Footprints at the scene led back to the border.

The killing terrified the local ranching community. Gun sales surged, and people demanded the border patrol step up enforcement in the area. Howard Buffett, son of billionaire Warren Buffett, donated walkie-talkies to ranchers whose land fronted the international line. (Buffett, who ran a research farm near Willcox, about seventy miles north of Douglas, went on to buy some border-front land of his own, and to write a book calling for more law and order on the border. He also fancied himself a sheriff's deputy: he donated millions in equipment to the Cochise County Sheriff's Department, and in early 2019 the *Phoenix New Times* published an investigation into his influence that showed at least four tickets signed "HBuffett.")

Despite intense focus on the case, including a forty-five-thousand-dollar reward, no one was ever arrested for Krentz's murder. (The prime suspect was reportedly killed in Agua Prieta in February, 2011.) His death became a rallying cry for Arizona politicians, and had a big impact on the push to pass SB 1070, a state statute aimed at cracking down on undocumented immigrants. Called the "show your papers" law, it required local police to call the border patrol if they encountered someone they suspected was undocumented. Governor Jan Brewer signed SB 1070 into law less than a month after Krentz's murder. This era was also the heyday of Maricopa County Sheriff Joe Arpaio, who later cost taxpayers an estimated $200 million in legal judgments and fees when his neighborhood sweeps targeting the undocumented were found to be unconstitutional.

In Cochise County an anti-immigrant militia group called the Minutemen got a lot of publicity in the early 2000s, though it had ceased to exist by the time of the Krentz murder. The group splintered in 2006 when its founder, a rancher who had bragged about detaining twelve thousand migrants on his land, was convicted of terrorizing a Mexican American family and ordered to pay nearly a hundred thousand dollars in restitution. The militia movement in Arizona was discredited even more after the leader of one group was arrested for and ultimately convicted of child molestation, and the leader of another was sent to prison for life for conducting a home invasion in Arivaca in May 2009, in which an alleged drug dealer and his nine-year-old daughter were killed.

Krentz's death prompted further calls to "build a wall" on the border. But the murder actually occurred after nearly twenty years of intense wall and fence building had driven migrants and smugglers away from cities and towns and into rural areas like his ranch. Border cities had come to resemble armed camps—crime rates dropped to record lows in places like El Paso and Nogales—but the vast stretches of empty land in between had become more dangerous. Even in areas with fencing or other barriers, smugglers used ultralights, drones, ramps, catapults, T-shirt cannons, migrants, and other means to get GPS-tagged bundles across, where they would then be picked up by other smugglers on the U.S. side. It appeared Krentz had interfered with one of these operations the day before he died.

Drug seizures held steady or increased as the crackdown went on, but migrant arrests dropped precipitously after peaking at 1.6 million in 2000. By 2010, the year of Krentz's murder, they had reached levels not seen since 1971. The decline prompted the border patrol to attempt to declare "full operational control" over at least part of the border. In the fall of 2011, border patrol chief Michael Fisher told Congress that his agency had about 873 miles of border under control, and that the already-constructed 650-mile fence was just two miles shy of what they believed was necessary. Experts agreed, in the words of Wayne Cornelius, director of the Mexican Migration Field Research Program at University of California–San Diego, that "no appreciable amount of additional deterrence can be wrung from more spending on border agents, hardware and technology."

At the same time, Princeton professor Douglas Massey said his research showed an end to cyclical migration. "We are at a new point in the history of migration between Mexico and the United States," he said at a news conference in Mexico City in 2011. There were more Mexicans leaving the country than coming in.

Massey noted the walls had helped end cyclical migration by making it too hard for people to cross back and forth. "Walls are terrible at keeping people out, but good at keeping people in," he said. The walls and related crackdown had a caging effect. The undocumented population in the United States, by then estimated at more than 11 million, about two-thirds of them Mexican, could not leave the country without risking never being able to return.

Long-term undocumented residents also faced an increased threat of deportation under Bush, and particularly Obama. Secure Communities, a program begun in 2008, trained local law enforcement to serve as "force multipliers" for immigration authorities. All fingerprints taken at local jails were run through an FBI database to identify undocumented people so they could be held for deportation after they would otherwise be released. Although canceled in 2014, Secure Communities was replaced by the similar 287(g) program, originally signed into law by President Clinton.

The idea of deporting criminal aliens sounded good, but the program also swept up many law-abiding and hard-working undocumented people, some with deep roots in the States, who were identified through traffic stops and other minor offenses. Prominent community leaders; successful businessmen; parents of young, U.S.-citizen children; people who'd never lived in their country of origin; and even veterans who'd served honorably in the U.S. military were all sent packing. By 2013, when deportations peaked at nearly 435,000, a new sanctuary movement was forming in response (see chapter 7).

Despite the mass deportations, the end of cyclical migration, the steep decline in arrests at the border, and the border patrol's assertions of operational control over hundreds of miles, what constituted a secure border remained subject to debate. In 2013 the Government Accountability Office again found there was no accurate way to determine the effectiveness of border security, and CBP announced that, due to budget cuts, it would no longer attempt to collect data on the effectiveness of border control.

That same year, apprehensions of undocumented crossers began to grow again after an eight-year decline. This time it was mostly Central Americans, including large numbers of teenagers traveling alone. By 2013 some 60 percent of migrants caught in the Rio Grande Valley were OTMs ("other than Mexicans"), although in the Tucson Sector it remained fewer than 20 percent. The year 2014 saw a slight rise to some 468,000 apprehensions, the first year ever that Central Americans outnumbered Mexicans. Obama opened two family detention centers in Texas, which together could accommodate more than two thousand women and children, as well as other shelters for unaccompanied minors, including one in Tucson. His administration was met with legal challenges concerning the treatment of these children, which became pertinent during the family separation crisis under President Trump.

In early 2017, not long after President Trump announced he intended to keep his campaign promise to "build the wall," the GAO reported on the current state of walls on the Mexican border. There were 654 miles of single-layer and 51 miles of double- and triple-layer fences already in place. Of the single-layer, 354 miles were pedestrian fencing, and 300 miles were vehicle fencing. Pedestrian fences cost about $6.5 million per mile to build, and vehicle fences cost $1.8 million, for a total of some $2.3 billion spent on border barriers between 2007 and 2015. Another $450 million was spent on the fences' operation and maintenance, including tactical infrastructure, drainage, and "vegetation control." In places where the walls crossed streambeds and washes, sections were frequently knocked down by rushing water and by backed-up debris during rainstorms. The government had spent millions in repairs, as well as in reparations to residents of Nogales, Lukeville, Naco, and other towns, due to wall-caused flooding and erosion. Millions more in damages went unreimbursed, after the Ninth Circuit Court ruled in 2013 that the government was not liable for harm caused by its wall building.

The report also looked at the cost of fixing holes in the fence. Smugglers and border crossers were constantly sawing through, wedging apart, driving over, and otherwise damaging and destroying the fences. The report said there were nearly 9,300 breaches in pedestrian fencing from 2010 to 2015, with an average repair cost of about eight hundred dollars each. Fences built in the 1990s were subject to an average of eighty-two breaching incidents per mile, while those built after the Secure Fence Act of 2006 had only fourteen breaches per mile. CBP also built and maintained some five thousand miles of roads along the fences. About a third of the border fence, some 211 miles, was in the Tucson Sector.

Nevertheless, Trump was adamant these walls were insufficient, and more were needed. He held a design contest and awarded bids for prototypes. Some of the winning designs were fanciful, with windows or artwork or a solar panel or two on top. Others were nearly identical to the existing walls, only much taller. Tucson and other border cities debated how to respond. Some voted not to do business with firms building the wall or the prototypes. Southern Arizona congressman Raúl Grijalva sued to stop further wall construction in his district. Lawsuits were also filed over the environmental impact of walls in New Mexico and California. But a Mexican American judge whom Trump had previously claimed was biased against him turned away the challenges and ruled wall building on the border could proceed.

In April 2017 Attorney General Jeff Sessions traveled to Nogales to announce there was a new sheriff in town. He stood before a podium on white stone steps in front of border patrol headquarters, with a pastoral background of a flag and trees and broad expanse of blue sky. Denouncing drug gangs that sneak into America to peddle their poison and "turn cities and suburbs into war zones," he ended his remarks with a dramatic flourish that veered from the press release: "It is here, on this sliver of land, where we first take our stand against this filth."

The prototypes went up that fall in Otay Mesa, south of San Diego. Once the scene of would-be migrants playing soccer on the Mexican side while they waited for night to fall, Otay Mesa had long since been sealed off to border crossers. But concerns about protests and vandalism by people on the U.S. side prompted San Diego County to spend three-quarters of a million dollars on security during the four weeks of construction. There were no demonstrations then, though a fight broke out at a protest at the site on December 9, and more protests occurred when Trump came to view the prototypes in early 2018. Church and border activists rallied in front of a mural of Mexican revolutionary heroes in San Diego, shouting, "We reject your hate! We don't need your racist wall!" City Councilmember Georgette Gómez addressed the crowd: "It's really important that as a region, as a city that has firsthand understanding of what the border wall means for our communities, that we stand against [this] and we send a strong message to D.C. to say this is something that we don't welcome."

Even with the hundreds of miles of existing walls and fences, the thousands of miles of roads to reach them, the squadrons of vehicles, the legions of agents, the lights, the cameras, the sensors, the helicopters, the airplanes, the drones, the radar, and all the other surveillance below ground, aboveground, and in the sky, smuggling still could not be stopped. On April 20, 2018—4/20, appropriately enough—the *Arizona Daily Star* published a story saying a man had been spotted on the Tohono O'odham reservation leading two horses loaded with burlap sacks containing 262 pounds of pot and six pounds of meth. The horses were captured, and the man got away (though agents later tracked him down and arrested him).

The more things changed . . .

Three

Where the Guns Go

On the night of December 14, 2010, U.S. Border Patrol Agent Brian Terry set out with three other agents to patrol Peck Canyon, a grassy, wooded ravine some eleven miles north of the border near Rio Rico, Arizona. The Peck Canyon exit off the I-19 freeway was for many years the site of a border patrol checkpoint, and agents routinely ran patrols to catch smugglers and migrants trying to circumvent the highway on foot.

Terry was forty and single, a muscular guy from Flat Rock, Michigan, who liked cars. He had previously been in the Marines and served as a policeman. He was the oldest graduate of the border patrol's training school in 2007 and a member of BORTAC, the agency's elite tactical unit.

Just before midnight, Terry and the others were standing on a hill overlooking a wash called Mesquite Seep when they got an alert that a ground sensor had gone off nearby. The agents positioned themselves in a line and a few minutes later, five men came walking up the wash. The agents yelled "Policía!" and fired a beanbag gun at them. The men—later found to be members of a rip crew intending to steal from migrants or smugglers—shot back. A firefight ensued. One of the men was wounded and captured, but the other four escaped to Mexico. Terry was mortally wounded and died the next day.

Terry's death sparked grief and anger, but beyond that, it sparked a major scandal when it was revealed that two of the guns used by the rip crew had been intentionally sold to drug cartels by agents of the United States Bureau of Alcohol, Tobacco, Firearms and Explosives (ATF). This "gunwalking" scandal, widely known as Fast and Furious, led to numerous investigations that exposed wrongdoing all the way to the top of the U.S. government. Since most of the gun sales and subsequent coverup took place during the Obama administration, Republican lawmakers on Capitol Hill and conservative agencies and groups, including Breitbart News, took up the torch.

But the investigations found plenty of blame to go around. Federal agents in Phoenix and elsewhere were allowing guns to be trafficked to Mexico as early as 2006, two years before Obama was even elected. Legal gun sales to the Mexican cops and military, as well as gun and ammunition smuggling and cartel money laundering, also proliferated under both Democratic and Republican administrations.

Fast and Furious

Only hours after the shootout that killed Brian Terry, authorities traced two rifles found at the scene to a Phoenix gun shop, and the Fast and Furious operation began to unravel. It was the biggest scandal for the ATF since the siege in Waco, Texas, in 1993. That tragic debacle began when four agents were shot and killed by religious zealots holed up in a compound. After a fifty-one-day standoff, the ATF and FBI tried to force the group out with tear gas and a tank, the cult members set the place on fire, and seventy-six of them, including twenty children, died.

Before Waco the ATF had a pretty spotless reputation. The agency's website described how it came into being in its current form, fighting Al Capone and his international empire built on illegal alcohol: "Criminal syndicates completely controlled the liquor industry. Assassinations, bombs, bullets and corruption were routine; every industry paid tribute, directly or indirectly, to bootleggers and gangsters who had forged such close ties with local authorities that anonymous prohibition enforcement squads became necessary in some cities. Chicago was one of those cities."

Confronted with such force, in 1930 the ATF (then called the Prohibition Unit) was moved to the Justice Department and, for a time, put under control of the FBI, where J. Edgar Hoover took a personal interest in it. (Previously, it had always been part of the Treasury Department, where its predecessor was established in 1791 to collect alcohol and tobacco taxes enacted to pay off Revolutionary War debt.) At Justice the ATF's reputation was solidified by Eliot Ness and his team of Untouchables, who took on Capone and his empire, eventually dismantling it and sending him to jail for tax evasion.

But the story didn't end with the end of Prohibition. The agency was renamed the Alcohol Tax Unit (ATU) and switched back to the Treasury Department:

> The newly organized ATU faced grave problems across the nation. The country was ill-prepared to re-establish the legal liquor industry as criminal syndicates continued to illegally produce and distribute distilled spirits. Organized crime escalated as gangs battled viciously for control of underground distilleries and distribution networks. Machine guns continued to be the weapon of choice. Gangsters killed each other on street corners, in social clubs and in restaurants. The massacres often resulted in the injury or death of innocent bystanders.

Eventually, with public support, the ATF got a hold of the situation. The process of finally stamping out the illegal liquor trade helped create respect for the integrity of federal law enforcement, the story said, as well as for its ability to defeat both organized crime and entrenched government corruption.

The ATF functioned as part of the Treasury Department until 2003, when it was caught up in the post-9/11 homeland security reorganization. The agency was split in two, with the taxation arm staying under Treasury and the law-enforcement arm again becoming part of the Justice Department. The word "explosives" was added to its title, and it became more focused on terrorism.

As of 2020, that's where the agency's official timeline ended. It didn't mention Fast and Furious, which unfortunately became the most infamous episode in the agency's post-9/11 history.

Fast and Furious was the code name of one of a series of gunwalking investigations conducted by the ATF Arizona field office between 2006 and 2011. These were sting operations, set up through gun dealers in Phoenix and Tucson, in which weapons were intentionally sold to people connected to drug cartels. The guns were supposed to be tracked to help lead authorities to the kingpin. Except it didn't work out that way.

The first such operation took place in early 2006, when a gun dealer in Tucson, Mike Detty, reported a suspicious buyer to the ATF. The agency responded by hiring Detty to continue selling guns to this and other disreputable characters over the next eighteen months. In total, Detty sold about 450 guns, including AR-15s, AK-47s, and Colt .38s, to buyers who then trafficked the guns to Mexico, where all but about sixty subsequently disappeared. A few low-level buyers were caught and convicted, but no kingpins were ever charged.

After a couple more unsuccessful operations involving Detty and other gun dealers, in which several hundred guns were lost after being sold to suspected criminals, Phoenix Field Division Special Agent in Charge William Newell inexplicably decided to launch a large-scale gunwalking sting. It was this operation that got the name Fast and Furious because some of the gun-buying suspects, like characters in the Fast and Furious movie series, were mechanics and street racers.

Starting in November 2009, the car buffs and other suspects were allowed to go on a gun-buying spree in Phoenix in which they eventually purchased, at a cost of more than $1 million, more than two thousand firearms. These included AK-47s, .50-caliber sniper rifles, and 5.7-mm pistols. One suspect alone bought more than six hundred guns. As this went on, some of the gun dealers and ATF agents began to protest vehemently, but Newell told them the sales were part of a high-level sting operation meant to take down an entire trafficking network and that other officials were supervising the situation. That turned out to not really be true.

By mid-2010 the ATF was facing a rising chorus of internal opposition. One of these voices was a whistleblowing agent named John Dodson. The

Brian Terry Foundation dinner in Tucson in 2017 featured Dodson as a guest speaker, along with the main honoree, Breitbart News founder Steve Bannon. (The foundation provided scholarships for people hoping to pursue law-enforcement careers.) Ignoring protestors who greeted him outside the Starr Pass Resort, Bannon spoke about Terry's sacrifice before turning to the threats posed by unrestricted immigration and global elites. Dodson also paid tribute to Terry and expressed gratitude to him. Terry's death in December 2010, he said, was what finally led to the exposure and end of Operation Fast and Furious.

Even though the operation had ended, the coverup was just beginning, and Fast and Furious morphed into a Washington scandal over what Attorney General Eric Holder knew and when he knew it. After first saying he didn't know anything about it, he later had to recant. He also became the first sitting member of the Cabinet ever to be held in contempt of Congress after refusing to release a number of documents related to the case.

Dodson and other whistleblowing agents faced retaliation and demotion, while Newell and others who led the operation were at first given transfers or promotions. That led to another scandal. Eventually, Newell lost his job, Detty and Dodson and another agent wrote books, and congressional investigations under Republicans Darrell Issa in the House and Charles Grassley in the Senate dragged on for years. Conspiracy theories abounded because, as Dodson famously said, "I cannot begin to think of how the risk of letting guns fall into the hands of known criminals could possibly advance any legitimate law enforcement interest."

The most popular theory of why and how this could have occurred is that Obama and Holder were frustrated in their efforts to achieve gun control, so they hatched a plan to take down law-abiding gun dealers. The legitimate dealers they targeted took the fall for selling guns to the cartels, which gave Obama and Holder the excuse they needed to close them down.

The gun shops at the center of the controversy were put on the hot seat. Some dealers faced charges and had their businesses closed, and in 2012 Brian Terry's family sued one, along with seven officials, for negligence and wrongful death. That case dragged on for years as well, with Terry's family stymied in their attempt to get access to documents related to Fast and Furious.

Although the U.S. attorney for the District of Arizona resigned, and that office as well as the Arizona ATF field office had to recuse themselves from the investigation, the men who killed Terry did not escape justice. A total of seven were indicted, five who were there that night and two who helped plan the crime. The one who was wounded and captured, Manuel Osorio Arellanes, pled guilty to avoid the death penalty and was sentenced in 2014 to thirty years in prison. Osorio Arellanes's two brothers were also charged; Rito, who was not at the scene, pled guilty to conspiracy and was sentenced to eight years. And after an extensive manhunt, Heraclio Osorio Arellanes, the suspected shooter, was caught on a ranch near the Sinaloa-Chihuahua border in April 2017.

The Osorio Arellanes brothers were from El Fuerte, Sinaloa, a picturesque Spanish colonial town at the foot of the Sierra Madre—the train to the Copper Canyon leaves from there—that had become a major drug trafficking locale. One of the four fugitive members of the rip crew, Iván Soto Barraza, was arrested in El Fuerte on September 11, 2013. He and another, Jesús Leonel Sánchez Meza, captured in Puerto Peñasco a year prior, were extradited to the United States, convicted of first-degree murder, and sentenced to life. In 2015 Rosario Burboa Alvarez, who helped plan the crime but was not at the scene, also pled guilty to first-degree murder and was sentenced to twenty-seven years. And in October 2017, the last of the four fugitives, Jesús Rosario Favela Astorga, was caught in Mexico. He was extradited to Arizona to stand trial in 2020.

In August 2018 suspected gunman Heraclio Osorio Arellanes was extradited to the United States with great fanfare. Announcing the event seven and a half years after Brian Terry's death, Attorney General Jeff Sessions said, "To anyone who would take the life of an American citizen, in particular an American law enforcement officer, this action sends a clear message: Working closely with our international partners, we will hunt you down, we will find you, and we will bring you to justice."

A thin man in his thirties with close-cropped hair and beard, Heraclio Osorio Arellanes appeared the next day before U.S. Magistrate Judge Eric Markovich in the Evo DeConcini Federal Courthouse in Tucson. The judge ordered him held without bond. In early 2019, after a five-day trial, Heraclio Osorio Arellanes was convicted of murder and sentenced to life in prison.

Of the 2,000 or so guns sold under Fast and Furious and allowed to enter Mexico, the ATF lost track of more than 1,400. Some 180 had shown up at crime scenes, and at least 150 Mexican civilians had been maimed or killed by them. One such shootout, which took place between the Mexican military and members of the Sinaloa cartel in November 2012, resulted in the deaths of five, including twenty-year-old beauty queen María Susana Flores Gámez.

In 2016 U.S. officials also confirmed that a Fast and Furious–connected .50-caliber Barrett M82 semiautomatic rifle discovered in the hideout of Joaquín "El Chapo" Guzmán had been used, as one source described, "to violently repel a May 29, 2011, assault by Mexican federal police against the drug kingpin's mountain redoubt in Michoacán in which four Mexican federal police Sikorsky Blackhawk helicopters were heavily damaged by .50 cal. gunfire." Investigators determined thirty-four of the approximately two thousand weapons sold under Fast and Furious were Barrett M82 .50-caliber rifles, including the one found in El Chapo's lair. But the whereabouts of almost all the others remained unknown.

When Fast and Furious was revealed, it also came to light that, due to fear of the investigation being compromised, Mexican authorities had not been notified about the flow of arms to the cartels. They were outraged. The brother of Chihuahua State Prosecutor Patricia González was tortured and killed by members of a drug gang in 2010, and two AK-47s found at the scene of a subsequent shootout with the gang were linked to Fast and Furious. González said she believed William Newell and the other officials who ordered Fast and Furious caused the death of her brother "and surely thousands more victims."

Where the Guns Go

About 6 p.m. on September 26, 2014, about a hundred students from the Rural Normal teachers' college in Ayotzinapa, Guerrero, commandeered some city buses to go to Mexico City. The student teachers were known for their activism and protest and would hijack buses every year to go to the capital to commemorate the Tlatelolco massacre. (An estimated two hundred to three hundred protestors were killed by armed forces in a plaza in the Tlatelolco neighborhood on October 2, 1968, ten days before the Mexico City Olympics.) In the nearby town of Iguala, the buses were stopped by municipal police. There was a skirmish, and six people were killed. Most of the student teachers escaped, but forty-three were rounded up.

This was not the first violent exchange between the student teachers and police. Two from the college were killed by state police during a protest on the highway from Cuernavaca to Acapulco in 2011.

After capturing the students, the Iguala police reportedly turned them over to members of a local drug gang, the Guerreros Unidos. Although the fates of all but two were still unknown as of 2020, the students were said to have been shot, taken to a nearby dump, dismembered, and incinerated, and their ashes thrown into a river near Cocula, Guerrero.

This shocking crime called international attention to the deplorable human rights situation in Mexico and became the biggest scandal of the Peña Nieto presidency. It also called attention to the issue of the legal sale and transfer of weapons, equipment, and training to Mexican police and military forces, after the Iguala police force was found to have been using guns and surveillance systems provided by the U.S. and other foreign governments. According to a 2016 American Friends Service Committee report called *Where the Guns Go*, "Documents from the Mexican defense ministry's arms registry included the weapons possessed by municipal police in Iguala, who carried out the crime. Among the arms listed: 20 assault rifles produced by Colt's Manufacturing, headquartered in Hartford, Connecticut. Colt sold the Mexican government those rifles, which arrived in Guerrero in 2013."

The report went on to say that an Israeli-made video surveillance system called C4, installed across Mexico after 2010 under the U.S.-financed Mérida Initiative, "allowed both local police and the Mexican military in Iguala, Guerrero, to follow the buses of the students from Ayotzinapa on the night that 43 were disappeared."

These guns and security systems were only a small part of a huge, multinational business in legal sales and transfers of weapons and surveillance equipment to the Mexican police and military. Although many countries were involved, and Mexico also had its own weapons industry, U.S.-based manufacturers were the biggest suppliers. *Where the Guns Go* and other investigations found weapons exports from the United States to Mexico grew by more than ten times between 2000 and 2015, mostly after the 2007 signing of the Mérida Initiative, a security cooperation agreement between the United States, Mexico, and Central America. Sales reached almost $122 million between 2015 and 2017, more than twelve times the amount sold in 2002–2004. The money was primarily funneled to U.S. gun manufacturers and other corporations, but funds were also granted to Mexico to directly purchase weapons, aircraft, surveillance systems, and other equipment, to operate and maintain them, and to train and support both military and civilian law enforcement.

Where the Guns Go was researched and written by investigators for the Philadelphia-based American Friends Service Committee, a nonprofit agency that promotes Quaker values of peace and social justice worldwide. The group of seventeen spent two weeks in June 2016 traveling to Mexico City, Cuernavaca, Chiapas, and Guerrero, where they met with military and government officials, activists, human rights workers, migrants, journalists, and families of the dead and disappeared. They went to Iguala to speak with survivors of the teachers' college disappearances.

"Ayotzinapa was the event that uncovered all that was happening in Guerrero," Alejandro Ramos of the Morelos y Pavón Human Rights Center told the delegation. "And the reality is that the Guerrero authorities, the whole state government, and the federal and municipal governments are in collusion with organized crime."

The disappeared students were reportedly planning to disrupt a speech by the wife of the mayor of Iguala, who, along with her husband, was later found to have ordered their arrest. The couple fled and were ultimately caught, along with the police chief, who had also fled. About eighty suspects were arrested in connection with the case, forty-four of whom were police officers. Mexican federal police and military personnel were implicated as well.

A mass grave initially believed to contain the charred bodies of twenty-eight of the students was discovered near Iguala on October 5, 2014. The corpses had been tortured and, it appeared, burned alive. Subsequent reports increased the estimate of the number of bodies found in the grave to thirty-four. A week later, police announced that forensic tests had shown none of the remains corresponded to the missing students. But on the same day, four additional mass graves containing unknown numbers of bodies were discovered.

On November 7, 2014, Mexican attorney general Jesús Murillo Karam held a press conference in which he showed a video of alleged gang members confessing to "an industrial-scale effort" to make the students disappear. The crime involved, according to NBC News, "piling their bodies like cord wood on a pyre that burned for 15 hours and then wading into the ashes to pulverize, bag and dispose of remaining teeth and bones." Murillo Karam also showed a video of "hundreds of charred fragments of bone and teeth that had been dumped in and along the San Juan River in the neighboring town of Cocula."

Although the fragments were degraded by fire and identification would be difficult, Murillo Karam said he would be sending them off to a lab in Austria for DNA testing. The results, however, proved embarrassing: among all the fragments tested, only one student could be identified. (In early 2020 the lab identified the remains of one other, who'd been found not in the dump or the river but in a ravine near Cocula called Butcher's Gulch.) The families were disgusted. Absent ironclad proof, many refused to believe their children were dead. Conspiracy theories abounded. At the same time, more mass graves were turning up.

According to *Where the Guns Go*, some 120 mass graves had been found in Mexico by the end of 2015, including at least sixty in Guerrero. Faced with official indifference or hostility, families of the tens of thousands who'd been disappeared were leading the searches. A man named Juan Carlos Trujillo, four of whose brothers had been disappeared, headed a group called Familias en Búsqueda (Families in Search). He told investigators his group visited churches to tell their stories and seek support. "After passing a collection jar, they would find a slip of paper someone had deposited that described in detail where a grave could be found. Using such outreach, the group located more mass graves than the government itself, in a shorter period," the report said.

Leading these searches could be extremely risky. Miguel Ángel Jiménez Blanco was a human rights activist from Xaltianguis, Guerrero, who'd formed a search group for the forty-three students. He was found shot to death behind the wheel of his taxi on the highway outside Acapulco on the night of August 8, 2015.

The ongoing discovery of mass graves and other crimes connected to the teachers' disappearances led to the resignation of the governor of Guerrero and several other high-ranking officials, including Attorney General Murillo Karam. He quit in disgrace only five months after the students disappeared. His reputation, already tarnished by the lack of DNA proof of the students' remains, became irreparably damaged when his response to repeated questioning at the November 7 press conference, "Ya me cansé" ("I'm tired," or "I've had enough"), went viral worldwide as a rallying cry for protestors outraged by the atrocity and the Mexican government's callous reaction to it.

The Mexican Secretary of National Defense (SEDENA) was in charge of all legal weapon imports, and sold the guns in turn to federal, state and local police, the military, and private security companies. There were no standardized purchases by police agencies, and individuals carried a variety of arsenals. The guns were not tracked, and many went missing. The American Friends Service Committee (AFSC) delegation saw numerous types of weapons for sale in display cases at SEDENA, including guns made in Israel, China, Italy, Slovakia, and the Czech Republic. The inventory highlighted the international nature of the arms trade. Many countries were involved in selling and transferring weapons and equipment, including Canada, Germany, Spain, the Netherlands, and France.

The Control, Command, Communication, Computer and Intelligence system, called the C4I or C4, was made by an Israeli security firm called Elbit Systems. Even after Ayotzinapa, the AFSC report said, officials from the Israeli defense ministry continued to work with police and military in Chiapas and other states to improve their C4 networks. Elbit Systems also made other kinds of surveillance equipment, including towers and drones used to provide border security for both the United States and Mexico. A string of white surveillance towers that stood guard by 2017 on wooded hillsides around Nogales—successors to the SBInet virtual fence—were made by a U.S. subsidiary of Elbit. These towers also started going up on the Tohono O'odham reservation in 2020.

Some countries that sold weapons to Mexico attempted to put restrictions on their use. Between 2006 and 2009, the German company Heckler & Koch sold nearly ten thousand G-36 assault rifles on the stipulation they not be sent to the contested states of Chihuahua, Jalisco, Guerrero, or Chiapas. But after the student teachers went missing, dozens of the German rifles were found in the possession of the Iguala municipal police force. German prosecutors charged six Heckler & Koch employees for their role in the gun sales, and in a remarkable move, German leaders visited Mexico to ask forgiveness from the families of the disappeared students.

It was a nice gesture to be sure, but the use of foreign guns to commit official abuses went on. While the AFSC delegation was in Mexico on June 19, 2016, federal police fired Belgian and Czech assault weapons at a teachers' protest in Nochixtlán, Oaxaca. At least nine were killed.

Although weapons and surveillance systems from Europe and Asia were part of the problem, investigators found the heart of it lay much closer to home. Many of the businesses profiting from legal arm sales to Mexico were based on or near the border, particularly in Arizona and Texas, across from the high-crime northern Mexican states of Sonora and Tamaulipas. One such business, Murphy's Guns and Gunsmithing, stood down the street from where I used to live in central Tucson. According to researchers for Global Exchange's Stop U.S. Arms to Mexico project, at least nine firearms, including assault rifles, recovered at crime scenes in Mexico between 2007 and 2010 were sold by this store.

Another Tucson company, Milkor USA, was located not far from Flowing Wells High School. In partnership with Abrams Manufacturing, Milkor produced grenade multi-launchers for the Mexican army's Special Forces Group (GFE). Global Exchange researchers wrote that "GFE officers based in Nogales ran a unit, 'Los Mecánicos,' that specialized in disappearing people. On the morning of November 14, 2008, the 6th Special Forces Battalion of Nogales entered the home of two brothers in Ciudad Juárez, took them to the military base, tortured and killed them and then 'disappeared' them in the desert. The Inter-American Human Rights Commission later found the Mexican military responsible."

Researchers also found that Scottsdale, Arizona–based Dillon Aero had sold to Mexico 44 mini-guns, which fired 125 rounds per second, at $67,000 apiece, between 2013 and 2016: "An investigation by Mexico's National Human Rights Commission found that Federal Police, who carried out the massacre of 22 persons in Tanhuato, Michoacán, in 2015, killed five of them with Dillon Aero guns mounted on Black Hawk helicopters."

"All of us in Mexico know that this is not a war against drug trafficking, but a war against the society, against our families, and above all against our children," María Herrera, the mother of Juan Carlos Trujillo and his four disappeared brothers, told the delegation. Those who sell arms to Mexico, she said, "should think about the damage and destruction brought by these weapons, and that eventually it will harm them as well, which in fact we are seeing."

Profiteers Big and Small

On May 31, 2018, prosecutors said, a nineteen-year-old U.S. citizen named Francisco Eduardo Santana López was driving down I-19 toward Nogales with 4,200 rounds of ammunition tucked around the engine of his Chevy Cobalt. Santana López, a man named Aaron Jazziel Córdova, and an unidentified woman were planning to smuggle the bullets into Mexico. As the car sped down the highway, loud bangs started coming from under the hood. Santana López pulled over at the Pilot Travel Center in Rio Rico. The three got out and ran away as the ammo continued to detonate and the car was engulfed in flames.

According to the indictment, Santana López and Jazziel Córdova had entered the United States by car through Nogales that morning and had driven to an ammo dealer in Phoenix. There they spent $2,300 on 200 rounds of .50-caliber, 2,000 rounds of 7.62x51-mm-caliber, and 2,000 rounds of 7.62x39-mm-caliber ammunition. Santana López also had several weapons and pieces of firearms equipment he intended to smuggle into Mexico. These included four M203 grenade barrels, which can be attached to a rifle to launch grenades, a parts kit and tripod assembly for a machine gun, and a Barrett .50-caliber rifle.

Santana López was caught two weeks after the incident, when he tried to enter the U.S. through the Deconcini Port of Entry. During his interrogation, he was asked where he had gotten the ammo. He said he'd bought it at a bulk ammunition store in Phoenix where they knew him well. He claimed he'd shopped there many times before. How many times? "Not more than fifty."

As you drive toward the border at Nogales, the signs are big, bilingual, and unmistakable: *Armas Prohibidas en Mexico.* Guns Prohibited in Mexico. The penalties for importing arms and ammunition without a license are supposedly severe. But as the Santana López and many other cases made clear, it was fairly easy for small-time operators to obtain large amounts of weapons and ammunition in the U.S. and smuggle them into Mexico. The ATF estimated 120,000 weapons were smuggled across the border between 2007 and 2015. It was a "river of iron," and U.S. authorities did almost nothing to stop it. Since there were no federal laws against gun trafficking, those arrested were charged with crimes like making false statements on government forms or exporting goods without a license. The *Arizona Daily Star* found that, in 2018, only thirty-two cases of gun smuggling to Mexico were filed in federal court in Tucson and Phoenix. This was in contrast to 750 cases of drug smuggling and thousands of cases of undocumented border crossings.

Some of the most notorious gun smugglers were current or former law-enforcement officers. One was former Tucson cop Joe Valles. He and a partner, a federally licensed firearms dealer named Timothy Veninga, ran a business called Ballistic Firearms out of a house on the northwest side. They were convicted of paying people, including family members, to act as straw purchasers for guns being trafficked into Mexico. Among the weapons purchased were 24 semiautomatic pistols and 7 rifles, including 1 semiautomatic assault rifle, 1 semiautomatic high-capacity rifle and 2 .50-caliber semiautomatic rifles. "Every family member had a .50 cal," including Valles's brother, sister, and sister's boyfriend, an investigator said.

A .50-caliber rifle connected to Valles was seized at an airstrip in Culiacán in September 2016. According to *Ríodoce* magazine, the Mexican military had learned about a scheduled drug delivery from a man arrested with weapons earlier that day in Mexicali. As they approached the airstrip, the Cessna pilot tried to take off, but a military truck driver crashed his vehicle into the plane's wing and disabled it. In addition to the Barrett, four AK-47s were seized.

Although the serial number was obscured on the Barrett, agents were able to trace it to a Tucson man who supposedly had bought it from Ballistic Firearms. The man turned out to be someone Valles had arrested in late 2014, not long before he resigned from the Tucson Police Department. The man was indigent and told agents he supported himself by selling his plasma. He scoffed at the idea he could afford an eight-thousand-dollar rifle. Another straw buyer, whose name appeared on more than two dozen sales records, was a mentally incompetent man who'd also been arrested by Valles. He lived with his mother and was only allowed to carry bus fare.

Valles and Veninga were each sentenced to six and a half years in prison.

In another case, in July 2016, a supervisory special agent for the Drug Enforcement Administration (DEA) named Joseph Gill was caught selling a Colt M4LE .556-caliber semiautomatic rifle to a suspected drug dealer. The rifle was smuggled into Mexico. Gill then sold a second rifle, similar to the first, to another trafficker. That gun was seized from a Mexico-bound shuttle van at the Nogales port of entry. ATF agents searched Gill's Tucson home and found thirty-five weapons and equipment including silencers. They also found records of firearms purchases and sales going back to 1998. He'd made 645 transactions, mostly buying guns online and reselling them to private buyers. He'd bought the Colt rifles for about $630 and sold them for about $1,000 each. He resigned from the DEA in June 2018 and pled guilty.

At his sentencing the following January, Gill said his gun-selling was a "hobby that I took to an extreme." U.S. District Court Judge Raner Collins responded that, although "torn," he was going to give Gill "the benefit of the doubt." The judge could have sentenced the ex-agent up to two years in prison but instead let him off with five years' probation, a fifteen-thousand-dollar fine, and five hundred hours of community service.

These cases highlight not only the ease with which guns and ammo could be obtained and smuggled but the slap-on-the-wrist nature of the penalties. In one case, the suspected leader of what prosecutors said was "one of the largest" gun smuggling rings in southern Arizona was sentenced to five years in prison in February 2018. It was the maximum allowed by law, despite the judge's protest that the sentence wasn't "sufficient for the conduct here." Sentences for the more than twenty others involved in the scheme ranged from probation to five years.

Another man, Richard Orozco, received five years in 2017 for recruiting his common-law wife and three others to buy a dozen firearms at gun stores in Tucson and Phoenix. His lawyer said the sentence was too harsh because there was no proof he knew he was buying guns for cartels, and his motives were "not at all or not entirely reprehensible" because he was a family man. One of Orozco's recruits got three years' probation. Two others had their charges dropped.

Piles of money from drug sales were also smuggled across the border into Mexico. Between 2005 and 2016, CBP seized about $211 million in illicit southbound cash. That amount was of course a small fraction of what was successfully smuggled, and an even smaller fraction of what big banks were laundering for cartels. In 2008 Wachovia Bank was found to have legitimized more than $378 billion in drug money—an amount equivalent to one-third of Mexico's Gross National Product—by, among other means, "failing to apply the proper anti-laundering strictures" to currency exchanges with Mexico between 2004 and 2007.

A two-year investigation by the DEA, IRS, and the U.S. Attorney's Office in south Florida found that a DC-9 jet belonging to the Sinaloa cartel, seized in April 2006 at an airstrip in the port city of Ciudad del Carmen, Campeche, had been bought with money laundered through Wachovia. The jet was loaded with 5.7 tons of cocaine, valued at $100 million, part of a total of 22 tons of coke found to have been transported using Wachovia-laundered drug profits.

Thorough *casas de cambio* (currency exchanges), investigators wrote, "persons in Mexico can use hard currency and . . . wire transfer the value of that currency to U.S. bank accounts to purchase items in the United States or other countries." The investigation also found that legitimizing cartel money was the only thing that kept Wachovia afloat during the 2008 financial crisis. Wells Fargo acquired Wachovia later that year for about $15 billion.

Wells Fargo settled the case against Wachovia for about $160 million in fines and forfeitures in 2010, a year in which it made $12 billion in profit. Officials at the bank and the *casas de cambio* promised not to do it again, and more oversight was put in place. However, no individuals were named, and no indictments were issued.

Government and independent investigations found many other cases of money laundering among big banks. In 2012 the *Wall Street Journal* reported on an FBI investigation that laid out how the Zetas cartel had used Bank of America to launder cash through a Texas horserace business. In 2015 Citigroup was fined $140 million for failing to monitor probable money laundering. It paid another $97 million in 2017 to settle similar charges against its Banamex subsidiary, which was subsequently closed.

The investigations and crackdowns caused many big banks to close branches and accounts in border cities to avoid the risk of being fined. Prior to this, several major banks, including Wells Fargo, Chase, and Bank of America, operated branches in Nogales, Arizona, with a population of about twenty thousand. They did a thriving business with clients from Nogales, Sonora, with some three hundred thousand residents, and other parts of northern Mexico. But that stopped after the U.S. government cracked down on cross-border money transfers. In 2014 Western Union agreed to increase oversight of money transfers on the border, and Mexican currency houses agreed to limit the size of dollar transactions. Nogales soon lost three of its nine bank branches and San Ysidro, California, lost five of twelve.

In a case of unintended consequences, the banking crackdown was hard on legitimate border businesses, especially the Nogales produce industry, which relied on quick, large cash transfers to buy and sell loads of perishable fruits and vegetables. Banks were found to be "de-risking" and harming border economies by refusing to serve customers there. But despite the closures, a February 2018 GAO report found that border banks were still more likely than banks in other regions to report large cash transactions and other suspicious activity.

While things were supposedly being improved, the money laundering seemed impossible to stop. Even people accustomed to the cartels' impunity were surprised at how openly it occurred. A National Public Radio report in 2014 described the results of another massive, years-long investigation into the financial dealings of the Sinaloa cartel, then estimated to be making between $19 and $29 billion annually in U.S. drug profits. ICE investigators found that in 2007 and 2008, the Sinaloa cartel and a Colombian cartel wired some $881 million into U.S. accounts of the British banking giant HSBC. HSBC was fined $1.9 billion in 2012. The NPR report said: "According to a subsequent investigation by the U.S. Senate Permanent Subcommittee on Investigations, . . . cartel operatives would sometimes deposit hundreds of thousands of dollars in cash in a single day using boxes designed to fit the exact dimensions of the teller's window at HSBC branches in Mexico."

NPR then quoted a local reporter: "'You see the building, the office, the cars, the papers, the men in suits. Everything looks legal. That's what frightens us,' says Javier Valdez, an author and journalist in Culiacán who writes about narcotrafficking."

II
Slavery

Four

All They Will Call You

U.S. marshals led the detainees into the courtroom in groups of seven. They were almost all young, male, dark skinned, and small, some five feet tall or shorter. A few had their hands clasped behind their backs and held them like that for so long I thought they were shackled, but they weren't. The marshals lined them up in a row across the front of the courtroom facing the judge, each with a lawyer standing behind and microphone in front. They wore their own clothes, mostly dark T-shirts, jeans, and sneakers, but appeared presentable, as if they may have had a chance to wash up and comb their hair before their appearance. They looked a little like contestants at an audition, except the microphone stands towered over them, and they were generally sorrowful in demeanor.

It was late May 2018, and I was attending an Operation Streamline hearing in the Evo A. DeConcini Federal Courthouse in downtown Tucson. Operation Streamline was a fast-track sentencing procedure designed to give all undocumented border crossers criminal records, so they could be more easily excluded in the future. Prior to its inception in 2005, undocumented entry was generally considered a civil violation. Most border crossers were "caught and released," or voluntarily deported without penalty, often the same day they were detained. But under Streamline, criminal prosecution of migrants caught at the border skyrocketed. These cases soon made up more than half of the federal docket, straining resources and overwhelming the court system.

While many politicians supported Streamline, the judges who administered the program were less enthusiastic, and doubts remained as to its effectiveness. A 2015 report by the Department of Homeland Security's Office of Inspector General found that neither Streamline's cost nor its deterrent effect could be accurately measured, and that it may violate international law by subjecting refugees to prosecution.

Streamline was just one aspect of an immigrant detention and deportation system built by the Bush and Obama administrations and put in overdrive by Trump. The first essay in this chapter describes two Streamline hearings I attended during and after the family separation crisis of 2018. The second essay looks at Southwest Key, a company that ran shelters for unaccompanied minors, and the migrant detention business overall. The third describes visits to two Nogales, Sonora, shelters that cared for deportees and asylum seekers.

Operation Streamline

The huge, light wood and fabric paneled courtroom was quiet and nearly empty, with bright but soft, recessed lighting in the high ceilings. The judge sat behind a high bench, faced by the detainees and their lawyers. The marshals and some others sat to the sides, and fewer than a dozen people sat in the spectator section. The detainees were given headphones so they could hear the translator, who sat in the witness box and whispered in Spanish into a small handheld microphone as U.S. Magistrate Judge Eric Markovich spoke in English.

Going from right to left, the judge read the detainees' names and had them raise their hands to make sure they were lined up correctly. The first group of seven included one woman, so the judge began, "Good afternoon ladies and gentlemen. You have been accused of a misdemeanor, that is, entering the United States illegally. The maximum sentence for that crime is six months in jail. If you plead guilty, you will be deported, and this conviction could result in a harsher sentence if you return to the United States and commit another crime."

Judge Markovich went on to enumerate the detainees' rights, including the right to talk to the consulate of their country of origin, and the right to remain silent, but they would have to give up that right if they pled guilty. He told them they had the right to a lawyer—you spoke to your lawyer this morning, he noted—and a trial, and to call witnesses, and to testify or not. But the government could also call witnesses, and all it had to prove was that they were not citizens of the United States, and that they had entered the country illegally.

He then spoke to them individually. Each question and answer was repeated by the translator. After addressing the first man by name, the judge said: "Are you thinking clearly today and are you pleading guilty of your own free will?"

"Sí," the man said.

"Yes," the translator said.

"Did anyone promise you anything or force you to plead guilty?"

"No."

"No."

"Do you understand the charges and the maximum penalty?"

"Sí."

"Yes."

"Do you understand your trial rights and are you willing to give up those rights to plead guilty?"

"Sí."

"Yes."

"Is it true that you are not a citizen of the United States and you entered unlawfully on May 29th near Lukeville, Arizona?"

"Sí."

"Yes."

"Do you plead guilty or not guilty?"

"Culpable."

"Guilty."

"You are sentenced to time served and will be turned over to immigration authorities for deportation."

Each group of sentencing took ten to fifteen minutes. Then there was a pause and the next group was led in. In the third group, one of the men was clearly more agitated than the rest. During his sentencing, he kept saying "Sí, culpable," when he was only supposed to be saying "Sí." He was older, perhaps in his thirties or even forties, and wore a white and orange striped rugby shirt, while most of the migrants were in their teens and twenties and wore dark clothes.

"Is it true that you are not a citizen of the United States and you entered unlawfully on May 24th [six days before] near Sasabe, Arizona?"

"Sí, culpable."

"Yes, guilty."

I was wondering if the man might have some mental problem until, after sentencing him to time served, the judge said: "I understand you were separated from your child. I will order that you be reunited."

"Una pregunta," the man said.

"One question."

"Yes?"

The man spoke in Spanish and the translator said: "The minor I came with, is he going to go over there too?"

"Yes, you'll be removed with your child."

The man spoke again so quietly I could barely hear him.

"My son wanted to come here to be with his uncle," the translator said. "His uncle is ready to receive him."

"If your son wanted to come to the United States to be with his uncle, he'll have to take that up with the immigration authorities where he is. I have no authority over that. I will order that you be reunited with him."

I later learned the agitated man was named Armando Ramírez Vásquez, and he was Guatemalan. His son was among more than 2,300 children taken during the ten weeks in 2018 when the Trump administration's stepped-up "zero-tolerance" policy on illegal immigration resulted in family separations and the parents' prosecution under Operation Streamline. Like Markovich, many of the federal judges overseeing these hearings repeatedly ordered immigration authorities to reunite the separated parents and children. But they had no authority to enforce their own orders.

Judge Markovich went on to the next person and finished the sentencing—all pled guilty, all received time served and all would be deported. He then asked the lawyers if anyone wanted to make a record. Of the twenty-one cases I witnessed, only one did, a woman in the same group as Ramírez Vásquez. Her lawyer said she was from Honduras and did have a credible fear of returning to her country, even though she had apparently signed a form saying she did not. She did not want to apply for asylum, the lawyer said. She just wanted a note made that she did have fear.

"Thank you ladies and gentlemen, good luck to you, safe travels," the judge said. "I hope you get home safely," he said to another group. The detainees were led out, Ramírez Vásquez in intense conversation with his lawyer. After a few minutes, more were led in.

By late September 2018, when I attended a Streamline hearing in the same courtroom but with a different judge, things had changed. This time, there were no separated parents, and there were more detainees. More than seventy people were sent in groups of ten or more. The judge spent less time with each one. Rather than individually asking the questions, the judge went down the line, addressing each person by name and then saying, "same question." She also used the generic "southern Arizona" as to where the migrants had tried to enter, rather than a specific place. The detainees looked scruffier and dirtier than the group I saw in May. They also were shackled. Their legs were bound by a chain long enough so they could walk, and their hands were cuffed to another chain that wrapped around their waists. One young man was in a wheelchair. He was handcuffed, but his stockinged feet were unchained.

There were more women—maybe one in ten instead of one in twenty—and more had Indigenous names, like Suk or Xhu. Although their countries of origin were not stated, the vast majority were evidently Guatemalan or Honduran. A few said they wanted to make claims of asylum when the judge asked if they or their attorneys wanted to make a record. They seemed to be asking to go back and make claims, after not being allowed to or being pressured not to. The judge said they would be remanded to the Department of Corrections while they made their claims.

Like those I saw in May, most of the migrants I saw sentenced under Streamline in September were first-time crossers from distant lands who'd been caught out in the desert. But this time, the docket also included a few locals from Nogales, Sonora—like a brother-and-sister pair who asked to be processed together—caught while riding the freight train across the border or trying to use fake documents at the port. There also were several groups of repeat crossers who'd been charged with felonies. They were convicted of misdemeanors and given prison sentences ranging from 30 to 160 days, depending on how many times they'd been caught before. The man in the wheelchair got 30 days, meaning this was probably his second offense.

Part of the post-9/11 crackdown on illegal immigration, Operation Streamline began in Del Rio, Texas, in December 2005 and expanded to other border patrol sectors, including Tucson, in 2008. Some three hundred thousand migrants were prosecuted during its first ten years. Those subject to prosecution under Streamline varied over time and in different sectors along the border, with the Del Rio Sector being known as one of the harshest. It served as model for Trump's first zero-tolerance policy against border crossers that took effect shortly after his inauguration. Family separations were evidently occurring in the Del Rio Sector long before they went border-wide in the spring of 2018.

In Tucson, Operation Streamline had come under scrutiny for removals of people without counsel. At first, only two out of a hundred migrants had a lawyer. Seventy or more shackled detainees received sentences at once. Lawyers and immigrant rights advocates sued to stop these practices, saying en-masse pleadings violated due process. After some legal wrangling, the Ninth Circuit Court of Appeals ruled that Streamline was constitutional but ordered modifications. Detainees were sentenced in smaller groups, and each had a lawyer and spoke individually to the judge, however briefly. Migrants also were supposed to be unshackled during their court appearance, as I witnessed in May 2018, if possible. But the ultimate decision on shackling was left up to the marshals, and by September, as the numbers of detainees seen at one time had grown, the chains were back on.

Another big difference between the May and September hearings was the size of the audience. In May the family separation crisis was just starting to hit the news, and the spectator section was almost empty. By September the benches were full of activists, journalists, and students. The marshals kept everyone to one side, away from the door where the detainees were led in and out. Anti-Streamline protestors also began to assemble more frequently in front of the courthouse.

The DeConcini courthouse had been the site of a couple previous high-profile protests against Operation Streamline. The biggest was on October 11, 2013, when about twenty activists had used plastic piping to tie themselves together and then blocked two buses carrying sixty-one detainees from entering the courthouse parking lot. Several protestors also crawled under the wheels of the buses and were dragged away by police. Operation Streamline was canceled for the day.

In 2015, after a two-day hearing, Pima County Justice Court Judge Susan Bacal convicted twelve of these anti-Streamline protestors of obstructing a highway and creating a public nuisance, both misdemeanors. But she acquitted them of numerous other charges and sentenced them all to time served. Several others who had blocked the courthouse parking lot were found guilty of disorderly conduct on federal property and failure to follow the direction of a federal police officer. They also were given time served. During their sentencing hearings, the protestors were unapologetic and spoke passionately about the suffering of the undocumented.

Before April 2018, in the Tucson Sector at least, Streamline was only applied to single adults. Unaccompanied minors (under eighteen) were supposed to be held in border patrol custody for no more than seventy-two hours, after which they were transferred to the care of the Office of Refugee Resettlement, which usually placed them in a shelter operated by a private contractor called Southwest Key. Families with kids under twelve detained at the border were generally allowed to stay together, as long as the adults were proven to be related to the kids and not criminals. After a few days in border patrol custody, if they were deemed excludable, they would be deported promptly or sent to a family detention center to await deportation.

If they were deemed to potentially qualify for asylum and had someone to sponsor them, they were released with a court date and an ankle monitor. People from a Catholic social service agency called Casa Alitas (Little Wings House) would show up to help them on their journey. In 2017, one volunteer told me, Casa Alitas helped about forty to sixty refugees a day who were released by ICE at the Greyhound station. The most had been one hundred in a day around Christmas.

Allowing migrant families to be cared for in this way—a policy Trump called "catch and release"—was far cheaper and more humane than family separation, but it wasn't having the desired deterrent effect. So in mid-April 2018, the zero-tolerance policy of criminal prosecution for undocumented entry as practiced in the Del Rio Sector was instituted border-wide. During the following ten weeks, children as young as one were taken and sent to a detention center for unaccompanied minors, while their parents were placed in Operation Streamline proceedings.

Kids in Detention

In early June 2018 social worker Antar Davidson was ordered to tell three Brazilian siblings taken from their mother the day before that they weren't allowed to hug.

"They were sixteen, ten, and eight," said Davidson, at the time the only Portuguese-speaking employee at the Southwest Key facility in Tucson. (Davidson, who is of Afro-Brazilian Jewish descent, also spoke Spanish and Hebrew.) "They thought their mom was disappeared. There was no bed for them, and they hadn't slept in eighteen hours. They were going to separate them from each other, and all three grabbed onto each other and were crying, 'Don't separate us.' The shift leader told me, 'You need to translate to the kids there is a no-touch policy. They can't hug.' I said. 'I can't do that.' She went to the kids and tried to tell them herself."

Davidson had been working at Southwest Key about four months when youngsters separated from their parents at the border began arriving. Even if it were possible for children to be treated humanely under such circumstances, he said neither the facility nor the staff was prepared to do so. The 283-bed shelter, called the Casa Estrella del Norte (North Star House), quickly became overcrowded and the staff overwhelmed. Most of the kids already in the shelter were teens eighteen and under who'd come to the border alone, but the seventy or so new arrivals were "tender age"—under twelve—and frequently terrified and inconsolable. Davidson said the children were not given adequate food, bedding, medical care, education, psychological support, or legal help. They were not allowed to communicate with their parents nor told when or if they would be reunited with them.

After refusing to carry out his boss's order, Davidson knew he would be fired. So he quit a few days later and took his story public. Interviewed by the *Los Angeles Times*, BBC, and more than a dozen other media outlets worldwide—he said he felt "like a national hero" in Brazil—Davidson helped spark a widespread movement of condemnation and protest that forced Trump to end the family separation policy on June 20, some ten weeks after it began.

The policy ended, but the media was onto the story, and the fate of the nearly three thousand separated children continued to dominate the news. A federal judge ordered them to be reunited with their parents by the end of July, but as that deadline came and went, more than five hundred remained in limbo and faced long-term, if not permanent, separation from their parents. The government said it could not reunite all of them because the parent had already been deported or failed a background check or other reasons. Reporters went to the border and took pictures of agents arresting families who'd just crossed, as well as children huddled under foil-like space blankets behind chain-link fences—kids in cages. While these things had been going on for years, headlines like "Border Crisis Families Torn Apart" on the cover of *People* magazine helped bring the treatment of migrants in detention to an unprecedented level of national attention.

In late June, First Lady Melania Trump came to Tucson to check on the condition of the separated children. Protestors waited for her in front of the Estrella del Norte shelter with signs reading, "I Really Do Care Don't U?," a reference to the words "I Really Don't Care Do U?" emblazoned on the back of a jacket she'd worn on her way to visit a child migrant shelter in McAllen, Texas, the previous week. (My daughter Lee, then twelve, said she liked Melania's jacket.) But Mrs. Trump never showed at Southwest Key. During her brief stay in Tucson, she visited a border patrol station that was also a temporary holding facility for undocumented parents and children. She met with officials and a local rancher. As she was touring the area where migrants were held, a child about three came out of a side room. "Hello!" she said brightly. "How are you?" The boy looked at her for a moment, then darted back into the room.

Opened by Obama to house an influx of Central American teenage migrants, the Estrella del Norte shelter had been operating unobtrusively in midtown Tucson since 2014. The building was a refurbished, two-story apartment complex that had formerly housed college students, shaped in an open square around a palm-tree-lined central courtyard. It was run by the Texas-based nonprofit Southwest Key, which began as a youth sentencing alternative program in the late 1980s before getting into child migrant shelters a decade later, after a court case called the Flores decision forced the government to open separate detention centers. (Authorities had in some places been jailing female migrant kids with adult male criminals.) By 2018, with more than thirty thousand in its care, unaccompanied minors had become the vast majority of Southwest Key's business. That year, the agency operated a network of a hundred shelters in fourteen states, with an annual budget of $458 million. Its founder and CEO, Juan Sanchez, made almost $1.5 million, prompting Latinx activists to charge he was profiting from morally bankrupt immigration policies. A petition was circulated against him, and he resigned in early 2019. Later that year, as revelations of abuses mounted, activists undertook another petition campaign, this time calling for Southwest Key to be put out of business.

Reporters are generally not allowed in Southwest Key shelters, but I was able to get inside Casa Estrella del Norte in late 2015, when Lee's elementary school mariachi orchestra was invited to play for the detainees.

Accompanied by Lee, then nine, who was wearing a black *traje* (suit) and sombrero and carrying her little violin, I entered a cavernous lobby furnished with a few overstuffed couches. A uniformed woman behind the front desk checked all our IDs, and then the parents waited in the lobby while our children, each wearing a name tag, performed in the cafeteria for a quietly seated group of about fifty, mostly teenage boys and staff. We were not allowed to have any interaction with the detainees, though we could stand at the cafeteria door and watch the twenty-minute show. The kids played and sang Mexican songs—"Víva Chihuahua," "De Colores," "Mariachi Loco"—that the audience seemed to enjoy but not really recognize. The place appeared orderly and well run and the staff friendly.

Around this time, in October 2015, Tucson police reported two teens had run away from Casa Estrella del Norte, and concerns arose over what was going on inside. City Councilman Steve Kozachik, who insisted on being accompanied by a reporter, was given a tour. The article in the *Star* described the place in physical detail: A swimming pool in the center courtyard had been covered by a soccer field. A ballroom had been converted into a gym and classrooms. The walls of the classrooms displayed maps of the children's home countries, drawings of flags, and national birds. The coffee shop had been converted to a game room with pool and foosball tables. At the entrance to cafeteria, a schedule board was filled with events like movie nights, church services, and dances. But no interviews with the kids were allowed.

Had they been, a different picture may have emerged. After the family separation policy went into effect, scrutiny by investigative journalists, government agencies, and others uncovered numerous reports of wrongdoing, including sexual, physical, and verbal abuse, forced drugging, and restraints, at Southwest Key facilities. A staffer at Casa Estrella del Norte was convicted of sexual abuse after touching a fifteen-year-old boy's genital area and pulling down his pants in 2015. An HIV-positive staffer at a shelter in Mesa, Arizona, was convicted in 2018 of abusing at least eight boys over an eleven-month period. A third worker at a Phoenix shelter was arrested and charged with molesting a fourteen-year-old girl the same year.

The Arizona Department of Health Services investigated Southwest Key and found numerous instances of employees not being given adequate background checks. In September 2018 the state threatened to revoke the agency's license to operate unless complete checks and other requirements were met. While they were negotiating, video emerged of another staff member dragging a child at a Southwest Key shelter in Youngtown, Arizona. The incident led to the closure of the facility and the relocation of its residents to other Southwest Key shelters.

Abuses at Southwest Key were part of a larger pattern of problems at privately run, for-profit immigration jails whose businesses boomed after 9/11. The two largest private prison companies, CoreCivic (previously Corrections Corporation of America) and GEO Group, received a combined $985 million from ICE to detain immigrants in 2015, up from $307 million in 2008. In addition to managing federal, state and local facilities used by ICE, these two companies also made money and avoided taxes by building and managing their own facilities. They each ran massive family detention centers in south

Texas, "nicknamed baby jails even before the current crisis," as *In These Times* reported in October 2018.

"Under private contractors," *In These Times* found, "allegations of inedible food, verbal and physical abuse, inadequate medical attention, children covered in lice, and forced ingestion of psychotropic drugs are commonplace." Sexual assaults also occurred. More than 1,200 allegations of sexual assault were filed between 2010 and 2017 in U.S. adult and child immigration prisons, the article said.

The vast majority of reported abuses were at private prisons, since they housed 85 percent of detained immigrants. But abuses, including "icebox" temperatures, were also found at border patrol facilities that held migrants temporarily. In 2017, after lawsuits over the treatment of unaccompanied minors detained by the border patrol, a federal court ordered the agency to provide mats and blankets to children held more than twelve hours. The lawsuits went on, however, as more evidence surfaced of inadequate care and abusive treatment.

In June 2019 a video went viral of a government lawyer arguing before incredulous judges that the border patrol was not required to provide soap or toothbrushes to children in custody. The lawyer said this was because, under the Flores settlement, minors were usually held fewer than seventy-two hours before being transferred. Some border residents responded by leaving bags of the items outside migrant holding facilities with notes saying, "Heard you needed these." The donations were not accepted. Former hostages also came forward to denounce the policy. One man who'd been held by the Taliban said even they had given him soap and a toothbrush. (The judges later ordered the border patrol to provide the items to detained children.)

That same month, more evidence came to light about deplorable conditions for migrants in detention. Investigators determined border patrol and ICE were keeping children and adults in crowded cells for days, with inadequate food, water, bedding, or sanitation. Kids as young as eight were taking care of babies and toddlers by themselves. Dozens were sick with the flu and other ailments. At least seven children and twenty-six adults had died in custody or shortly after release since December. The American Civil Liberties Union (ACLU) found more than nine hundred children had been separated from their parents in the year since the practice was ordered stopped. Twenty percent were under age five. Psychologists interviewed the separated children and said irreparable harm was being done.

In 2020 more shocking allegations surfaced when a doctor at an ICE facility in Georgia was accused of performing unnecessary hysterectomies and other gynecological surgeries on unsuspecting detainees. Preliminary investigations confirmed at least two cases, and the Mexican Foreign Ministry announced it might file a class-action lawsuit.

Besides Melania Trump, several Democratic politicians made site visits to child and family detention facilities during and after the family separation crisis. Southern Arizona congressman Raúl Grijalva visited Casa Estrella del Norte in Tucson and emerged saying, "It's clean, but it's still a place where kids can't leave." Oregon Senator Jeff Merkley visited a border patrol processing facility in south Texas where scenes of fenced-in children, he said, became "seared in my mind." He said kids were being held in "dog-kennel style" pens. The visits led these and other progressive politicians across the country to introduce legislation requiring more local, state and federal oversight of Southwest Key and other private companies, as well as border patrol and ICE detention facilities.

But migrant detention was big business, and many politicians, particularly Republicans, vigorously defended it. In addition to the private prison companies themselves, *In These Times* reported some of the country's biggest banks, technology, communication, transportation, food service, medical, consulting, and other companies were profiting from the criminalization of migrants. Monitoring and oversight functions were farmed out to subcontractors as well, shielding the industry from public scrutiny. Even educational institutions were getting a piece of the pie, as they helped design IT and other parts of the detection, detention, and deportation system.

As awareness of corporate and academic involvement in migrant detention grew, protests occurred. In July 2018 hundreds marched in Boston to protest a $7.8 million ICE tech contract held by Northeastern University. Twelve were arrested for lying down in front of the university president's house. Amazon, Microsoft, Deloitte, Salesforce, and others faced protests by their own employees. While these companies continued to work with ICE, the consulting firm McKinsey canceled its contract with ICE in 2018, partly in response to employee concerns over the family separation policy.

In June 2019 protestors again took to the streets of Boston, when employees at Wayfair staged a walkout over the furniture company's refusal to cancel a contract to sell detention beds to ICE. The action sparked a lot of discussion, and Wayfair donated $100,000 to the Red Cross. But the contract remained in force.

Under public pressure, airlines and hotels also took stands against ICE. In 2018 American and United Airlines announced they would not fly migrant children separated from their parents. The following year, after Trump proposed that migrants arrested in sweeps be held in hotels, Marriott, Hilton, Choice Hotels, Best Western, Hyatt, Wyndham, MGM Resorts, and others issued a statement saying their properties would not be used to house detainees. At the same time, Motel 6 suffered a public relations disaster when numerous locations were found to have been sharing Latinx guests' private information with ICE—some 80,000 people between 2015 and 2017. The chain apologized and ended up paying nearly $20 million to settle class-action lawsuits against motels in both Phoenix and Washington state.

The issue of ICE using hotels to hold children came up again during the pandemic. Trump enacted an emergency public health order requiring immediate expulsion of all migrants, regardless of circumstances, and ICE was found to be housing families and unaccompanied minors in hotels, sometimes for weeks, before deporting them. Activists decried the secrecy, lack of due process, and potential health and safety threats. The practice continued in the spring of 2021, when CBP used hotels, among other places, to detain the many asylum-seeking families then arriving on the border.

But there were signs the tide was turning. In the summer of 2019, Illinois became the first state in the nation to pass a law preventing local governments from contracting with private prison companies to detain immigrants. The law was intended to prevent a 1,300-bed facility from being built outside Chicago. Democratic governor J. B. Pritzker called the move "a firewall against Donald Trump's attacks." California enacted a similar ban in October, and other states were expected to follow suit.

Deportees

One place on the border that received asylum seekers and deported migrants was the Jesuit-run Kino Border Initiative (KBI), informally known as the *comedor* (dining room), in Nogales, Sonora. The simple, whitewashed concrete-block building sat alongside the line of cars waiting to enter the United States at the Mariposa Port of Entry, the commercial truck crossing west of downtown and the place where deportees were released. Most weekday mornings, several dozen of them descended from big, white buses, walked a short distance down an open-air, metal-mesh-topped concrete corridor, and passed through a revolving gate into Mexico.

On a sunny but chilly morning in March 2018, I visited the comedor with three No More Deaths volunteers from Tucson. All were in their late sixties and early seventies, with long histories of social activism. Rick was a retired software engineer; Dorothy was a nurse; Lynda had been a teacher. In addition to volunteering at the comedor, they went out in the desert with the Samaritans, and Rick, who had lived in Chile as a child, helped translate for migrants in detention.

Migrants gather in front of the Kino Border Initiative comedor. (April Wong)

Above a low, bright white wall and up a short flight of stairs was a small square room where people were already seated at four long tables. On that day, three of the tables were filled with men and one with women and children. (Later in the year, the tables would be filled mostly with Central American women and children.) The migrants were waiting for breakfast, which was being prepared by more than a dozen staff and volunteers, mostly Mexican nuns and church workers, plus some Catholic high school students from Tucson on a spring-break service project.

Opposite the windows facing the street, a large mural of the Last Supper was painted on the cinderblock wall. Male and female migrants joined Jesus at the table. Men's and women's toilets, just single stalls with handwashing sinks, and a storage closet had been built against the wall. There was a tiny kitchen to one side, and a giant tank of drinking water stood in one corner near the stairs down to the street. The room was clean, neat, and quiet, especially considering it was full of people, maybe seventy-five in all.

On the refrigerator was a picture of a seventeen-year-old Guatemalan boy who'd disappeared near Altar, Sonora, the previous June, and a plea for information in finding him.

The migrants were warmly dressed in dark clothes, some with baseball caps (one man wore a new Red Sox one, with a B on it), with their backpacks and belongings at their sides. They were mostly young and dark skinned. The few young children stayed close to their mothers and were well behaved.

Sister María Engracia Robles, who oversaw the comedor, spoke into a cordless microphone to welcome everyone and ask how many were there for the first time. Only a few raised their hands. Most, presumably, had been deported or had come through on their way north before.

While they waited for breakfast, the migrants played a game. Sister María distributed laminated Mexican *lotería* cards depicting various people, places, food and objects related to the migrants' journey and the comedor. Pictures included the desert, tortillas, and the special *ponche* (punch) Sister María made at Christmas from a secret recipe.

Sister María handed me the first key card. It was a picture of Donald Trump, with the caption El Diablo ("The Devil"). She asked me to hold it up and read it. (All the following conversation took place in Spanish.)

"El Diablo," I said loudly, holding up the card. There were a few low chuckles and hisses, but not many. Donald Trump was not funny to them.

"Who has El Diablo on their card?" Sister María asked.

A couple people raised their hands.

"How does he relate to the migrants' journey?"

Sister María took the mic over to a young man who'd raised his hand.

"He wants to keep us from crossing over to the United States."

Taking turns, Sister María asked for another volunteer to read the second key card. It was a picture of beaded earrings: Los Aretes.

"How do these relate to the migrants' journey?"

A woman raised her hand.

"They are a way you can identify people."

"Maybe where they are from," said someone else.

"Yes," said Sister María. "Also because the women in the shelter make them to sell." KBI had a small women and children's shelter but at that time no men's shelter. Male migrants could stay for three days at another place across town, Casa San Juan Bosco.

Next was La Guitarra—the guitar.

"What does this have to do with the migrants' journey?"

"To sing and play songs to accompany you."

"Yes, and also because Father Sam plays the guitar and sings when he says Mass. Didn't anyone go to Mass?" chided Sister María.

The next card depicted El Migrante—the migrant.

"Who wants to say something about the migrant?"

One man raised his hand. Sister María handed him the mic.

"The migrant must suffer to make a better future for his family," he said quietly.

After the game, the windows were shaded and a screen pulled down, and a video from the Mexican Commission on Human Rights was shown. It was upbeat and reassuring, and exhorted migrants to stand up for their many rights and feel free to file complaints. The migrants watched politely.

When the five-minute video was over, the curtains were opened and Sister María spoke again, this time about security precautions. She said there were cameras everywhere, including inside the comedor, and while the migrants could trust the staff and volunteers, they needed to be aware that the place could be "infiltrated" by bad people.

"Be careful if someone offers to help you," she said. "Don't give them your personal information." She asked for other suggestions.

"Speak in a low voice," one man said.

"Don't loan your cell phone to anyone," added a woman.

Sister María introduced the No More Deaths volunteers and the students from San Miguel High School, and urged everyone to think and talk about what the United States could do to change the situation.

Then Father Sean Carroll, the Jesuit priest who directed KBI, said the blessing, and the students served breakfast. Each plate was filled with *birria* (stewed, shredded beef), beans, rice, macaroni salad, potatoes cooked with tomatoes and onions, and tortillas. Lots of food. The comedor served two meals a day, at 9 a.m. and 3 p.m.—about 46,000 meals a year since it opened in 2008. During the Central American migrant crisis of 2018–2019, people were being fed in five shifts a day, and in that time KBI served 100,000 meals in one year.

After the migrants ate, some left, and others fanned out around the room to get help. Most wanted to talk to the staff social worker, Marla Conrad. While they waited, she had them fill out half-page forms, preprinted in Spanish, with their name, age, sex, nationality, reason for leaving home, deportation status, if they're searching for someone, and detailed questions about whether they had been victimized by authorities or others.

On the back of the form, types of perpetrators and abuses were listed: the green *migra* (border patrol, who wore green uniforms), the blue *migra* (ICE, who wore blue), Mexican local, federal, or migration police, the guide or coyote, and the "organized mafia." Among the crimes people could check were theft, physical mistreatment, bad conditions in detention, illegal detention, kidnapping, extortion, threats, and not returning personal belongings.

Conrad met each migrant separately. Some needed help getting to the bus station or the Casa San Juan Bosco. Conrad said she or Grupo Beta frequently drove people over there. Other migrants lined up for clothes—there were boxes of clothes and shoes of all sizes stacked neatly to one side. The three No More Deaths volunteers went to work. Dorothy ministered to people with medical problems in a corner where the medicines and first-aid treatments were kept. Lynda helped people make phone calls. She later told me she was able to connect a distraught woman to a family member in central Mexico. The woman had two young children with her and cried as she spoke about having to return to her hometown.

Rick usually worked cashing checks for people who'd been in U.S. detention. (Migrants who had money were given it back in check form when they were released; No More Deaths maintained a bank account to help them avoid check-cashing fees.) That day, he found himself talking to a Honduran teenager who wanted to know about where and how to enter the United States. Rick showed him a map of the region west of Nogales, made by Humane Borders, that had lines drawn in half-circles indicating distances in terms of days walking, as well as blue triangles marking water stations and red dots marking where bodies had been found. Some areas were just seas of red. The map said at the bottom in Spanish, "Don't Go! There's not enough water! It's not worth it!!" *No vale la pena.*

"You could die in the desert," Rick said. *Podrías morir.*

"If I go back to Honduras, I die. If I stay here, I die. I might as well try," the boy said.

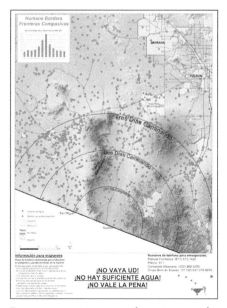

Poster warning migrants about crossing the southern Arizona desert. (Humane Borders)

Around noon, the volunteers finished seeing all the migrants and packed up to leave. We walked back into the United States along a long, concrete walkway lined by walls made from gabions, large rocks piled tightly inside wire cages that also were used to prevent erosion elsewhere on the border.

The port of entry was new, huge, and empty. Other than the customs inspectors, we were the only people there. We carried several bags and backpacks, which were given cursory inspection. No trouble at all. Same with the checkpoint on the highway to Tucson—we were waved through.

Since I was supposed to be filling in for a No More Deaths volunteer (and doing a bad job of it at that), I didn't get to interview any migrants at the comedor. But the previous year I spoke to some while helping lead a group of University of Arizona Honors College students on a daylong border-study trip. In April 2017 I accompanied a class of eight, their professor, and a graduate student to several places in Nogales, Sonora, where migrants congregated, including Casa San Juan Bosco and Grupo Beta headquarters.

Grupo Beta polices both the U.S. and Guatemalan borders, focusing on internal and external migrants. At the time we visited its Nogales office, on a hot morning in late spring, there were no families or non-Mexicans, just a dozen or so single men sitting on shaded benches out front.

Deported the previous day from the United States, the men ranged in age from late teens to mid-fifties. The ones we talked to were making plans to either return to their hometowns or try to reenter the States through the desert.

Teodoro was thirty-eight and had been working in construction in Las Vegas for twelve years. He had a wife and nine-year-old daughter in Vegas. He said he'd paid seven thousand dollars to get his papers fixed but was ripped off. He spent nine months in immigration prison before being bused to the border. He was going back to his hometown in Veracruz and then would somehow try to get back to the United States.

Javier, twenty, was also picked up while working construction in Las Vegas. He said he had been bitten by a border patrol dog and had not been allowed to see a judge before being deported.

Inside the Grupo Beta office, a cheerful, English-speaking young woman gave a presentation on the local migrant population. Depending on the season, she said, Grupo Beta agents in Nogales encountered between fifteen and eighty migrants a day.

Some were Mexicans deported from the United States, some were Mexicans who found themselves in trouble before crossing the border, and, at that time, about half were from countries other than Mexico. Most of these were Central Americans, but a few were from South America, Cuba, Haiti, Africa, the Middle East, and other faraway places.

If these foreigners did not have proper papers to be in Mexico, they were sent to an immigration prison to await deportation. As for the rest, Grupo Beta told us they helped people with bus fare, but the migrants we spoke to out front said that wasn't true. They said Grupo Beta just took people to shelters and left them there.

Later that afternoon, we visited one of the places where Grupo Beta took people: a clean, orderly, hilltop migrant shelter called Casa San Juan Bosco. Migrants could stay in bunkbeds, shower, and eat for three nights, then had to move on. The place also had facilities for about thirty women and children. Those rooms were empty when we visited, but by the following year, they would be filled with Central American families waiting to apply for asylum at the port.

At Casa San Juan Bosco, we met in small groups with about a dozen men in a small chapel, facing a simple altar and a statue of the Virgin of Guadalupe. Most of the men were from southern states embroiled in turmoil. Several were from Guerrero, the state where the forty-three student teachers had disappeared. "Four of them were from my village," one man said. He had been working in Salt Lake City for two years. Another young man from Morelos had lived and worked in Redwood City, California, for three years and was anxious to get back to his family in Los Angeles.

"There's no work, just violence," he said of Mexico. "The mafia have control of everything."

Another young man described how migrants were accosted on the streets of Nogales. "They come up to you and tell you to take a package across for them or they'll kill you."

In his book *Deported to Death*, University of Texas at El Paso sociology professor Jeremy Slack documented the threats cartels posed to deported migrants. Slack and his researchers interviewed hundreds of deportees at

Casa San Juan Bosco and other shelters on the border over several years, starting in 2014. At a presentation at the University of Arizona Latin American Studies Department in October 2019, Slack said the U.S. policy of busing deportees to a different part of the border from where they'd been apprehended—a practice intended to break up their relationship with a smuggler—was putting them in mortal danger, since they were suspected of being spies for rival cartels. In addition to being forced to serve as drug mules and lookouts, migrants reported being kidnapped for ransom or made to identify others who'd been living in the States many years (*es un pocho*). Although bereft by American standards, these deportees were likely to have family in Mexico or undocumented family still in the States who were willing to pay several thousand dollars to get them released. Their relatives also wouldn't dream of contacting authorities in either country.

In 2019 the situation took a turn for the worse after Trump instituted a policy that forced tens of thousands of Central Americans and other asylum seekers to "remain in Mexico" while their claims were adjudicated. Although some border residents objected, Mexico acceded to Trump's demands. Migrants were kept in camps and shelters, made to feel unwelcome, and sent home if at all possible. Many became victims of crimes, including sexual assault. Those who ran shelters were also targeted. In early August Aaron Méndez, a priest who ran a migrant shelter in Nuevo Laredo, told an Associated Press reporter that the policy of returning asylum seekers to Mexico was "undercover deportation," and "Mexico has not said one word." Two weeks later, gunmen came into the shelter and abducted Méndez. Staffers said he was taken after he refused to allow the gunmen to kidnap some Cuban migrants. (Cubans were thought to have rich relatives who would pay ransoms fast). He was not seen again.

Despite the danger, migrants continued to arrive on the border, and Mexican and international humanitarian aid groups continued to try to care for them. Among those who offered support was Pope Francis, who gave $500,000 to help migrants in Mexico; KBI received $21,000 of that for operating expenses. During these years, KBI also instituted a $3 million capital campaign to build a migrant service center across the street from the comedor. With big donations, such as a $300,000 gift from Arizona Cardinals owner Michael Bidwill and the

Cardinals Charities, the campaign quickly succeeded. Father Sean gave me a tour of the new building in December 2019.

A converted former warehouse, the shelter featured a two-story central atrium with natural light pouring in from skylights overhead. The floor of the atrium served as a dining area. Also downstairs was an intake room, industrial kitchen, laundry room, a sleeping area for men, showers, and bathrooms. Upstairs were more showers and bathrooms, sleeping areas for women, children, and trans people and places where migrants could receive clothing, first aid, legal aid, pastoral aid (a chapel), and other forms of assistance. Three floor-to-ceiling murals, painted by local artists of biblical themes, served to divide the atrium from the sleeping areas. In all, the new building could accommodate about 150 for a meal and about one hundred overnight.

The new KBI shelter opened to serve food to go and offer aid to migrants in the spring of 2020, though no overnight guests were allowed until the COVID-19 pandemic subsided. While the virus posed a threat to people living in camps and shelters, the migrant situation in Nogales was in many ways more manageable than in the previous year. The crackdown in southern Mexico had discouraged or prevented people from reaching the border, and after the pandemic broke out, the United States started expelling undocumented crossers at the nearest port of entry, which usually was not Nogales. With the courthouse closed, Operation Streamline was temporarily suspended. But shelters in Sasabe, Sonora, reported being overwhelmed with expelled migrants, and as the summer went on, desert deaths went way up.

Five

Death in the Desert

O
n a hot day in May 2017, my friend Mary Whitehead encountered a man dying in the desert.

Whitehead was a volunteer with the Samaritans, one of many groups that worked to prevent desert deaths in southern Arizona. On this day, she and other Samaritans from Tucson had gone out to the desert with Álvaro Enciso, an artist and activist who made crosses and placed them where migrants had died. They were accompanied by a van of college students on a border-study trip, and an older couple in their truck.

To get to the spot, the group drove two hours west of Tucson, to the far side of the massive Tohono O'odham reservation. As they approached the old mining town of Ajo (pronounced "ah-ho," Spanish for "garlic"), the two-lane highway curved south. The caravan followed the highway briefly toward the border before turning off onto a dirt road heading further west. Driving slowly to keep the dust down, the three vehicles ventured across the desert another eight or so miles, until finally reaching a mesquite grove where a migrant's body had been found. They parked at the desolate spot and got out to pray, plant the cross, and take photos.

When they were done, the group climbed into their vehicles and started back. They were still a few miles from the highway when they came across a man sitting by the side of the road.

Samaritans like Whitehead, Enciso, and the older couple were among hundreds of border residents who, from the late 1990s on, worked to prevent desert deaths. These activists and volunteers were young and old, students and teachers, church people and medical professionals, of varying races, ethnicities, and socioeconomic status, mostly Democrats and Independents but Republicans too. They went to great effort and took many risks, both individually and collectively, to save lives. No doubt they saved quite a few. Yet the difficulties and limitations of providing humanitarian aid in the desert proved considerable, and despite all their efforts, the death toll kept rising. This chapter looks at these attempts to save lives and their consequences, intended or not. It also looks at border patrol attitudes and actions toward migrants and humanitarian aid, as well as the work of people who care for the remains, and the families, of those lost in the desert.

The Man in the Road

When they saw the man, the Samaritans stopped short, jumped out, and ran to him. He was young, tall, and thin, dressed in dusty jeans and a T-shirt. He carried a near-empty water jug that had been blackened to prevent reflections visible to overhead surveillance. He gasped in Spanish he was from Honduras, had been in the desert about two weeks, and had run out of food days before.

The college students offered some food from their supplies. The man ate a little but was disoriented. "He pointed south toward Mexico and asked if that was the way to Phoenix," Whitehead said. Fearing he would die without medical attention, the group talked about what to do. Transporting him in the van with the college students was out of the question. The students could all be arrested, their electronics seized, and their program shut down.

Álvaro Enciso was adamant the Samaritans couldn't take him either. Maintaining the organization's reputation for staying within the law was essential to the border patrol's continuing to allow the group to operate. It quickly became clear that, if aid were to be rendered, it would have to be by the older couple.

The couple debated quietly. Being caught driving the man, even taking him to the hospital to save his life, could result in felony charges and loss of their truck. One thought perhaps they shouldn't chance it, and they should call the border patrol. But the other said calling the border patrol would only cause more suffering for the man and for themselves.

There was a pause. A decision was made.

"We're taking him."

The couple helped the man into the cab of the truck. The caravan started slowly back down the dirt road. Whitehead said the tension grew palpable as they approached the highway. "We had seen their cameras on towers coming in." They anticipated being met at the intersection by a phalanx of border patrol agents.

By some miracle, they were not. The paved road was empty in both directions. The vehicles turned north and headed back to Tucson. The couple with the truck went another way to avoid the checkpoint. A few days later, Whitehead texted them to find out what happened. "All okay" was the response.

Southern Arizona writer and activist Byrd Baylor faced a similar decision. The author of *Yes Is Better than No* and many other books, Baylor had lived since the early 1980s on twenty acres near Arivaca, a small town about twelve miles north of the border. In the late 1990s, after the crackdown sealed off more direct routes, her property became a migrant corridor. Baylor responded by offering water, food, and shelter to people passing through. She also posted a "Border Patrol Keep Out" sign on her driveway.

On July 4, 2003, Baylor found the body of a young man lying near the road not far from her home. She wrote about it in the *Arivaca Connection*:

Face up to the early morning sun, he lay only a foot or so from the road, his few belongings rolled up in a bundle beside him. He had taken off his shirt. His ribs showed, and he was covered with scratches from cat's claw and mesquite.

Remember, this happened on the Fourth of July, the great American holiday. It's one of those times—between the cookouts and the fireworks and the beer—when we like to give a moment's thought to the founding of our nation. . . . We know our ancestors were not casual or careful in seeking better lives. They thought that it might be their only chance. I suppose the young man lying by the road was doing the same thing.

The experience moved Baylor to try to do more to prevent desert deaths. She invited the humanitarian group No More Deaths to set up a traveler's way station on her land, where migrants could obtain water, food, rest, and medical attention. The aid station, named Byrd Camp, opened in 2004.

As desert deaths began to spike in the late 1990s, southern Arizonans were already organizing a response. People who had been active in the sanctuary movement and other social justice causes began holding meetings about what to do. The meetings were well attended, and everyone showed concern and alarm. But few could imagine what lay ahead.

One of the first groups to get organized, in the fall of 2000, was Humane Borders. Founded by Robin Hoover, a United Church of Christ pastor from Texas, this Tucson-based nonprofit placed and maintained water stations in the desert. The stations were fifty-five-gallon drums, painted sky blue, with tall flags sticking up from them.

Over the next few years, Humane Borders grew into a major operation. But as deaths continued to mount, it became clear that more and different approaches were needed. Two other church-based groups, the Samaritans and No More Deaths, soon formed. The Samaritans, a Presbyterian group cofounded by sanctuary pastor John Fife, conducted search and rescue operations. Churches in Tucson, Green Valley, and Phoenix established chapters. Some volunteers had medical training. They hiked in the desert with food, water, and first-aid kits, looking for people in distress. They picked up empty water jugs and other trash. They also accompanied those looking for remains of the missing.

In addition to these activities, No More Deaths, founded in 2004 and connected with the Unitarian Universalist church, left food and water jugs near migrant trails. This practice soon brought the group into conflict with authorities. No More Deaths also set up aid stations, like Byrd Camp, and helped migrants at the comedor in Nogales, Sonora, make phone calls, receive medical care, and recover money confiscated during detention.

Similar migrant aid groups formed in California and Texas. In Southern California John Hunter, brother of former Republican congressman Duncan Hunter (who resigned in 2020 after a felony conviction for stealing campaign funds), started a Humane Borders–type group called Water Station. Hunter also worked with others to reduce drownings in the All-American Canal. This concrete irrigation channel, which parallels the border for eighty miles between Yuma and Calexico, was estimated to have taken at least 550 migrants' lives by 2009. Under pressure from Hunter's group and others, in 2011 the Imperial Valley Irrigation District added warning signs and about a hundred lifesaving buoys. More fencing, sensors, and agents also helped reduce the number of migrants entering the canal, though drownings continued to occur.

Search and recovery groups also formed, like the Ángeles del Desierto and the Águilas (Eagles) del Desierto in the San Diego area, and the Armadillos Búsqueda y Rescate (Search and Rescue) in San Marcos, California. In Falfurrias, Texas, a group called the South Texas Human Rights Center formed to provide water stations, search and rescue, and care for dead migrants, after scores of bodies started turning up in Brooks County, about seventy miles north of the border. Some of these bodies—evidently remains of people who died trying to circumvent a checkpoint—had to be exhumed after being surreptitiously buried by local officials.

In addition to local aid workers, each one of these groups received support from all over the nation and world, including thousands of donors, a steady flow of church, retiree, and student volunteers, and a great deal of media attention. Yet provision of humanitarian aid to undocumented border crossers remained controversial.

Some even questioned whether it was doing more harm than good. That was the border patrol's position. They maintained that, by enticing migrants into the desert who would otherwise give up and stay home, water stations and aid camps were causing more deaths than they were preventing. The agency's acting special operations supervisor in Tucson, Steven Passement, said leaving water in the desert for migrants was "giving them false hope."

Other government officials agreed. Land managers at the patchwork of agencies overseeing the borderlands were in general unenthusiastic about water stations, and Humane Borders found the process of getting permission agonizingly slow. The requests also often resulted in rejection. In addition to the concern the water would attract migrants, officials cited damage to the environment and protection of endangered species as reasons for denying the permits.

Humane Borders faced logistical complications as well. The water could only be placed in areas accessible by truck, and it was expensive and time-consuming to keep the far-flung stations filled and maintained year in and year out. Sabotage of the water stations and the group's trucks in Tucson also occurred with depressing frequency.

Nevertheless, there were indications the water was saving lives. It was certainly being used. By 2008 there were more than one hundred water stations, including some in the Buenos Aires National Wildlife Refuge, Ironwood Forest National Monument, Organ Pipe Cactus National Monument, and on Bureau of Land Management and Pima County land near Arivaca and Three Points. Some were also on private property, like Byrd Baylor's. Humane Borders reported more than fourteen thousand gallons of water were dispensed between May and September that year.

In addition to operating water stations, Humane Borders collected data on where human remains were found and plotted the locations on maps. The maps seemed to indicate that deaths were fewer near migrant trails where water stations were located. But the evidence was inconclusive, as some migrants could have died because they intentionally avoided water stations out of fear the blue barrels were being watched by the border patrol.

Although their sixty-plus miles of border was rapidly becoming a smuggling hot spot, the Tohono O'odham also resisted having water stations, aid camps, and Samaritan patrols on their land. Given how much smuggling and migrant traffic they were enduring and how much sovereignty they had already surrendered to the border patrol and other authorities, their desire to not want more outsiders running around was understandable. Tribal officials pointed out that many residents, and the hospital in Sells (the nation's capital) helped migrants, as did the border patrol. But the decision to refuse outside humanitarian assistance proved increasingly controversial as migrant deaths became concentrated on the reservation.

Meanwhile, aid workers were beginning to run afoul of the law. The first felony arrests took place in 2005. Two No More Deaths volunteers were stopped near Arivaca and charged with transporting and human-smuggling conspiracy for having three undocumented people in their vehicle. The volunteers said they were taking the migrants to receive medical care at a Tucson church. They were able to convince U.S. District Court Judge Raner C. Collins that they were following protocol they believed had been agreed to by the border patrol, and he dismissed the charges in September 2006. But the judge left the door open to prosecution, saying in the future, aid workers should be aware they could be charged, "at the least, with reckless disregard for the law."

In 2008 and 2009, fourteen No More Deaths volunteers were cited for littering for leaving water jugs and other supplies in the Cabeza Prieta refuge. Also in 2008, an aid worker named Dan Millis, who went on to head the local Sierra Club chapter, was charged with littering for leaving gallons of water in the Buenos Aires National Wildlife Refuge. Millis was cited just two days after he and others had discovered the body of a fourteen-year-old Salvadoran girl during a search for her on the refuge. He refused to pay the $175 fine and was convicted at trial, though the Ninth Circuit Court of Appeals later reversed the decision on the grounds that sealed gallons of water are not necessarily trash. Judge Sidney Thomas wrote, however, that Millis could have been charged with abandonment of property or failure to obtain a special-use permit.

After 2009 there was a hiatus in arrests of humanitarian aid workers until Trump took office. Then in 2017 several took place. In separate incidents in June and August, nine No More Deaths volunteers were arrested on misdemeanor charges for driving in a wilderness area and littering. Both arrests occurred after volunteers had left water jugs and food in the Cabeza Prieta National Wildlife Refuge, where that year about half of all the sets of human remains recovered in Arizona's deserts had been found.

June 2017—the hottest June ever recorded in southern Arizona—also saw a border patrol raid on Byrd Camp. Midafternoon on June 15, about thirty agents in trucks, quads, and a helicopter descended on the site. Armed with arrest warrants, they searched the camp and took away four undocumented migrants. Officials later said they'd tracked the men for four days from where they'd tripped a sensor some eighteen miles away. The agents had followed the men to the camp, staked it out, and waited two more days for a judge to sign the warrants. They said the delay gave the men ample time to turn themselves in, thus preventing the raid. But the men had failed to leave.

The camp had been raided once before, in 2005, but this time activists said agents' actions violated International Red Cross guidelines the border patrol had agreed to abide by. The border patrol said it had made no such agreement. Either way, after the raid few people sought refuge at Byrd Camp, and it was closed for a while.

Four of the nine people arrested for littering in the Cabeza Prieta National Wildlife Refuge in August 2017 went on trial before Judge Bernardo Velasco in January 2019. The judge listened to three days of testimony before finding them guilty of failing to obtain a permit to enter a wildlife refuge, driving in a restricted area, and abandoning property. The aid workers said they could not have obtained a permit, since leaving food and water was prohibited. Judge Velasco sentenced each one to fifteen months' probation, a $150 fine, and permanent banishment from the refuge. Another four pleaded guilty to entering the refuge without a permit and paid about $280 each in fines. The ninth, Scott Warren, was set to be tried later in the year.

As these cases played out, signs appeared in front of hundreds of Tucson homes, churches and businesses saying, "Humanitarian Aid Is Never a Crime." But just like during the sanctuary movement thirty years before, government officials disagreed.

Water Poured Out

In January 2018 No More Deaths released a series of video clips of border patrol agents dumping water and other supplies left for migrants in the desert. The first clip, taken from a hidden camera, shows a woman agent walking down a trail between two men agents and enthusiastically kicking over five full water jugs as she passes by. The male agents don't join in but don't stop her either. In the next clip, also taken by a hidden camera, a male agent looks into a plastic bag containing clothes and blankets before carrying it away like the Grinch who stole Christmas.

Border Patrol agent kicking over water in screenshot from secretly recorded video. (No More Deaths)

In the third clip, the agent knows he's on camera, and he's belligerent. He pours out gallon after gallon of water while he taunts and threatens the No More Deaths volunteer filming him. "Picking up this trash someone left on the trail," he says. "It's not yours is it?" He accuses the aid worker of "helping felons enter the country."

The clips go on for several minutes. In addition to scenes of agents directly destroying food and water, they show aid workers finding dozens of water jugs smashed and slashed and cans of beans dumped out, right after seeing border patrol agents in the area.

This video, along with an accompanying report, was released by No More Deaths and the Tucson-based legal rights group Coalición de Derechos Humanos (Human Rights Coalition) on the morning of January 17. It went viral, racking up thousands of views on YouTube within hours. The border patrol response was equally swift. That same afternoon, federal agents in Ajo arrested No More Deaths volunteer Scott Warren, thirty-five, and charged him with alien smuggling and harboring. Warren, who had also been cited for leaving food and water in the Cabeza Prieta refuge the previous June, was accused of bringing water, food, and clothes to two undocumented men hiding in a building known as The Barn.

The border patrol insisted Warren's arrest was not in retaliation for the video. They said The Barn, which was owned by a local doctor known to be sympathetic to border crossers, had been under surveillance since April 2017 as a potential "stash house" for human smuggling. The day before Warren's arrest, the border patrol said, agents had detained a Central American man near a church in Ajo, who told them two more were hiding in The Barn. The border patrol staked the place out, and the next afternoon, Warren showed up. He went inside for a while before emerging, and agents confronted him in the driveway. At least five border patrol and Pima County sheriff vehicles surrounded the fenced property during his arrest.

Whatever the timing of Warren's arrest, activists saw it as an escalation of tactics. More than two dozen southern Arizona humanitarian aid workers had been charged with littering and trespassing and other minor offenses over the previous fifteen years. But this was the first time one had been arrested for human smuggling since 2005. Indicted for three felonies, including conspiracy, Warren pled not guilty and was released.

The report accompanying the video tracked what happened to 31,558 gallons of water left by migrant trails in an eight-hundred-square mile area around Arivaca between March 2012 and December 2015. More than 86 percent of the water was found to have been used by migrants, possibly saving the lives of hundreds. Of 4,119 gallons destroyed, 533 were by birds, cattle, and other animals, and 3,586 by humans. Researchers found a total of 415 incidents of human vandalism, about twice a week throughout the study period. While some of the sabotage could be attributed to hunters, militia members, and other private parties, border patrol agents were determined to be the likely culprit in the destruction of some 3,500 gallons of water.

Border patrol officials disagreed with the report's methodology and findings. They pointed out that some of the images on the video were from as long ago as 2011, after which a specific policy prohibiting agents from tampering with or removing humanitarian supplies was adopted. But the practice had continued—two clips were from 2017—and no agent had ever been punished, or even accused of wrongdoing, for destroying food, water or other supplies. Activists said the lack of accountability was evidence of a border patrol culture that dehumanized migrants.

As Scott Warren's trial approached, more evidence of that culture surfaced. Court papers revealed border patrol agents had referred to the two Central American men hiding in The Barn as "toncs." (This was border patrol slang for undocumented people, an onomatopoeia of the sound made by clubbing them on the head.) "Toncs at the barn," read one text. Also, "Make sure those toncs are isolated so we can get good mat wit [material witness] interviews."

At the same time, court papers filed in a separate case revealed another Nogales agent had sent text messages referring to migrants as "disgusting subhuman shits unworthy of being kindling for a fire." Agent Matthew Bowen had also joked about frying "fucking beaners" in oil. He wrote supportive texts to agent Lonnie Swartz in November 2017, while Swartz was awaiting trial for the killing of Mexican teen José Antonio Elena Rodríguez (discussed in chapter 6). In one, Bowen called perpetrators in a different rock-throwing incident "mindless murdering savages."

The texts came to light when Bowen, thirty-eight, was indicted by a federal grand jury in May 2018 for "deprivation of rights under color of law" and falsifying records by hitting a man with his border patrol vehicle and then lying about it. The incident took place around 7:30 a.m. on December 3, 2017, in a semitrailer parking lot near the Mariposa Port of Entry. A man later identified as twenty-three-year-old Guatemalan Antolín López Aguilar had just jumped over the wall and was trying to escape arrest by running back toward the port of entry when Bowen rammed him repeatedly with his Ford F-150. According to video recordings and other agents on the scene, Bowen, who had had several previous complaints against him for excessive force, knocked López down and came within inches of running him over. Bowen drove away after handcuffing the prostrate man. Other agents took López to Nogales Hospital, where his injuries were documented. The next day he was processed through Operation Streamline. The judge, who sentenced López to thirty days, recommended he receive immediate medical care.

Making matters worse was Bowen's lawyer's defense of the texts. Sean Chapman was a Tucson criminal defense attorney who often represented law-enforcement officers accused of wrongdoing, including Lonnie Swartz. Chapman (who died of cancer in June 2020) wrote in court papers that such language was "commonplace throughout the Border Patrol's Tucson Sector, that it is part of the agency's culture, and therefore says nothing about Mr. Bowen's mind-set."

Chapman's frank assessment confirmed what critics had long said about the border patrol: casual cruelty was so rampant it was considered normal. In 2019 an investigation by ProPublica uncovered a secret border patrol

Facebook page containing many crude, racist and sexist jokes about migrants, members of Congress, and others. More than 9,500 agents belonged to the group, including then–agency head Carla Provost (who said she was unaware of the "completely inappropriate" posts). And in his 2018 memoir of moral awakening *The Line Becomes a River*, former agent Francisco Cantú described seeing agents destroying water, food, and clothing and burning and urinating on belongings of migrants who'd scattered as they approached.

Yet Cantú also described agents' acts of humanity and kindness, not least of which were by himself. There were acts of heroism as well. The same week as the Bowen texts came out, an agent jumped into the raging Rio Grande near Eagle Pass, Texas, and saved a seven-year-old Honduran boy whose family had tried to cross the river in an inflatable wading pool. Ten days before, although one man and three children, including a ten-month-old, drowned when their raft capsized near Del Rio, Texas, the border patrol rescued several other adults and children. Agents also jumped into the All-American Canal to save people.

Border patrol agents risking their lives to rescue people who were risking their lives to avoid the border patrol was another tragic consequence of the crackdown. After migrant deaths began to spike in the late 1990s, the agency greatly expanded its search and rescue capabilities. It formed the BORSTAR (Search Trauma, and Rescue) unit, installed rescue beacons in remote areas, and took other measures credited with saving at least several hundred lives a year. I saw one border patrol helicopter pilot describe how he arrived on the scene too late and witnessed the death of a young woman. The experience had clearly shaken him.

By 2018 the border patrol had thirty-four rescue beacons in Arizona, some of which had satellite phones that migrants could use to call for help. The blue-lit towers were visible from ten miles away. There were seven on the Buenos Aires refuge. But aid workers said the distance to the lights could be misleading and disorienting, some were hidden, as in Charlie Bell Pass, and in any case, they were inadequate.

"It's like if you have a sea full of drowning people and you throw out one life vest and say that it's the solution," aid worker Geena Jackson said. "It's not."

The felony smuggling and harboring trial of Scott Warren—the first smuggling trial for a border aid worker in Tucson in more than ten years—took place at the Evo DeConcini Federal Courthouse in May and June 2019. The trial received a lot of national and international media attention. The courtroom seats were full, people lined the halls, and TV crews positioned themselves out front. After three days of testimony and three more days of deliberations, the jury announced it was hung eight-to-four for acquittal, and the judge declared a mistrial.

Those who attended the trial said there was no smoking-gun evidence, like texts or transcripts of Warren coordinating with others, so the jury probably never even considered thorny issues like Warren's motives, the "toncs" texts, or the underlying moral dilemma of the situation. Nonetheless, the outcome showed that, after twenty years of official inability to stop desert deaths, a majority of jurors—in Tucson at least—were reluctant to brand as a criminal someone who was just trying to save lives. Perhaps they were influenced by Warren's comment on the stand that, since his indictment, eighty-eight sets of human remains had been recovered in the desert.

Warren was retried on the harboring charge in the fall, and in a strange twist of border justice, his case was decided on the same day and in the same courthouse as the case of the border patrol agent who almost ran over a migrant and sent the "mindless murdering savages" texts. On November 20, 2019, in the DeConcini courthouse, U.S. District Court Judge D. Thomas Ferraro went against the government's recommended six months' jail time and sentenced Matthew Bowen to three years' probation, 150 hours of community service, and an $8,000 fine. Bowen also resigned from the border patrol as part of the plea deal.

That same day, in U.S. District Judge Raner Collins's courtroom, a jury took only two and a half hours to reject the government's characterization of Warren as a human smuggler and acquitted him of harboring. After the jurors were excused, Judge Collins convicted Warren of driving without a permit in the Cabeza Prieta refuge in August 2017, but acquitted him of abandoning property in a wilderness area because he was following his religious beliefs.

Not only jurors but judges as well were beginning to be receptive to the idea of acquitting aid workers. In early February 2020 U.S. District Judge Rosemary Marquez overturned the convictions of the four arrested with

Warren in Cabeza Prieta in 2017. She wrote in her decision the government seemed to be

> reasoning that preventing clean water and food from being placed on the Refuge would increase the risk of death or extreme illness for those seeking to cross unlawfully, which in turn would discourage or deter people from attempting to enter without authorization. In other words, the Government claims a compelling interest in preventing Defendants from interfering with a border enforcement strategy of deterrence by death.

After this ruling came out, the government dropped its pursuit of Warren, since his conviction for driving without a permit would also likely be overturned. But the Trump administration wasn't done yet with No More Deaths. In what was largely a replay of the June 2017 incursion, the border patrol raided the reopened Byrd Camp on July 31, 2020. Agents—some of whom were BORTAC units fresh from quelling protests in Portland—had surrounded the camp the day before, circling it with ATVs and setting up a checkpoint to stop anyone coming or going. The following night, they raided the camp and arrested some thirty migrants. No aid workers were arrested, however, which may have contributed to a lack of media coverage. The nation was also then too preoccupied with the pandemic to pay much attention. In October the border patrol staged another raid employing a low-flying helicopter, which resulted in the arrest of twelve migrants and near-destruction of the camp. And in one last act of intimidation before Trump left office, agents on horseback surrounded the camp two days before Christmas, though they later withdrew without incident.

Naming the Dead

By the early 2000s, the remains of those who'd died trying to cross the Arizona border were stacking up in the Pima County Medical Examiner's Office. The office received all the dead migrants from Pima, Santa Cruz, and Pinal counties, increasing their workload (which focused primarily on Tucson, a city of more than one million) by one-third. Homeland Security paid for an extra storage cooler, but staff could not keep up with the additional autopsies and time and effort it took to try to identify the dead and return them to their families.

For many years, Assistant Pathologist Dr. Bruce Anderson conducted most of the autopsies on the border crossers. He documented scars, tattoos, missing organs, and dental work. Some bodies were still fresh and fully clothed and looked as if they might sit up and walk away. Others were little more than fragments of bone, or teeth, their clothes just bits of fabric and metal. Corpses decayed quickly in the desert, desiccated by the sun, eaten by animals, and scattered by the wind until nothing was left.

Anderson took bone fragments, catalogued belongings, and tried to contact family. A few of the dead carried their actual IDs, photos, letters, even phone numbers. Most however, carried no ID—smugglers told them not to—or fake Mexican IDs so they would be deported right back across the border if caught.

Identified remains were returned to their families, at Pima County taxpayer expense. As for the unidentified, after collecting their biological and material effects, and making a good faith effort to find out who they were, Anderson released the remains to the Public Fiduciary, which cremated and buried them in the pauper's graveyard, a dirt field behind Evergreen Cemetery in central Tucson.

Every year on December 18, International Migrant's Day, activists and church people gathered at the unknown migrants' graveyard for an ecumenical prayer service. By 2018 the remains of about nine hundred were interred.

At the same time as the medical examiner's office was being overwhelmed by the bodies of the dead, Anderson was getting calls from people looking for someone who went missing while trying to cross the border. He filled out forms with the information he collected about their loved one's physique and personal effects. He added little details in the margin that might help with the search. I saw some of these handwritten notes when I visited the office in 2018. One lost woman, Anderson wrote, "wore traditional dress." Another "did not bite her nails."

In 2006 Seattle native Robin Reineke, twenty-four, came to Tucson to study forensic anthropology at the University of Arizona. After learning from Anderson about the crisis at the medical examiner's office over a beer at the Shanty (a campus-area bar), she volunteered to help. Reineke's work grew into the basis for her dissertation and eventually into a nonprofit called the Colibrí Center for Human Rights. (*Colibrí* is Spanish for "hummingbird." These tiny powerhouses, who migrate between Central America, Mexico, and the United States, took on special significance for the Pima County Medical Examiner's Office in 2009, when, during examination of a deceased border crosser, a small dead hummingbird was found in the man's pocket.)

In 2013 Reineke cofounded the Colibrí Center, which continued to operate out of the medical examiner's office, and served as its executive director until 2019. Recognized internationally as one of the most important human rights organizations established since the turn of the century, the Colibrí Center focused on caring and advocating for dead and missing migrants and their families, as well as on working to prevent future deaths in America's killing fields.

Some 46,000 migrants died worldwide between 2000 and 2018, according to the International Organization for Migration. About 10,000 of them died along the U.S.-Mexico border, 2,900 on the Arizona border alone. A 2009 report by the ACLU found that, of nearly 400 people who died or were found dead on the border the previous year, 118 died of heat exposure, 54 drowned, 44 were killed in vehicle accidents, 9 died from cold, and 5 from trains. Seventy-one died from other causes, including homicide, 27 were undetermined, and 62 were skeletal remains.

Two other studies of migrant deaths on the border found that about three-quarters of the decedents were men, and of those whose ages were known, 81 percent were under forty. Nearly half were between the ages of eighteen and twenty-nine, and about 10 percent were under eighteen. In terms of nationality, of the 1,824 sets of remains identified by the Pima County ME's office between 2000 and 2017, 83 percent were Mexican, 10 percent Guatemalan, 3 percent Salvadoran, and 4 percent other nationalities.

In contrast to U.S. citizens, more than 99.5 percent of whom were identified after death, only 64 percent of border crossers were. At the Pima County

ME's office, of the 2,816 total sets of remains recovered between 2000 and 2017, 992 were *desconocidos* (unknowns). In 2018 the Colibrí Center was working on about 1,000 cases of dead and missing border crossers, most from southern Arizona but also some from Texas and California.

Even though, border-wide, there were thousands of unidentified people who'd died and thousands of families looking, it turned out to be really hard to match them up. Collaborating with local medical examiners, law enforcement, the Mexican consulate, forensic experts, and many others, Reineke was only able to identify about twenty a year. This was not only because it was unknown when or where the loved one perished, but because the U.S. government was making it difficult for the families to get access to the main FBI database of the DNA of those who died unknown in America.

"There are many barriers, some intentional," to matching dead migrants with families, Reineke said. "Several parts to the work, including the forensics—biological death—are relatively straightforward. But the question of the disappearance, and the struggle of grieving families to get answers from an indifferent or intentionally cruel system, makes the loss even harder to take."

As Reineke explained, there were two parts to the process of identifying the dead and connecting them with families. DNA needed to be extracted from both the deceased and their family and matched through a database. Extracting the DNA from the dead and putting it in a database was expensive, more than a thousand dollars per sample, but doable. These samples were all sent to the FBI database and, depending on where the remains were found, to private databases maintained by Colibrí and the University of North Texas.

Extracting the DNA from a family member was more problematic. The FBI insisted that law enforcement take the sample for it to be checked against its database. Families were understandably reluctant to do that. Relatives of missing migrants in the United States, afraid of being identified and deported themselves, often did not even report the disappearance to authorities, let alone give DNA samples.

The situation was further complicated by the fact these people died trying to "enter without inspection." There was shame associated with the death, and as Reineke said, "when society doesn't know what to do, it can compound shame." People searching for lost relatives endured depression, chronic health problems, guilt, blame, isolation, and stigma. As one woman told Reineke: "Someone whispered to me, 'My aunt disappeared too.'"

Over the years, Reineke found that a lot of Colibrí's work involved supporting not only those who had lost loved ones but those who would never find out what happened. The organization evolved into three components: the Missing Migrant and DNA program; the Family Network, through which relatives and friends of the dead and missing could connect; and Historias y Recuerdos (Stories and Memories), a testimony project.

In hopes of matching relatives with remains despite the FBI restrictions, the Calibrí Center raised $1 million to expand its DNA database. Investigators traveled to Los Angeles, San Francisco, New York City, Washington, D.C., Chicago, Salt Lake City, Mexico, Guatemala, and many other cities and countries where families of missing migrants were living. Samples were primarily taken from people who believed their loved one died crossing the Arizona border because those were most likely to match someone in the Colibrí database. But Reineke also continued to follow up on a few cases from Texas and California she had taken on years before.

"I was just in Seattle collecting DNA from a woman whose daughter disappeared in Texas in 2014," Reineke told me in the spring of 2018. "I remembered the story when I was reviewing the notes. The daughter had crossed. There was a snow storm and it was cold. She got hypothermia, felt feverish, shed clothing, and died. The group had to leave her behind. They wrapped her body in plastic. The mom showed up for her DNA sample and said, 'You are the person I originally talked to.' She expressed gratitude I was still there and still caring."

On February 17, 2018, Reineke spoke at a symposium on desert deaths at the Global Justice Center in South Tucson. The Global Justice Center was a former dance hall called the Stardust Ballroom that'd been converted into meeting and office space for progressive organizations. Its walls had been painted with colorful murals, including one of a river, a jaguar, and women with babies in their arms breaking down a border fence. To the side of the stage hung a stark reminder of how slow progress had been on the issue of migrant deaths. A large black-and-white poster announced a *gran marcha*, or big march, calling for an end to the loss of life. The poster was dated December 11, 1999.

The symposium was held to follow up on the 2016 book *Migrant Deaths in the Arizona Desert*. Panelists, several of whom had contributed to the book, addressed the three types of death happening on the border: the "social deaths" of the deported, "ambiguous deaths" of the disappeared, and biological death.

Reineke, whose work dealt with the second and third types of death, told a story illustrating the obstacles faced by families trying to find out what happened to their loved ones.

Nancy Lucía Ganoza Córdova, forty-four, left Peru in October 2009 to come to the States to join her daughters, for whom her ex-husband had obtained visas, in New York. Ganoza took buses from Peru to Mexico and crossed into the United States through the desert north of Altar, Sonora. She was in a speeding van going north on Mission Road on the Tohono O'odham reservation just south of Tucson that was pulled over by the border patrol. Everyone ran into the desert. The other migrants later regrouped and tried to look for her but Ganoza had disappeared.

After not hearing from her for several weeks, Ganoza's daughters, Karen and Johanna, launched a search. Despite the cost and difficulty, they came to Tucson, traveled to Mexico, spoke to dozens of people, hired a private investigator, and combed the desert near where the other migrants said they had been pulled over.

"They did everything right, but they were turned away, discriminated against, given no funding, and denied access to information because it was 'confidential,'" said Reineke, who took on the case. "They were treated horribly by Mexican consular officials. The Pima County sheriff refused to take a missing persons' report. The border patrol said, 'If we find her, we're going to deport her.'"

The search went on for eight years. "It's something that haunts you every day," said Karen, who was nineteen when her mother disappeared. "I only feel alive when I'm searching for her."

Finally, on December 1, 2017, Reineke called Karen and Johanna with heartbreaking news. A piece of human skull found in the desert in 2011 near milepost seven on South Mission Road—not far the San Xavier del Bac Mission—had been positively identified as their mother's. Although only recently tested at Colibrí's request, Ganoza's cranium had been in the possession of the Pima County Sheriff's Department the entire time.

The sisters wondered how a strong woman like their mother could have died so close to a well-traveled road on the outskirts of a major city. Was she murdered? They would never know.

The following spring, Karen and Johanna came to Tucson to hold a small ceremony at the place where the cranium had been found. They set it on the ground and gathered around. Bruce Anderson and Robin Reineke were there, as was Tohono O'odham activist Mike Wilson, who gave a Native blessing. John Fife, the sanctuary pastor, said a Christian prayer. Karen and Johanna handed out papers with "Nancy facts" on them: "Nancy was caring." "Nancy was resourceful." "Nancy didn't like to wear makeup."

Colibrí wasn't the only group pressing for access to the FBI database. At a conference sponsored by the Inter-American Commission on Human Rights in Boulder, Colorado, in October 2018, an umbrella organization called the Forensic Border Coalition formally requested that the database be cross-checked with four thousand samples collected from relatives of people presumed to have died along the border. Among the groups making the request was the Argentine Forensic Anthropology Team, which formed after that country's Dirty War and had gone on to help identify victims of Mexico's drug violence as well as migrants who died on the U.S. border. Another requestor was the South Texas Human Rights Center, which also was working to exhume and identify migrant remains and return them to their families. The FBI responded that the national database was only accessible to law enforcement, not private groups or researchers, but would look into it.

Large pictures of lost loved ones were held up in the audience during the hearing, and one woman wept as she testified about her two children who went missing on the Arizona border more than twenty years before. Irma Carrillo of Sinaloa said her sons, aged twenty-five and twenty-seven when they disappeared, were never heard from again.

"We only want to know what happened to them," Carrillo said.

"Bruce has said something over the years," Reineke told me. "If the deaths were to stop tomorrow, we would still have a decade of work in front of us. Until every family has answers, there's work to be done."

And the day the deaths stop is still a long way off. In 2020 the medical examiner's office and Humane Borders reported the highest yearly total ever for human remains recovered in the Arizona desert. Some 227 sets were found, a 58 percent increase over the 2019 total of 144, bringing the number of documented migrant deaths in Arizona in the previous twenty years to nearly 3,400.

Six

Under Color of Law

Around 11:30 at night on October 10, 2012, Nogales, Arizona, police responded to a report of suspicious activity at the border. A couple of athletic youths, wearing what looked like loads of marijuana on their backs, were climbing a downtown stretch of the wall into the United States.

The wall that divided Nogales from Nogales, Sonora—its much larger Mexican twin—snaked across the valley in various forms, with the section where this event took place among the more formidable. It was a twenty-two-foot-high barrier of square iron poles, anchored diagonally in concrete about four inches apart, connected by metal plates welded across the top, and perched atop a hill sloping another fourteen feet down into Mexico. It was difficult, but not impossible, to climb.

Shortly after the police arrived that night, someone on the Mexican side began throwing rocks over the fence, evidently to provide cover for the smugglers, who'd hidden their load on the Arizona side and were in the process of scaling the fence back to Mexico.

Since it was a downtown street, the scene was lit and under surveillance. A video camera recorded what occurred next.

A border patrol vehicle pulled up and an agent later identified as Lonnie Swartz got out. A couple minutes passed. Two figures could be seen dangling from the U.S. side of the fence, and a police K-9 officer brought his dog below them before retreating when the rocks started flying.

Rock throwing was a routine occurrence along populated stretches of the border, and the Nogales cops seemed relatively unconcerned. The rocks appeared to be golf-ball sized pieces of concrete that smashed when they hit the ground. As one investigator noted, to accurately and forcefully toss a large enough projectile to do damage from where the rock throwers stood—uphill, some thirty-six feet in the air and ninety feet away—you'd have to have an arm like a major-league pitcher.

The video showed the Nogales cops get behind their vehicles while the suspected smugglers finished scrambling over the fence. At about the same time, Swartz strode toward the barrier. He aimed his gun between the bollards and fired three rounds. He moved down the fence, aimed, and fired again, this time ten shots. Then he reloaded, went to a third position, and fired three more times.

Across the border, at the bottom of the ravine and against a building on the opposite side of a narrow street, ten of those bullets hit the back of the head and torso of sixteen-year-old José Antonio Elena Rodríguez. The teen, who wore a gray T-shirt, blue jeans, and gray Nikes, died face down on the sidewalk, with, a photo taken shortly after showed, his arms under his body.

The killing prompted outrage in Nogales, Sonora, and some protest in Arizona. Candlelight vigils and marches were held. A large mural of Elena Rodríguez's placid face, painted in the style of the Obama "Hope" poster, appeared at the base of the Mexican side of the fence near where he died. But for two and a half years, the border patrol wouldn't even release the name of the man who shot him. A *New York Times* article on the case, published in March 2016, revealed an interagency struggle, with the border patrol closing ranks around Swartz, first transferring him to Nevada and then placing him on paid leave, while CBP's internal investigative arm and other federal oversight agencies sought to prosecute him. No progress was made until Elena Rodríguez's parents sued in civil court and won the right to proceed.

In the fall of 2015, federal officials charged Swartz with second-degree murder. It was just one of a number of cases in which border patrol agents were charged with serious misconduct, ranging from corruption and bribery to rape and murder. While these cases were extreme, they raised questions about the qualifications and training of border patrol agents in general, especially after the agency went on a hiring spree starting in the 1990s. They were also symptomatic of deeper issues posed by the massive influx of border patrol agents to the border, issues that involved not only misconduct by individual agents but financial waste and excess, as well as systemic, legalized violation of rights of citizens and non-citizens alike.

Border Agents on Trial

On Monday morning, April 16, 2018, I attended the closing arguments in the Lonnie Swartz trial. They took place in a large, tall-ceilinged windowless courtroom on the fifth floor of the Evo DeConcini Federal Courthouse in downtown Tucson. Not a lot of spectators were in attendance. A few border activists, the Elena Rodríguez family, and local reporters sat on one side. About a half-dozen border patrol agents, out of uniform, who had warmly greeted Swartz outside the courtroom, sat with his family on the other side, behind the defense table. Swartz, tall and redheaded, sat facing the jury, and wrote on a legal pad the whole time.

Elena Rodríguez's grandmother, who lived in the United States but still owned the family home in Nogales, Sonora, made a brief appearance on the stand. She talked about the last time she saw the boy, earlier in the afternoon on the day he died, at her house on the Mexican side. The prosecutor wanted to show her some photos of Elena Rodríguez as a child, but the judge refused, and she was excused after about ten minutes of testimony.

The prosecution's closing argument was gruesome. A gray mannequin of a male figure stood in front of the courtroom throughout. The figure had ten long knitting needles stuck in it, each showing the trajectory and point of impact of the bullets Swartz had put in Rodríguez's back and head. The video was played repeatedly, with digital blobs of color used to highlight the different positions of Swartz, Elena Rodríguez, and others there that night. Still photos on large screens on both side of the room showed Elena Rodríguez's body lying face down on the sidewalk, his head in a pool of blood, as well as a close-up of his face after someone rolled his body over. One side of the face was a mass of bloody pulp. The prosecutor talked at length about abrasions on the other side, which he said were evidence of Elena Rodríguez's inability to break his fall. Which one of Swartz's shots had killed him was in question. Did the agent really need sixteen bullets to neutralize the threat?

The prosecutor pointed out the deadly accuracy of the shots. Swartz had been an expert marksman at the Border Patrol Academy. Despite the distance, the darkness, and Swartz's alleged fear for his life, thirteen of the sixteen bullets went into Elena Rodríguez or the wall right behind him. Swartz "was not firing his pistol wildly," the prosecutor said.

The defense's closing argument was simple. Swartz was a law-enforcement officer trying to protect himself and fellow officers against potentially deadly projectiles. Swartz had testified he'd heard the dog had been hit, although that turned out not to be true. (According to the *New York Times*, the initial Nogales police report named only the dog as having received injuries.) He'd heard a rock smash, and a piece of it rolled near the foot of one of the cops. He did not know how many people were throwing rocks or how long the barrage would last. He was battling members of lawless drug cartels. I saw the heads of a few jurors nod slightly during this argument.

The judge allowed the jury to consider lesser charges than second-degree murder, those of voluntary and involuntary manslaughter. After five days of deliberation, the jury announced it was hung. The judge told them to try again. One day later, they came back. Swartz was acquitted of second-degree murder, but the jury deadlocked, seven to five, over acquitting Swartz of voluntary manslaughter.

After the verdict, protestors briefly blocked Congress Street and the freeway on-ramp. Darkness fell, and they dispersed. Another protest took place in Nogales, at the spot where Elena Rodríguez died.

Juror interviews showed how differently people can perceive the same evidence. One juror said on TV that everyone had agreed right away to acquit on second-degree murder. "He did not intend to kill the kid," this juror said.

Another juror was quoted saying the killing wasn't "personal."

"We really tried to take José's name and face and everything away from it and look at it as a blue blob on the screen," juror Heather Schubert told the *Arizona Daily Star.*

A third juror said he could not understand how anyone could look at the same evidence he did and think the killing was justified. He and a couple others had refused to acquit Swartz, forcing a deadlock on the manslaughter charges. "We fought and fought and fought for José and for justice," juror Kevin Briggs said. "I'm all for securing the border, but not by killing people who are lying on the ground helpless."

Swartz was tried again on manslaughter charges in November 2018. This time, the jury acquitted him of the lesser charge of involuntary manslaughter but could not agree on the more serious charge of voluntary manslaughter. As the verdicts were being read, a border activist in the spectator section, Richard Boren, stood and shouted "Justice for José Antonio!" before being hustled out of the courtroom. A small protest followed in front of the courthouse. Boren was arrested for disturbing the peace after repeatedly shouting "Justice! Justicia!"

A couple weeks after the second partial acquittal, the prosecutor announced the government would not be trying Swartz for a third time. No one was surprised at the outcome. Only a handful of border patrol agents had ever been charged with murder for killing someone in the line of duty, and none had ever been convicted.

An estimated fifty people were killed by border patrol agents on duty in southern Arizona in the twenty-six years between 1992 and 2018. Prosecutors considered filing charges against the agents in about a half-dozen of these cases, including the death of Carlos LaMadrid, nineteen, shot and killed by a border patrolman while attempting to scale the fence in Douglas, Arizona, in 2011. The government ultimately declined to prosecute in the LaMadrid and several other cases, on the grounds they couldn't prove the killings weren't justified. But in addition to Swartz, three were criminally charged.

The first was Border Patrol Agent Michael Elmer. Around dusk on June 12, 1992, Elmer killed a twenty-six-year-old man named Darío Miranda Valenzuela in the hills eight miles west of Nogales, Arizona. The case became known as "Rodney King of the Border" because it paralleled, in many ways including its outcome, the 1992 trial of the four white Los Angeles cops who beat Black motorist Rodney King. I wrote about it in *Lives on the Line*.

Miranda had several things in common with José Antonio Elena Rodríguez. Both grew up with absent fathers in working-class barrios of Nogales, Sonora. (José's father was imprisoned and, shortly after his release, murdered when José was thirteen.) Both were acquainted with street life, and evidence indicated they were involved in drug smuggling when they were killed, although they were unarmed and shot in the back from a considerable distance.

There were also parallels between Elmer and Swartz. Elmer had spent seven and a half years in the army before joining the border patrol. He supposedly had bragged about killing people, even though he spent the Persian Gulf War refueling tanks in Kuwait. Swartz, for his part, had gone AWOL from the army and been "less than honorably" discharged in lieu of court-martial. His attorney successfully fought to keep that information from the jury, as well as the fact that on his border patrol application, Swartz had lied about going AWOL and being arrested for it. He wrote he had left military service "after my immaturity won out."

The circumstances of the killings were different: Swartz killed Elena on a city street, under video surveillance, and with numerous eyewitnesses present. Elmer killed Miranda on a remote hillside with only his partner for a witness. He then hid the body and did not report the shooting. According to the partner, who turned him in the next day, Elmer had wanted to plant a gun on Miranda, and failing that, drag him into Mexico and bury him there.

Despite his egregious conduct, Elmer was acquitted on all charges. The jury was evidently swayed by signs that Miranda was operating as a scout for drug smugglers, and not just crossing to find work, as his family claimed. The Elena Rodríguez case turned on similar evidence. Although the teen's family insisted he was just on his way home, the government conceded before the trial even began that he had been one of the ones throwing rocks.

After Elmer, the next southern Arizona border patrol agent charged with murder was Denin Hermosillo, who shot an unarmed marijuana smuggler named Julio Cesar Yenez Ramírez west of Rio Rico in 2005. The prosecutor filed charges of negligent homicide, but the case was later dismissed, after it was determined the shooting was accidental. A civil suit filed against agent Hermosillo by Yenez Ramírez's father in Mexico was also unsuccessful.

The third case was that of agent Nicholas Corbett, who in 2007 killed a Mexican immigrant named Javier Domínguez Rivera in Cochise County, near the border between Bisbee and Douglas. Corbett said Domínguez Rivera tried to smash his head with a rock; prosecutors contended he was kneeling to surrender when killed. Corbett was charged with second-degree murder. His two trials both ended in hung juries, and the charges were dropped. In 2011 the U.S. government paid Domínguez Rivera's family $850,000, despite no admission of wrongdoing.

A similar lawsuit ultimately resulted in a settlement for Darío Miranda's widow, although Elmer was also acquitted of violating Miranda's civil rights in a second trial in Phoenix in 1994. The widow, and Miranda's two young children, received lifetime annuities equaling the amount paid to Domínguez Rivera's family. Elmer's lawyer called it "a gift from the U.S. government," adding, "legally, they aren't entitled to anything."

Although the outcome was the same, the José Elena Rodríguez case differed from these others in one respect: Swartz was the first agent ever charged for a cross-border shooting. The circumstances raised legal questions about the rights of people killed on foreign soil by law enforcement on U.S. soil. Darío Miranda and the others were all killed in the United States, where they presumably had rights under the Constitution (though there was ongoing debate about that too). But what rights did Elena Rodríguez, a Mexican citizen killed in Mexico, have under U.S. law? As it turned out, the courts had already been wrestling with this question in the case of another border patrol shooting, which took place across the Rio Grande in 2010.

In that case, border patrol agent Jesús Mata Jr. shot from the U.S. side and killed fifteen-year-old Sergio Adrián Hernández Güereca, who was standing on the Mexican side of a culvert separating El Paso from Ciudad Juárez. Mata was not criminally charged, but the teen's parents attempted to sue in civil court for violation of their son's constitutional rights. Both the Obama and Trump administrations argued the family had no right to sue, since Hernández was Mexican and in Mexico at the time of his death. Lower courts agreed, and so did the Fifth Circuit Court of Appeals. Then, in 2018, the Ninth Circuit Court of Appeals issued an opposite opinion in the José Elena Rodríguez case, ruling the family's wrongful death suit against Swartz and the border patrol could proceed. Given the conflicting decisions, the U.S. Supreme Court took up the case.

In February 2020, in a major blow to the Elena Rodríguez family, the Supreme Court ruled 5–4 that Hernández's family had no right to sue in U.S. courts. It called the shooting an "international" dispute. Justice Ruth Bader Ginsburg sharply criticized the decision. Noting in her dissent that the act in question took place on U.S. soil, she wrote, "It scarcely makes sense for a remedy trained on deterring rogue officer conduct to turn upon a happenstance subsequent to the conduct—a bullet landing in one half of a culvert, not the other." The decision meant the Elena Rodríguez family's case against Swartz was likely to be thrown out as well.

A couple of weeks after the final acquittal and mistrial of Lonnie Swartz, a former border patrolman turned academic named Chris Montoya published an op-ed on the case in the *Star*. He described visiting the scene of the shooting (as had both juries). From the U.S. side, it was clear Swartz had shot from an elevated position, giving him considerable advantage over his target. From the Mexican side, Montoya wrote, the distance was so far, and the fence and embankment so high, he could not imagine how anyone could have thrown a rock capable of endangering Swartz or anyone else on the U.S. side. Montoya wrote about being on the receiving end of "rockings" many times, and never feeling in danger. The rocks were so small and slow-moving that he once saw an agent catch one in his hand.

The question of how much danger border agents actually were in was important because it was often used to justify use of lethal force and ever more border security. There was no doubt border patrol agents were assaulted. They were bitten in the leg, punched in the face, hit and dragged by cars, kicked, stabbed and shot. They were pelted with rocks, bottles, pieces of concrete, and other objects.

But there was also evidence attacks on agents were exaggerated. In November 2017 two agents were found severely injured at the bottom of a culvert by the I-10 near Van Horn, Texas, about thirty miles from the border and a hundred miles east of El Paso. One later died, and the other said he had no memory of what happened. Conservative media like Breitbart News and others, including President Trump, jumped on the case as evidence of the danger posed by undocumented immigrants. But the FBI report found the injuries were more consistent with a fall from the highway overhead, and there was no evidence anyone else was at the scene.

At the same time, reports of a sharp upward trend in assaults on border patrol agents were examined and questioned by investigators from *The Intercept*. In 2016 Customs and Border Patrol data cited a 20 percent rise in assaults over the previous year. In 2017 it reported an even greater rise, to 786 assaults, a 73 percent increase over 2016, despite a drop in apprehensions from 415,816 to 310,532.

But *The Intercept* found that those statistics were inflated. The magazine determined that almost all the increase was from a single event in the Rio Grande Valley, on February 14, 2017, when seven agents were assaulted by six subjects throwing rocks, bottles and tree branches. This was counted as 126 assaults.

In fact, as Montoya pointed out in his op-ed, the border patrol was the safest of all federal law-enforcement agencies. Not only officers of the FBI and U.S. Marshals Service, but National Park Service and Bureau of Indian Affairs police were all more likely to be killed or injured on the job than border agents were. According to *The Intercept*, FBI statistics from 2016 showed that "Border Patrol agents were about five times less likely to be assaulted than officers in local police departments—and only half as likely to be killed on the job by homicide or by accident." After the Van Horn overpass death, the conservative Cato Institute did a study and determined, in any year since 2003, "regular Americans" were more than twice as likely to be murdered as border patrol agents.

Moreover, agents were supposed to be trained and equipped to respond appropriately to threats, by, for example, moving out of the way, as the Nogales cops did. Border patrol use of force in response to rock attacks came under scrutiny after a 2011 Department of Homeland Security inspector general report found that, the previous year, agents were attacked by rocks 339 times and responded with gunfire 33 times and with less-than-lethal force, such as beanbag guns, pepper spray, and batons, 118 times. A subsequent police review recommended ending the policy of allowing agents to respond to rock attacks with lethal force, as well as the policy allowing them to shoot at people in moving vehicles. Both those recommendations were rejected in 2013, although agents did receive more equipment and training in how to respond to rock attacks, and recorded uses of lethal force went down.

Knowing all this, and after studying the facts of the Lonnie Swartz case, Chris Montoya wrote he believed that if the jury been entirely made up of "seasoned, thoughtful and honest Border Patrol agents," Swartz would likely have been convicted.

Checkpoints

Just after Christmas 2016, a forty-seven-year-old Tucson pastor named Abran Tadeo pulled his RV up to a border patrol checkpoint near Three Points, about twenty-five miles down the road from Tucson toward Ajo. Tadeo was returning from a trip to Rocky Point with six other family members, including his seventy-seven-year-old mother and fifty-year-old sister, Andrea.

Tadeo and family had already stopped and been questioned at a border patrol checkpoint about twenty miles north of the border, in addition to having been thoroughly inspected at the border crossing in Lukeville.

"I drove up to the checkpoint and opened the window to say, 'We're U.S. citizens,'" Tadeo later told the *Star*.

The agent insisted on hearing it from everyone.

"I said, 'We're all U.S. citizens. This is the third time. We're getting harassed.'"

The agent didn't like that, and an argument ensued. Another agent approached the other side of the RV. Things got heated. At one point, after Tadeo was told he was being sent to secondary inspection, he took his foot off the brake and the RV lurched forward a couple feet before stopping. The agent standing on the passenger side later claimed Tadeo had tried to run him down. He said he'd been hit by the side mirror as the pastor accelerated and was in fear for his life. Tadeo ended up getting arrested for assaulting a federal officer, as did Andrea, after she got out to help, saying, "Leave my brother alone, what the hell?" Legal papers filed by the government said she'd "pushed," "pulled," "grabbed," and "dragged" a third agent, who subsequently took a week off work for neck pain.

After the arrests, the whole family—Tadeo, his sister, mother, two brothers, sister-in-law, and niece—were put in a holding cell overnight. He said they had to stand because so many people were brought in. The border patrol had claimed a drug dog alerted on the RV, and it took time to do a thorough search, though no contraband was found.

The case dragged on for ten months, hurting the Tadeos financially and professionally. Finally, their lawyers were allowed to view border patrol video of the incident. As one wrote in the request to dismiss the charges, the video "unquestionably refutes the allegations made by the Border Patrol agents in this case." According to *Star* reporter Tim Steller, who viewed videos of the event, the RV did lurch forward and stop, but the side mirror barely brushed the agent and he did not act in fear for his life. Steller also said video of Andrea Tadeo's supposed assault on the other agent looked more like she touched his shoulder as she attempted to move past. The allegations of her attacking and dragging him were ludicrous.

On November 2, 2017, Judge Raner Collins dismissed all charges against both Tadeos.

This case touched a nerve in Tucson, for a couple of reasons. First, it raised questions about the truthfulness of border agents who claimed they'd been assaulted or were "in fear for their lives." It cast additional doubt on the accuracy of statistics about assaults on agents. Second, the Tadeo case called attention to the increasing prevalence and intrusiveness of immigration checkpoints in the border region. As one of the few places where border patrol agents regularly interacted with local residents, checkpoints generated a lot of friction. Perhaps not surprisingly, although the vast majority of people the border patrol encountered were undocumented, the *Star* found that nearly one-third of alleged assaults (eleven of thirty-five) on Tucson Sector agents in 2016 and 2017 were committed by U.S. citizens. Some of these people, like the Tadeos, were no doubt upset by their treatment at checkpoints.

Increased immigration enforcement, which also included checkpoints and roving ICE patrols far inland, raised a number of constitutional questions. ICE was supposed to be in charge of legal entries at the ports and "internal" enforcement, and border patrol was in charge of unauthorized entries and "external" enforcement, but their jurisdictions overlapped. Both had the authority to detain and search people without warrants, and to search and seize property, within a hundred miles of any border, land or sea. As investigative journalist Todd Miller pointed out in his 2014 book *Border Patrol Nation*, this region encompassed nine of the ten largest cities as well as ten entire states, or about two-thirds of the entire U.S. population. Border patrol agents were also authorized to enter private property anywhere within twenty-five miles of any border.

While abuses occurred on the Canadian border that led to lawsuits, immigration enforcement was concentrated on the Mexican border, and dark-skinned people were singled out. Courts had allowed the practice when, in rulings on Arizona's SB 1070 and other "show your papers" laws, they'd said race or ethnicity could be a factor in deciding who was stopped. An October 2018 *Harper's Magazine* article revealed CBP even used "a complexion code chart, which categorized skin color on a scale from 'white to sallow to olive and black.'"

The acceptance of racial profiling at checkpoints meant that people whose families had lived on the border for generations were routinely stopped and questioned, and not infrequently detained and searched, while white-skinned Canadian snowbirds, for example, were waved through with barely a glance. I know from personal experience this was the case.

One notorious incident took place on June 12, 2012, when, on his ninety-sixth birthday, former Arizona governor Raúl Castro was made to sit outside in ninety-seven-degree heat for more than half an hour. The elderly Castro, ambassador to three countries as well as Arizona's first and, as of 2020, only Hispanic governor, was being driven from his home in Nogales to a birthday luncheon at the Mountain Oyster Club in Tucson. A border patrolman stopped the car at the I-19 checkpoint because it was emitting a small amount of radiation. (After 9/11, border agents got radiation detectors.) The radiation was apparently related to a heart procedure Castro had had the previous day. He was sent to secondary inspection and told to get out of the car and wait. He was given a chair in the shade with a fan blowing, but the heat was oppressive and his condition delicate. His friend told the agents who Castro was and asked if he could sit in the air-conditioned car instead, but they refused. After a while, he was told to go inside to submit to a body scan and fill out forms. As Castro was heading back to his car, an agent stopped him in the sun and made him show ID. He got flustered and dropped his wallet.

Castro eventually made it to his birthday lunch, but the experience was a stark reminder that, when it came to border patrol checkpoints, peoples' constitutional, civil, and even human rights could be ignored.

The issue of racial profiling at checkpoints came to a head in Arizona the following year, when residents in Arivaca, sick of the checkpoint near their town since 2007, began trying to monitor what was going on. One of the reasons the courts had okayed the practice was because there was no data to prove Hispanics were being singled out. The ACLU and others had tried to get Customs and Border Protection to release the relevant data, but the agency had refused, citing privacy and security concerns or, alternatively, arguing that the data didn't exist. So the Arivaca activists, dressed in reflective vests, went out to the checkpoint with clipboards and cell phones and started collecting their own data. The border patrol objected. Citing privacy and security concerns, it set up ropes and cones to keep the activists a hundred feet back or more, preventing them from seeing what was going on. The activists sued, arguing they had a constitutional right to observe the checkpoint.

At first, the case was tossed out. The judge ruled the border patrol could keep people as far back as it wanted. But the Ninth Circuit Court disagreed, ruling in 2018 that the border patrol did not have an unlimited right to keep people at a distance and that people had a right to monitor public police activities. The case was sent back for reconsideration.

At same time, the courts also agreed with the ACLU over the release of data on checkpoints. After suing to get the data released in 2014, the civil rights group had issued a report in 2015 that documented widespread abuses at both checkpoints and by roving patrols. CBP responded by releasing some data, but argued the rest was private.

But in a rebuke to the government, federal magistrate Bernardo Velasco wrote in a January 2017 ruling that CBP couldn't claim Hispanics weren't unfairly singled out if it refused to release the data proving they weren't. Velasco wrote a fifty-five-page recommendation that CBP should release statistics on the nationality and skin complexion of those stopped. He said people's privacy wasn't threatened if their identities were kept anonymous. About false alerts by drug dogs, the judge wrote: "As long as the government asserts that its canines are reliable, it should not be able to avoid producing records about their reliability." Velasco also wrote the government should make available locations of checkpoints where its data was collected, since, "in this day and age, with the use of cell phones, and other electronic means . . . the location of a checkpoint can hardly be kept secret."

Waste, Fraud, and Abuse

By the late 1990s, the border patrol's reputation for lack of accountability was growing as fast as it was. In 2001 the Justice Department's Office of Inspector General announced it was investigating some forty-five agents at the Douglas Station for engaging in kickbacks and other schemes to defraud the government. While the report detailed "troubling practices," no one was ever prosecuted, and some of these agents later went on to serve in the top ranks of the border patrol. The post-9/11 hiring surge led to more cases. An average of one CBP officer a day was arrested between 2005 and 2012, 144 of them for corruption, according to the *New York Times*. By 2018, when CBP had grown to become the nation's single largest law-enforcement agency, with an annual budget of more than $15 billion and some 60,000 employees, it reported about 500 employees had been arrested for a variety of crimes over the previous two years. A July 2019 analysis found 176 arrests of CBP employees in the previous ten months. If continued at that pace, the report said, CBP arrests would amount to an annual rate of 0.5 percent, about five times higher than the arrest rate for other U.S. law enforcement.

In addition to agent misbehavior, government waste and fraud was also associated with the hiring spree:

HOUSES IN AJO: In 2011 Customs and Border Protection spent some $17 million to build twenty-one homes for agents stationed in Ajo, Arizona—a cost of more than $680,000 each. The homes ranged from 1,276 to 1,570 square feet and featured award-winning, energy efficient design and luxury touches including quartz countertops, stainless steel appliances, wireless ceiling fans, and three-car garages. They ended up being only half occupied, as the rent cost of $1,000 to $1,300 per month was too high for the area, and most agents were single or preferred to live elsewhere. Ajo was a depressed town with nearly 30 percent of the houses vacant. CBP also bought twenty park-model mobile homes for $2.4 million to temporarily house agents in Ajo. But, according to a 2014 Office of Inspector General audit, the mobile homes sat almost entirely unoccupied. A local official named Tina West told the *Arizona Republic*: "You could buy any house in town for $100,000. It's just another multimillion-dollar waste."

ACCENTURE: In November 2017 the Trump administration awarded the professional services firm Accenture a five-year, $297 million contract to recruit and hire five thousand border patrol agents. The Treasury Department employees' union immediately objected, saying the money could be better spent on in-house recruitment and retention. A few Accenture employees also circulated a petition demanding the contract be canceled, after the family separation policy came to light the following summer. "We joined Accenture because we want to work for a company that does good in the world, a company that helps vulnerable immigrants, not facilitates putting them into cages," the petition said.

CBP did cancel the Accenture contract in April 2019, just seventeen months after it was awarded, but not because of any protests. While it was officially canceled "for convenience," meaning Accenture was not found to be at fault, a Homeland Security Inspector General's report at the end of 2018 determined the company had fallen way short of its lofty goal of hiring six hundred new agents in its first year. According to Axios, the report found "Accenture had been paid $13.6 million, and had only produced 2 frontline hires for CBP within the first 10 months of the contract." Accenture ended up being paid about $61 million, for a grand total of fifty-six people who accepted job offers with CBP.

Accenture's failure underscored the problems CBP was having hiring and retaining border patrol agents. The agency could not fully meet Congress's requirement of 21,370 agents (there were about 19,500 in 2018), let alone hire the 5,000 more ordered by Trump. Every year between 2013 and 2016, more people had quit or retired from the border patrol than were hired (an average of 904 agents left, while 523 came in). Among the reasons, a CBP statement said, were "changing generational values, the statewide legalization of marijuana and a growing distrust of law enforcement."

The statement seemed to imply applicants couldn't pass drug tests, yet as it turned out, they couldn't pass lie-detector tests either. The Associated Press reported in 2017 that some 65 percent failed. The polygraph requirement had been put in place by Congress after several high-profile corruption cases were linked to lowered standards during the post-9/11 hiring surge. The failure rate renewed debate about how to bring in more agents without lowering standards again. One proposed change was to waive the polygraph requirement for all former military and law enforcement who'd passed background checks or polygraphs within the past three years. But as noted in chapter 3, a lot of people involved in crime and corruption on the border have military or law-enforcement backgrounds. Exempting them from scrutiny could make the problem even worse.

OPERATION STONEGARDEN: This federal grant program, which funded local police to help CBP fight drugs and secure the border, was controversial from its inception in 2009. Critics said it turned local cops into immigration agents, and a November 2017 DHS Office of Inspector General report found widespread financial mismanagement including lack of accounting, misappropriation of funds, and excessive overtime resulting in unfunded pension increases.

Reacting to these concerns, the Pima County Board of Supervisors voted in February 2018 to turn down about $1.4 million in Stonegarden funds. The board had never previously rejected these grants, and response was swift and negative. Under pressure from its own sheriff's department, state lawmakers, and others, the board changed its vote—only to change it back again three times over the next two years. The vacillation illustrated the dilemma Operation Stonegarden posed to border communities.

A week after the first vote, amid criticism from Republican sheriff Mark Napier that they were undermining public safety, the Democratic-majority board reversed itself and voted to conditionally accept the grant. But by August, after a summer of family separations at the border, and its conditions not having been met, the board voted again to reject the money. Besides the financial issue, and concerns over county employees participating in racial profiling and other civil rights violations, board members said deputies were wasting time at remote locations when they should be in town.

"If our officers are sitting at the border patrol checkpoint on the road to Sells, somebody's not being covered," Supervisor Ramón Valadez said after the second vote to reject Stonegarden.

Then circumstances changed again. In May 2019, with Tucson overwhelmed by hundreds of Central American refugee families released on the streets by ICE, the board of supervisors decided to accept Stonegarden money. This time they did so with the caveat that $200,000 of the $1.8 million grant would be used to reimburse the county for expenses related to caring for the refugees. An old Benedictine monastery in midtown had served as a temporary shelter that spring and summer, but with the building slated for redevelopment, the county voted to move the shelter, operated by Casa Alitas, to three unused wings of the juvenile jail. (The juvie had been built during a time of fear over a future full of delinquent "super-predators," who never materialized.) The cost was estimated at $530,000 for six months.

Supervisor Richard Elías, however, stuck with his original vote to turn down the grant, saying there was no way to ensure any of it would go to humanitarian aid. Elías, who died of a heart attack the following March, was right. Homeland Security refused to redirect the money because shelter operations provided "no border security operational benefit." After that, the Tucson Police Department announced it would no longer be accepting Stonegarden grants either, and the county board of supervisors voted for a third time to reject the money.

In 2020 Sheriff Napier was defeated for reelection, so Operation Stonegarden may have been finished in Pima County. But his Democratic successor and the Democratic majority on the board were likely to continue to struggle with the conflicts this program represented, including police cooperation with ICE, rights violations at checkpoints, border militarization, and others.

As for criminal behavior, border patrol agents have been charged with and convicted of crimes ranging from smuggling, bribery, and forgery to child porn, rape, and murder. Among the more notorious recent cases were:

SAWMILL FIRE: In April 2017 an off-duty Tucson Sector border patrol agent sparked a massive wildfire when he blew up a box of explosives during a gender-reveal party on state land in the Santa Rita foothills south of town. The Sawmill Fire burned for more than a week, blackened forty-seven thousand acres, and caused more than $8 million in damages. Video of the blue box exploding in a cloud of blue smoke (indicating the expected baby was a boy) went viral. The forty-nine-second clip recorded agent Dennis Dickey shooting up to seven bullets from a high-powered rifle at the target before the box exploded and ignited the surrounding dry grass. The video also recorded the sound of the wind gusting to forty miles per hour at the time. Dickey, who pled guilty, was given five years' probation and ordered to pay about $220,000 in restitution.

SEXUAL ASSAULT: In May 2019 a Tucson Sector border patrol agent was arrested for sexually assaulting a woman he met through a dating app. Police said the investigation revealed several more potential victims of Steven Charles Holmes, thirty-three, from January 2012 to January 2019. An agent for seven years, Holmes was placed on administrative duties pending outcome of the case. That same month, an internal scandal unfolded when a junior Tucson Sector agent reported that Gus Zamora, an assistant chief in the Yuma Sector, had sexually assaulted her. Zamora was indicted on three counts of felony sexual assault and one of kidnapping. The border patrol allowed Zamora, fifty-one, whose wife of more than twenty years was acting chief of the El Paso Sector, to retire quietly. He pled not guilty and was scheduled for trial.

Agents were also charged with sex crimes against children. In October 2017 Kyle Mrofka, twenty-nine, a supervisory agent at the Ajo Border Patrol Station, was arrested for "lewd acts in which the defendant was at least ten years older than a fourteen or fifteen year old child." The incident allegedly took place in 2013, in the Picacho State Recreation Area, along the Colorado River about twenty-five miles north of Yuma. Mrofka was originally from Yuma and had been with the border patrol nine years.

MURDER: The Laredo Sector saw two sensational murder cases in 2018. In April a border patrol supervisor was arrested for killing his girlfriend and her one-year-old son. Then, over a ten-day period in September, another Laredo Sector supervisor named Juan David Ortiz went on a killing spree, murdering four people he picked up near San Bernardo Avenue, a part of town frequented by sex workers. Authorities said Ortiz, thirty-five, knew all his victims. After the first two were found shot and dumped on rural roads, a third potential victim managed to get away and alert police. Ortiz killed twice more before being caught. Police said he eluded them throughout the rampage by using his law-enforcement training, experience, and equipment to track their movements and cover his own. After his capture and confession, authorities found an arsenal in his tidy suburban home, where he lived with his wife and two children.

The murders, and the arrest of a border patrol agent as the killer, shocked Laredo. People wondered how a person like Ortiz could have been hired in the first place, let alone serve as an agent for ten years and be promoted to supervisor. They wondered what other crimes he might have committed.

A central question underlying these cases, as well as all the other problems attendant to the exponential growth of the border patrol, was whether so many agents were actually needed. In July 2017, for example, there were around 3,800 agents in the Tucson Sector, and 2,177 migrant arrests. That's almost two agents per arrest. By way of comparison, in July 2007 there were around 2,600 agents in the sector and 30,373 arrests. Another comparison found in 2018, "on average, each of the 19,437 Border Patrol agents nationwide apprehended a total of only 19 migrants," or fewer than two per month. Apprehension figures fluctuated seasonally and annually, of course, and went up sharply again in 2019, when agents effected 851,508 arrests border-wide. But as the increase led to renewed calls for more agents, critics asked: if fewer than 10,000 border patrol agents were able to make 1,643,679 apprehensions in 2000, why, twenty years later, were nearly twice as many agents still not enough to make about half as many arrests?

III

The Peaceable Kingdom

Seven

The Triumph of Sanctuary

O n the afternoon of March 24, 1982, about a dozen people of various faiths and nationalities—including one with a bandanna hiding his face—gathered on the front porch of Southside Presbyterian Church in Tucson. Banners in Spanish on either side of the church door behind them read *La Migra No Profana el Santuario* and *Este Es el Santuario de Dios para los Oprimidos de Centro America* ("Immigration police don't profane the sanctuary" and "This is the sanctuary of God for the oppressed of Central America").

Speaking in English and Spanish and addressing a sparse crowd, the pastors and refugees declared the unimposing building a sanctuary for people fleeing civil wars and death squads in Central America. As the banners indicated, they knew they were being watched. That was one of the main reasons for declaring sanctuary. At one point, John Fife, the lanky pastor of Southside, gestured to the plainclothes immigration agent watching them from his car across the street.

"We thought they might come arrest us all right then," Fife said later.

The *migra* did ultimately come and arrest the sanctuary workers, but not until almost three years had passed. The day of the declaration, the mood remained celebratory.

"Today, in this church, human solidarity is out in the open, and oppression is in hiding, waiting for another time without witnesses," said border rancher, Quaker philosopher, and intellectual architect of the nascent movement, Jim Corbett. After the press conference, Southside was filled to overflowing for an ecumenical service that lasted well into the evening.

Thirty-eight years later, sanctuary was resurgent. Founded on the narrow premise that refugees fleeing wars and political persecution deserve protection under international law, by 2020 public awareness and the practice of sanctuary had spread far and wide. The movement had grown in so many ways that it was beginning to resemble the idealized form once envisioned by Corbett: "Sanctuary in its broadest sense," he wrote, "extends far beyond Central America and specific human refugees to the need for harmonious community among all that lives."

Sanctuary Established

In the late 1970s, people fleeing death squads and civil unrest in El Salvador and Guatemala began arriving at the border. U.S. authorities maintained the vast majority were economic migrants, not political refugees, and sent them back to their home countries. Subsequent investigations by the ACLU and others showed many deportees later turned up dead.

The only way for these refugees to get in was to sneak in, but that path was also perilous. In one notorious incident in July 1980, eleven middle-class Salvadorans died of sunstroke in Arizona's Organ Pipe Cactus National Monument after being abandoned by a smuggler.

Jim Corbett, an arthritic, retired rancher and librarian, lived in Tucson with his wife, Pat, and a small menagerie of dogs, cats, goats, chickens, and a mule. In May 1981 Corbett got a call from a friend, who, like Corbett, was a Quaker, or a member of the Religious Society of Friends.

I describe Corbett's story in my book about the sanctuary movement, *Convictions of the Heart*. He had grown up in a nonreligious family in Wyoming, married young, and had several kids before divorcing. He studied philosophy at Colgate and Harvard and embraced Quakerism as an adult when he became opposed to the Vietnam War. In addition to its tenets of pacifism and belief in "that of God" in every person, Corbett was attracted by the faith's emphasis on social activism. He and Pat, his second wife, lived for a while in California, where he taught at a Quaker school. There he took students on goat walks, exercises in nomadic pastoralism in which they had to wander in the wilderness for several days, living off oatmeal and warm goat's milk. (One of Corbett's students told me it was awful.) He learned Spanish while working with Mexican goatherds in Baja and running a small ranch with Pat near the border in Cochise County. He also worked as a librarian at Cochise College in Douglas. Stricken by rheumatoid arthritis, he had to retire, and the couple moved to Tucson.

Corbett's friend called to tell him he had picked up a Salvadoran hitchhiker, who had then been taken away at a border patrol checkpoint. Corbett called the border patrol and learned the man had already been deported.

At first, Corbett tried to work within the system. He visited Central Americans in detention in California and worked with lawyers bailing people out and fighting for their rights. But after realizing that even those with good cases for asylum were being detained and deported without their cases ever being heard, he decided to help them avoid detection.

He began coordinating with other locals, including John Fife, and several Catholic priests and nuns on both sides of the border, to vet refugee claims by Salvadorans and Guatemalans. They interviewed people in prisons or migrant shelters on the Mexican side. If the migrant was found to have a well-founded fear of persecution, the group would then help him or her cross the border and get to safety in the United States.

Corbett knew rural parts of the border from his years as a rancher, and he brought some particularly traumatized refugees through the mountains on mules, but in those days, it was still pretty easy to cross through holes in the fence in downtown Nogales. The main danger was street kids armed with knives demanding money to let people go through the fence. Once the refugees were in Nogales, Arizona, a priest and parishioner at Sacred Heart Catholic Church gave them shelter until a time when the Peck Canyon checkpoint was closed (like during a rainstorm), and they could safely travel to churches and houses in Tucson, and from there to churches, monasteries, synagogues, and other places around the country.

The group tried to operate in secrecy, but word soon got around. The border patrol let them know they'd been "picking up aliens with Corbett's number in their pocket," as Fife said, and that the sanctuary workers were due to be arrested.

Hoping to bring attention to their cause and perhaps shield themselves and the refugees from arrest, the group decided to declare the church a public sanctuary. They picked March 24, 1982, the second anniversary of the assassination of Salvadoran archbishop Oscar Romero, for the event, and in the short run, going public worked. They were not arrested, and the sanctuary movement received a flurry of favorable media attention. Profiles of Jim Corbett appeared on *60 Minutes* and in *People* magazine. He led border crossings accompanied by sympathetic reporters, including one in which he helped a woman with the pseudonym Juana cross into the United States through a rural area of Cochise County in 1984. Juana had been raped by Mexican cops and almost bled to death after fleeing her Guatemalan home when death squads killed her husband. A photo appeared in the *Arizona Daily Star* of Corbett helping Juana climb over the border fence, which in that place and time was a rusty chain-link cattle fence about five feet tall, topped by a single thin strand of barbed wire. The photo would soon figure in the federal trial of the sanctuary workers.

In January 1985 the U.S. government indicted Corbett, Fife, and fourteen others on charges of smuggling, transporting, and harboring illegal aliens. Defendants included priests from Nogales, Sonora, and Nogales, Arizona, nuns from Nogales and Phoenix, and young volunteers and activists from Tucson. Unindicted co-conspirators included other sanctuary leaders and Central American refugees. Other sanctuary workers were charged around this time—activists Jack Elder and Stacey Merkt in south Texas and writer Demetria Martínez in New Mexico, who had had her poetry used against her on the stand—but this case was big, aimed at the movement's leaders, and meant to show that, when it came to immigration policy, federal law held sway.

The indictments helped renew public interest in sanctuary. A defense fund was set up, and millions rolled in. Celebrities like Bonnie Raitt and Joan Baez, both Quakers themselves, came to Tucson to perform at a benefit concert. High-priced lawyers were hired, some local, some from out of town, one each for the eleven defendants who went on trial in Tucson's old downtown federal courthouse in October, 1985.

The magistrate, U.S. District Judge Earl Carroll, was a white-haired man from a prominent Arizona family. Although affable, he seemed unsympathetic to the defendants from the start. During jury selection, one young man with a tattoo on his arm (unusual in those days) said he'd gone to the benefit concert, but he'd never heard of the sanctuary movement.

"I thought sanctuary was something for birds," he said.

Amid laughter, Judge Carroll said, "There is a comment there but I won't pick that up either."

The young man was impaneled.

Judge Carroll also showed flashes of humor sympathetic to the defense. When the prosecutor tried to impugn a refugee's character by saying the man had boasted he was coming to America to get "a car, a house, and a wife," the judge quipped, "Well, shouldn't a man's reach exceed his grasp?"

Another prospective juror said he'd heard about the Salvadorans who perished in Organ Pipe Cactus National Monument in 1980. "I told my family—it's terrible that people have to die like that. They should be able to get in in an orderly fashion." But the man assured the court the memory of what happened wouldn't affect his ability to be impartial, and he was impaneled as well.

The trial lasted six months. It featured few dramatic moments. One came early on, when a young man in the gallery suddenly stood up, yelled, "The blood of Central America is on our hands because we are our brothers' and sisters' keepers!" and slapped two red handprints on the wall. He was quickly hustled out and the wall washed off. The judge did not declare a mistrial because the jury was not in the room when it happened.

A handful of Central American refugees testified, but they were not allowed to say why they had fled their homes. The judge ruled that question inadmissible. "We're not going to get into ears and eyes and individual tortures," he warned the defense.

Carroll also rejected the defense's contention that the Central Americans helped by sanctuary were, in fact, political refugees with "a well-founded fear of persecution" who deserved asylum under U.S. and international law. Corbett had written several papers to that effect. He said sanctuary workers were attempting to uphold laws the U.S. government was violating and were therefore committing "civil initiative" rather than "civil disobedience." But the judge forbade even the mention of the idea. (During pretrial hearings, when one of the defense lawyers had compared sanctuary to the movement led by Martin Luther King Jr., Carroll responded these defendants weren't of the same character of King, and in any case, King had done his time in jail.)

The only relevant question, Carroll ruled, was whether sanctuary workers had helped certain people to "enter without inspection," at such-and-such a time and such-and-such a place, and to "further their illegal presence" in the United States.

As a result, the trial was mostly a tedious recitation of endless meetings at Southside Church about travel arrangements for refugees. The star witnesses for the prosecution were two undercover informants who'd secretly recorded the discussions while posing as sanctuary workers. (Both men, one Mexican American and one white, looked like alien smugglers from central casting, and the churchy sanctuary workers had been suspicious. But Corbett convinced the group to let them stay. He thought it the principled thing to do, and that the informants might even be converted—a naïve hope he'd come to regret.)

Arguments gutted and evidence denied, the defense team decided not to put on a case. The day it was set to begin, all eleven lawyers stood up one after another to announce that, on behalf of their clients, they were resting. It was dramatic, and a huge relief, given the trial had gone on too long already. But some jurors later said they were surprised and let down.

During closing statements, one of the defense lawyers brought up the Virgin of Guadalupe. Judge Carroll stopped him, sent the jury out, and then banned any reference to her, saying her story was irrelevant, prejudicial, and not in evidence. I remember wondering about it at the time. "It's a sign he knows the power of our Holy Mother," explained Socorro Aguilar, a church worker in her late fifties from Nogales, Sonora, who was one of the defendants.

The jury spent nine days deliberating before convicting eight of the eleven defendants on eighteen counts of conspiracy, transporting, and harboring in May 1986. John Fife and Socorro Aguilar were among the convicted, but

Corbett was not. This was mainly because the *Star* photographer who had taken the picture of Corbett helping Juana cross the border had, on First Amendment grounds, refused to testify.

Corbett was surprised at the verdict. He thought at least one juror would side with sanctuary enough to resist the pressure to convict. But the forewoman, a staunch Christian, did not see the requirements of her faith the same way the defendants did.

"Render therefore unto Caesar the things that are Caesar's; and unto God the things that are God's," she said after the verdict. "You see what the Lord says about government. You can protest your lot on this Earth, but in the end, you have to respect your government and its laws."

Although Fife and all the others who were convicted received probation, they remained convicted felons and could not vote or own guns (which was a problem for Fife, a hunter). But later court rulings somewhat vindicated the sanctuary movement. Salvadoran and Guatemalan refugees were given temporary protected status, and undercover recordings in churches were outlawed.

Not long after the trial, the Corbetts left Tucson to found an intentional community, the Saguaro-Juniper Project, thirty miles northwest of Benson near the San Pedro River. The couple and their menagerie were joined by a few other Quakers and like-minded people, who signed a contract agreeing to live in harmony with the land. They built straw-bale houses, generated their own power, and raised organic beef.

Corbett published one book, a philosophical and spiritual memoir called *Goatwalking*, and was working on another when he was stricken with a rare, microscopic form of brain cancer. After a brief illness, he died in his house on the Saguaro-Juniper land on August 2, 2001. He was sixty-seven. Pat Corbett continued to live on the land, and coordinated the 2005 publication of his manuscript, *Sanctuary for All Life: The Cowbalah of Jim Corbett* (a pun on the Jewish mystical text the Kabbalah). But Corbett did not live to see the resurgence of sanctuary and the fulfillment of his prophecy.

※

Sanctuary Revived

As the border crackdown intensified throughout the 1990s and 2000s, the meaning and purpose of *sanctuary* began to change. The term had no legal definition, and in a realization of Jim Corbett's vision, it came to represent a whole host of pro-immigrant policies and practices. These included churches and individuals sheltering people, public and private organizations declaring themselves off-limits to immigration authorities, local and regional law enforcement refusing to cooperate with ICE, and local jurisdictions passing laws to prevent police cooperation with ICE.

The new sanctuary movement came about primarily in response to the stepped-up enforcement against America's long-term undocumented population after 2008. Mass detentions and deportations of tens of thousands for minor offenses or for immigration offenses alone served to expand public acceptance of the idea that undocumented people in general, and not just political refugees, may need and deserve sanctuary. By 2014 scores of cities, counties, states, universities, and other public and private entities were pledging to protect everyone in their care from heavy-handed immigration enforcement.

Declaring sanctuary meant taking on political, and potentially legal and financial, consequences, and a few places balked at the idea. Big cities like Chicago and Portland had no trouble designating themselves as sanctuaries, while Tucson, a liberal city in a conservative state, had to tread more carefully. It declared itself "immigrant welcoming" in 2012 but consistently rejected the "sanctuary" label. Concerned about legal and financial implications, the city opposed the designation even after Tucsonans successfully petitioned to get it on the ballot in 2019. (The initiative failed by a two-to-one margin.) And unlike dozens of other schools nationwide, Arizona's three public universities, the University of Arizona, Arizona State University, and Northern Arizona University, also all refused the sanctuary designation, though they said they had policies in place to protect students and staff from immigration raids.

Churches around the country responded to the mass deportations, as they did during the original sanctuary movement, by sheltering people. Some were doing so quietly. But others, for the same reasons as the original movement, decided to declare themselves sanctuaries. By the end of 2014, about a dozen immigrants had publicly taken sanctuary in churches in cities including Boston, Philadelphia, New York, Kansas City, Denver, Oakland, and Seattle.

In Tucson, public sanctuary was revived at the same place it had begun: Southside Presbyterian Church. The first person to be offered shelter, in May 2014, was Daniel Neyoy Ruiz. He and his family were welcomed in a ceremony in the round, wood-beamed adobe kiva, which had replaced the original square, whitewashed church years before. The pastor during the original sanctuary movement, John Fife, had retired. But the new pastor, Alison Harrington, was a leader of the new sanctuary movement, and she proudly led the congregation in reclaiming Southside's historic role as the nation's first sanctuary church.

Neyoy Ruiz and his wife had come to the United States in 2000, and they had a thirteen-year-old American-born son. In 2011 Neyoy Ruiz was pulled over on I-19 for excessive smoke coming from his vehicle, was found to be undocumented, and was slated for deportation. He went into Southside after receiving his final removal order. He spent about a month inside before ICE granted him a stay.

The second person to take sanctuary at Southside had a much different experience. In August 2014 a Mexican woman named Rosa Robles Loreto entered the church and ended up staying for more than a year. This was hard on her, her family, and the congregation because, for her safety, church members provided round-the-clock accompaniment the entire time. They held nightly vigils for her there—461 in all.

Originally from Hermosillo, Sonora, Robles Loreto came to the States on a visa in 1999 but never returned to Mexico. Mother of eleven- and eight-year-old U.S.-citizen sons, she was pulled over for an incorrect lane change while driving her employer's van in 2010. She was turned over to the border patrol, spent two months in custody, and released on three thousand dollars' bond. When she received a final deportation order on August 8, she went into the church. ICE said she was low priority but refused to close her case.

During the fifteen months she was in the church, some nine thousand "We Stand with Rosa" signs appeared throughout Tucson. People wrote letters and protested. She finally received a stay of deportation and work permit that allowed her to resume her life without fear of arrest on November 11, 2015.

Another Tucson church that had supported the 1980s sanctuary movement, Saint Francis in the Foothills United Methodist Church, also declared itself a public sanctuary in 2014. On September 26 Francisco Pérez Córdova, thirty-seven, a father of five U.S.-citizen children, went into sanctuary at Saint Francis. Also originally from Hermosillo, Pérez came to Tucson to help support his family after his father died when he was sixteen. He was discovered to be undocumented when his brother-in-law reported a burglary at their home to the Pima County Sheriff's Department. Pérez Córdova was placed in removal proceedings and, rather than be permanently separated from his family, went into sanctuary. He spent ninety-four days in the church before ICE closed his case. He got out just in time for Christmas.

In Colorado the interfaith Metro Denver Sanctuary Coalition came together to offer shelter to a fifteen-year Denver resident and married father of two. Mexican-born Arturo Hernández García went into a Unitarian Universalist church on October 21, 2014. A subcontractor, Hernández had been arrested by local police after getting into a fight at work. Although he was acquitted at trial, deportation proceedings began. He went into sanctuary when he received his final deportation order. Eighty-one clergy members wrote a letter to ICE on his behalf, and other supporters started an online petition and funding campaign to help his family because he couldn't work while in sanctuary. Nine months later, in July 2015, Hernández received assurances his case was not a priority. He left the church and went back to work.

While these and other cases played out, the stage was being set for another major showdown between the U.S. government and the sanctuary movement. This time, however, the battleground would not be, as it was in the 1980s, over the legality of small private entities such as churches and individuals providing sanctuary. (That case had been decisively won by the government, which established that people cannot set up their own immigration service.) This time, the battle was much larger and the implications greater. This time, it was over the complex jurisdictional questions raised by large public entities, such as cities, counties, and entire states declaring themselves sanctuaries, and the degree to which local law enforcement should be made to cooperate with immigration authorities. The battle was within government itself.

Sanctuary Everywhere

On January 20, 2017, Trump's inauguration day, Sally Hernandez, the recently elected Democratic sheriff of Travis County, Texas, announced that county jails would no longer automatically grant requests to hold immigrants for deportation if they were otherwise eligible for release.

The announcement made Travis County, which surrounds the city of Austin, a focal point in the fight over sanctuary. Governor Greg Abbott withheld $1.5 million in state grants in response, and Hernandez faced a Texas-sized mountain of criticism. The situation heralded similar fights that took place all over the country after Trump took office.

Shortly after the election, Trump moved to stamp out sanctuary on several fronts. In April 2017 Department of Homeland Security Secretary John Kelly issued a memorandum ordering the expansion of the 287(g) program and the resurrection of Secure Communities, both programs that paid and trained local law enforcement to cooperate with ICE. The same month, Attorney General Jeff Sessions sent letters to nine jurisdictions, including the cities and counties surrounding New York, Chicago, Philadelphia, Miami, Milwaukee, Las Vegas, and New Orleans—places identified as having limited law enforcement cooperation with ICE—threatening the loss of federal funding if they didn't comply. Sessions noted that, in 2016, the Obama administration had issued similar threats to these jurisdictions for their sanctuary policies.

Churches offering public sanctuary were also put on notice. The same month of April 2017, Arturo Hernández García, the Denver man who had spent nine months in the Unitarian Universalist church in 2015, was detained and placed in deportation proceedings when he went to pick up tile for his job. His arrest, as well as the increasing number of arrests of undocumented people in or near hospitals, courthouses, and schools—places previously avoided by ICE—prompted some churches to avoid making public declarations while still practicing sanctuary in secret.

On the question of local law enforcement cooperation with ICE, policies differed from agency to agency, even in the same town and within the same jurisdiction. Confusion reigned. Border sheriffs said they didn't need to participate in Secure Communities or 287(g) because the border patrol was already in their jails. And the cities of Baltimore, Maryland, Albuquerque, New Mexico, and Stockton and San Bernardino, California, all of which had applied for federal grants to confront gun violence and drug trafficking, were surprised to receive letters from Attorney General Jeff Sessions telling them they would not be eligible for the money unless they gave ICE access to their jails. They wrote back saying they weren't sanctuary cities; further, the city of Albuquerque had no control over the Bernalillo County jails, which apparently weren't cooperating to ICE's satisfaction.

In Tucson the issue of local police cooperation with ICE came to the fore in 2013, when city cops stopped a man driving near Southside Church, suspected he was undocumented, and called the border patrol. A "flash mob" of nearly one hundred people appeared and surrounded the border patrol vehicle, refusing to let it leave with the man inside. Several crawled under the wheels of the vehicle and were dragged away and arrested. The episode prompted the police chief to clarify the policy. Chief Chris Magnus wrote in a *New York Times* op-ed on December 6, 2017, that his department cooperated with the feds "to go after drug cartels, human traffickers and transnational gangs." But Tucson Police Department officers were not going to check immigration documents. He added that "Justice Department grants and other federal support funded through our taxes should not be tied to immigration policies."

Officials in Pima County, a 9,189-square-mile region that included Tucson and 125 miles of border, were split over the issue. The Republican sheriff wanted ICE in the jail and working with deputies in the field, but the Democratic majority on the board of supervisors did not. For about a year, ICE had an actual desk in the Pima County jail, but in 2018, amid conflict with the board over Stonegarden funds (discussed in chapter 6), Sheriff Mark Napier said it wasn't needed because there were so few undocumented people being held. While the desk was removed, the tough policy remained: the immigration status of everyone was verified, and ICE was notified when an undocumented person was set to be released in time to pick the person up.

With billions at stake, the standoff between the Justice Department and sanctuary jurisdictions over the withholding of federal grants quickly became a legal battleground. In 2016 the Office of Justice Programs extended almost three thousand grants, totaling $3.9 billion, to states, counties, cities, and other jurisdictions for things like victim services, body cameras, community involvement, and rape kit testing. Just days after Sessions sent the letter threatening to withhold the money, the city of San Francisco and Santa Clara County, California, sued to stop him from enforcing it. U.S. District Judge William Orrick promptly issued a preliminary injunction against Sessions's order, and in November, after finding the order was too broadly written and could potentially affect hundreds of grants that had no connection to immigration, Orrick made the injunction permanent.

Other targeted jurisdictions also responded with lawsuits. A sanctuary city since the 1980s, Chicago had one of nation's strongest policies against cooperation with ICE. It prohibited police from providing info or access to people in custody unless they were wanted on a criminal warrant or had serious criminal convictions. It also had received $33 million in Justice Department grants since 2005, which it had used to buy nearly a thousand police cars, radios, and SWAT equipment. In August the city filed a forty-six-page lawsuit against the Justice Department over the denial of federal funds. More than thirty other jurisdictions filed briefs in support.

In September the courts again sided with sanctuary jurisdictions when U.S. District Judge Harry Leinenweber ruled that Attorney General Sessions couldn't withhold federal grants from Chicago, Cook County, and surrounding suburbs. Sessions responded he would not "simply give away grant money to city governments that proudly violate the rule of law and protect criminal aliens at the expense of public safety."

Meanwhile, the states of Texas and California were engaged in their own internal battles over sanctuary. In May 2017 the Texas legislature passed Senate Bill 4, banning local jurisdictions from enforcing sanctuary policies. It created criminal penalties for police chiefs, county sheriffs and constables in violation, and ordered fines of up to twenty-five thousand dollars a day for jurisdictions that refused to comply. Public officials who violated the ban were also subject to removal.

Although the chiefs of every major police force in the state opposed the measure, Governor Abbott signed it into law. The next day, the state sued Austin city officials for being in violation. The town of El Cenizo and Maverick County, pro-sanctuary areas, sued the state a day later, and El Paso County and the cities of Austin and San Antonio followed a few weeks after. In June the ACLU and LULAC (League of United Latin American Citizens, a Latino civil rights group) sued to stop the law from going into effect. They argued it was "unconstitutionally vague" and violated the First, Fourth, and Tenth Amendments. Activists called it the "show your papers law," like Arizona's SB 1070.

On August 31, 2017, the day before the law was set to take effect, U.S. District Judge Orlando Garcia blocked most of it. But on September 25, the Fifth U.S. Circuit Court of Appeals upheld the part of the law that required local authorities to honor immigration detainers on people otherwise eligible for release.

Travis County Sheriff Sally Hernandez, who had been requiring warrants to hold people, said she would comply with the unanimous, three-judge ruling. However, lawyers representing the cities of San Antonio and El Paso in their suits against the state said the ruling did not necessarily require strict compliance with all requests.

With an estimated 2.3 million undocumented residents, the most of any state, California was the epicenter of the battle over sanctuary. Under Democratic leadership, the legislature had enacted laws to issue driver's licenses and offer in-state college tuition to the undocumented. Los Angeles and many other cities had declared themselves sanctuaries. The California attorney general had led the fight against the Justice Department's attempt to cut federal grants to sanctuary jurisdictions. And in September 2017 the legislature voted to make California a sanctuary state.

The vote came after a late-night compromise between law enforcement and immigrant rights advocates over which offenses would be considered serious enough to trigger an ICE referral. Some eight hundred were named, including some nonviolent ones, as well as crimes that could be charged as either misdemeanors or felonies. It allowed cooperation in jails to continue.

The law barred local police from asking about immigration status. Other laws signed at same time limited ICE from entering schools or workplaces without warrants, prohibited landlords from calling ICE on tenants, and prohibited local governments from contracting with for-profit companies to hold ICE detainees.

"These are uncertain times for undocumented Californians and their families, and this bill strikes a balance that will protect public safety, while bringing a measure of comfort to those families who are now living in fear every day," Governor Jerry Brown said at the signing in October.

The sanctuary laws took effect in January 2018, and by March the Justice Department had filed suit. The government contended that, by enacting laws usurping the federal government's power to enforce immigration law, the state had violated the supremacy clause of the U.S. Constitution. Legal experts said the conflict was between the supremacy or sovereignty clause—the feds have total power to enforce immigration law—and the Tenth Amendment, which gives the state the authority and the duty to protect its residents from harm.

This argument could cut both ways, as the state of Arizona learned in its legal battle over SB 1070. Advocates had sued to stop the law's enforcement on the grounds the state had no authority to make immigration policy. The Supreme Court agreed and in 2012 struck down most of SB 1070. (The court did, however, let stand the law's most controversial provision, which allowed state and local officers to question people about immigration status. Ongoing instances of people being turned over to ICE after traffic stops were, in part, what led Tucson activists to push for sanctuary city status in 2019.)

If California was the epicenter of the national split over sanctuary, Orange County was ground zero for the statewide split. The county had 3.2 million people, with 30 percent of the population immigrants, mostly Latinx and Asian. Three of the five county supervisors were Asian American, and all were Republican. In March 2018 the board voted unanimously to condemn the state's sanctuary law and join the Trump administration's lawsuit against it. The vote prompted vehement protests, with people carrying signs saying "Melt ICE" and "Shut Down Detention Centers."

After the vote, the Orange County seat, Santa Ana, reasserted its status as a sanctuary city, and officials said they planned to join the lawsuit against

California on behalf of the state. Another town in Orange County, Los Alamitos, voted to opt out of the state law, raising the threat of lawsuits against it as well. It joined Escondido in San Diego County and Ripon in the Central Valley, other communities that voted to opt out of the state's sanctuary status.

As the battle played out in California, sanctuary won another round over the denial of federal grant money. On June 6, 2018, U.S. District Judge Michael Baylson ruled the Justice Department could not cut off grants to Philadelphia. He wrote the order was "arbitrary and capricious" and that the city's policy of requiring a warrant to hold people for immigration authorities was reasonable and appropriate. The judge went on to say the stipulations for grant spending were unconstitutional and would require city police to serve as the arm of immigration enforcement. After hearing of the decision, Mayor Jim Kenney called it a "total and complete victory" and did a little dance in honor of his Irish immigrant ancestors outside his office.

The year ended with the short-term future of the sanctuary movement up in the air. On one hand, sanctuary had won legal victories in every case litigated over the withholding of federal grants. In December seven more states and New York City won their lawsuit against the Justice Department, and by the spring of 2019, the agency reported that twenty-eight of the twenty-nine jurisdictions threatened with the loss of grant money had, in fact, received the funds. The one jurisdiction with funds still being withheld was Oregon, which way back in 1987 had become the first state to declare itself a sanctuary for the undocumented.

But the state of Texas continued with its tough anti-sanctuary policies, and California's first year of being a sanctuary state wasn't a huge success. Many advocates felt the declaration had actually made things worse, by emboldening roving ICE patrols in areas where migrants congregated. The death of one farmworker couple, while being chased by ICE around six in the morning on March 13, 2018, prompted particular outcry.

Santos and Marcelina García had lived in the States for sixteen years and had five U.S. citizen children. They'd just dropped off their daughter at Robert F. Kennedy High School in the town of Delano when ICE agents tried to pull them over. Terrified, Santos sped away, and in the ensuing chase, he hit a pole and the car flipped. The ICE agents stopped down the road but did not render aid. Forty minutes passed before an ambulance arrived. A woman on her way to work at a nearby prison stopped and held Marcelina's hand while she died. The couple, originally from Oaxaca, were undocumented, but they weren't wanted by ICE. Agents were actually after Santos's brother, who had an old DUI conviction that made him deportable.

Nationwide, ICE also continued to arrest people in sensitive locations, including courthouses, despite pleas by judges not to do so. It also continued to arrest people who'd been in sanctuary, as well as their supporters. On November 23, 2018, ICE arrested an undocumented Mexican man who'd just left a United Methodist church in Greenville, North Carolina, after being in sanctuary for eleven months. Samuel Oliver-Bruno was originally from Veracruz and had been living in the States for twenty years. He had a wife and son. He was ordered deported when his appeals ran out over a 2014 arrest in El Paso for using a fake Texas birth certificate to reenter the United States.

Oliver-Bruno and several dozen supporters had gone to Raleigh to meet with immigration officials, who detained him. As he was being driven away, the church people locked arms around the van and refused to let it leave. For about two hours, they sang "Amazing Grace" and other spirituals and shouted, "Let him stay!" and "Let your people go!" Twenty-seven were arrested. Oliver-Bruno was deported. His fate taught a lesson to others in sanctuary: don't leave the church.

Despite this case and the fallout from various struggles, sanctuary was still ascendant across the nation and the world. It was being practiced in a variety of places and contexts. In one noted example, a church in The Hague, Netherlands, held a worship service continuously for ninety-six days between October 2018 and February 2019 to protect an Armenian family facing deportation. More than a thousand pastors of various denominations participated. The service ended after the Dutch government agreed to consider this family, and seven hundred others who had lived in Holland for more than a decade, for an asylum policy called *kinderpardon*.

And back on the U.S.-Mexico border, sanctuary was being revived in its purest sense. In late 2018 and early 2019, churches, social service agencies, and local governments mobilized to offer temporary housing to migrant families released by the thousands on the streets of border cities. One of the places where refugees stayed in Tucson, fittingly enough, was a former

Benedictine monastery. The Sisters of Perpetual Adoration had sold the Spanish colonial-style building to a local developer who, before turning it into apartments, opened it to Casa Alitas in the spring and summer of 2019. Scores of volunteers from Tucson and elsewhere organized to provide food, clothes, beds, laundry, medical care, transportation, travel assistance, psychological support, and other services. One volunteer told me she loved hearing the children laughing as they played under the orange trees in the old orchard out back.

Eight

The Jaguar

The video's opening shot shows the jaguar walking right by the camera at night, ghostly and surreal. He glances to the side and for a moment his eyes shine bright yellow, as if from an inner fire that also radiates white from his cheeks and neck and undercarriage. His ears are cocked forward, his stride purposeful but unhurried. His paws look big and brown and almost clownish, like he's wearing dirty leopard-print slippers. His movements convey stealth, yet a complete lack of fear. After a few seconds, he pads away, the dark rosettes on his spotted tan coat shimmering in the dark. Then the scene changes to daytime, and the jaguar is caught twice more, first by one camera as he strolls down a forest trail in dappled sunlight, and then by another on a cloudy day as he steps over a shallow, rocky pool and saunters off into the distance. In all, he's shown for about forty-one seconds.

This video, of a jaguar nicknamed El Jefe ("The Boss") roaming the Santa Rita Mountains near Tucson between 2012 and 2015, caused a sensation when it was released in February 2016. It went viral, quickly garnering tens of millions of views. The images received worldwide news coverage not only because they revealed El Jefe's magnificent self, but because they proved jaguars were coming from Mexico as far north as sixty miles into the United

States. El Jefe joined six other distinct jaguars photographed with remote cameras between 1996 and 2016 in the Santa Rita, Chiricahua, Huachuca, and Dos Cabezas, as well as in other adjoining mountain ranges in southeast Arizona and New Mexico.

El Jefe and his kind were the first wild jaguars to be documented in the United States in many years, and their discovery was not met with unmitigated joy. Government authorities in charge of the border buildup and supporters of an open-pit mine planned for jaguar habitat in the Santa Rita Mountains dismissed the cats' presence as "biologically insignificant." They contended that because no females had been found north of the border, the mine and border wall would not affect jaguar recovery currently underway in Mexico.

Jaguar defenders, however, saw the cats' presence in the States as both a legal justification and a powerful symbol for their battles against border militarization and the Rosemont open-pit mine. They said protection of undisturbed wilderness and wildlife corridors between habitats that straddle the border was essential to the long-term health of both the jaguar and the entire ecosystem. Federal agencies and courts went back and forth in this decades-long struggle, and key decisions tended to side with the wall-builders and mine owners, including crucial permits for the Rosemont Mine issued by the U.S. Forest Service in 2017 and the Army Corps of Engineers in 2019. But the fight was not over, and in 2020 jaguars were still out there, crossing the line. This chapter describes some of their stories and struggles, as well as conservationists' efforts to protect them, other animals, and the land they inhabit.

El Jefe

Ironically, proof that jaguars were coming into the United States from Mexico was provided in part by funding from the border buildup. About two-thirds of the $1 million study that documented the presence of El Jefe, for example, came from Department of Homeland Security funding for studying the effects of existing border barriers. The rest was from the University of Arizona. Two university researchers conducted the three-year study

El Jefe, photographed by remote camera in southern
Arizona. (U.S. Fish and Wildlife Service)

using remote cameras placed at 250 sites across sixteen mountain ranges.
Cameras were placed so that jaguars could be photographed on both sides,
enabling researchers to identify individual animals, since each has a unique
spot pattern.

The remote cameras captured 118 photos and videos of a lone male jaguar
in the Santa Rita and Whetstone mountains from fall 2012 to June 2015. Students at Valencia Middle School dubbed him El Jefe, and he became locally
famous. He lent his name to a cat lounge (where customers paid to hang out
or do yoga with shelter cats), and his image to a twenty-foot-long, ground-
level mural on the side of a building downtown. A mariachi band played
and people cried "Viva!" at the unveiling. El Jefe was not seen in the States
after October 2015 and was presumed to have gone back to Mexico in search
of a mate.

Further evidence that jaguars were taking up long-term residence in Arizona surfaced in September 2017. Two nonprofit groups, the Center for Biological Diversity and Conservation CATalyst, released a fifteen-second video
of another young, male jaguar blinking and looking and walking away, taken
in the Dos Cabezas Mountains near Willcox, in November 2016. The same
cat was photographed in the Chiracahuas the following April, and then again
back in the Dos Cabezas in May. Kids at the Paulo Freire Freedom School
named him Sombra ("Shadow").

A third jaguar was repeatedly spotted in the Huachuca Mountains in
December 2016 and January 2017. He was named by students at Hiaki High

School on the Pasqua Yaqui reservation. They called him Yo'oko, the Yaqui word for "jaguar."

These jaguars were almost certainly all born in Sonora and crossed into the States through the mountains that straddle the border. Male jaguars have big ranges—between nineteen and fifty-three square miles—and young males leave their mothers to seek out new territory. Jaguars live solitary lives and only come together to mate, with males visiting several females in their range. Female jaguars have smaller ranges, between nine and fifteen square miles, and usually stay close to their mother's range. While some biologists say a female jaguar is unlikely to come up into the United States on her own until Sonora reaches carrying capacity, others are more optimistic.

The jaguar (*Panthera onca*) is, after tiger and lion, the third largest of the big cats, and the only non-extinct member of the *Panthera* genus native to the Americas. (The word *panther* is a generic term for all big cats. Leopards, which also come in spotted and black varieties, are smaller and native to Asia and Africa. Florida panthers are actually a subspecies of cougar, or mountain lion.) Jaguars are stocky and low-slung, with a barrel chest and broad shoulders. Adults typically weigh between one and two hundred pounds, but like humans, big males can weigh more than three hundred. They stand about two and a half feet tall and are between three and a half and six and a half feet in length, with the tail another two to two and a half feet. They have a square-shaped head and proportionally the most powerful jaws of the roaring cats. They are expert at ambushing their prey and typically kill by crushing the skull. (One of the other mothers in my son's mariachi group told me about a cattle rancher she knew in Sonora who was riding his horse down a mountain trail when, all of a sudden, a jaguar leaped up, landed on his shoulder, and bit him on the head. He survived, but tales like that help explain why poaching still occurred in Mexico.)

Unlike most cats, jaguars love to play, bathe, and hunt in water. They are said to have evolved eating sea turtles on the coast of what is now Central America. They are crepuscular, meaning they like to hunt at dawn and dusk, and broad in their tastes, eating everything from crocodiles and monkeys to deer, peccary, sloths, tapirs, rodents, eggs, frogs, and fish. In one study, researchers identified dozens of animal species in a jaguar's habitat, and every one but the jaguar itself was considered prey.

Their camouflage coats are typically yellow and tan but range from orange and reddish brown to black. Regardless of color, all jaguars have ghost striping on their faces and spots that are solid on the neck and leg and rosette patterned on the body. Black jaguars are the result of a dominant gene mutation affecting about six percent of jaguars, almost none of whom live north of the Isthmus of Tehuantepec in southern Mexico. Unlike black varieties of Old World leopards, black jaguars are never born to spotted parents or have spotted litter mates. Although black jaguars were once thought of as a separate species that was even fiercer, biologists now know them to be the same cat.

Jaguars feature prominently in the stories, songs, poems, and myths of many Native peoples. They were central to Olmec and subsequent Mesoamerican cultures. The Mayans believed the Jaguar God of the Night battled underworld forces so the sun could rise in the morning. Aztec warriors were named after jaguars, and priests wore jaguar skins. The Comanches used their pelts for arrow quivers. Jaguars are still considered sacred to many tribes, and they maintain symbolic power. In the 2017 hit movie *Coco*, a Mexican folk-art spirit guide, or *alebrije*, appears in the form of a giant, colorful flying jaguar and saves the day. And in a lawsuit filed in 2018, the jaguar's spiritual significance to the Tohono O'odham was cited as legal justification against the Rosemont Mine. As reporter Tony Davis wrote, "the jaguar is known to the O'odham as *ooshad*, the spotted one, and is regarded as part of the spirit world that appears to give tribal members strength and access to the world's animating spirit."

Though by 2018 there were only an estimated fifteen thousand left in the wild, jaguars still roamed many parts of South America, Central America, and Mexico. They once ranged farther north, into what is now the southwestern and southern United States, from California to Louisiana. But by the mid-twentieth century, they were hunted to extinction in the States, mostly as the result of a U.S. government predator control program that paid bounties for dead jaguars. The last known female jaguar in the United States was shot at Big Lake in the White Mountains of Arizona—some 175 miles north of the border—in 1963.

The question of how prevalent jaguars once were in Arizona—which goes to the question of whether the population could be revived—is in dispute. One study said there were 70 credible sightings between 1900 and 2015, all but 4 prior to 2001. ASU biology professor David Brown wrote in his 2001 book *Borderland Jaguars* that more than 60 jaguar killings had been documented in Arizona from the 1900s through the 1970s. But other experts disputed those numbers. They said the number of jaguar sightings and killings was much lower, and that credible sightings alone numbered no more than 33. According to these experts, of the 21 credible sightings prior to 1963, only 4 were female, and, of the 12 since, none were.

"Having a jaguar in Arizona is neat, but from a population standpoint it is completely insignificant," said Jim deVos, assistant director of wildlife management for the Arizona Game and Fish Department, which issued a report saying construction of the Rosemont Mine would not affect critical jaguar habitat. Experts like deVos argued that jaguar recovery should focus on Mexico, where there was a viable population. It was a good point. While some said it might be possible to reintroduce jaguars in Arizona, Diana Hadley, co-founder of the Northern Jaguar Reserve in Sonora, told me that would be extremely difficult for the relocated animals.

Mine proponents also argued that the site was not critical habitat because it was at the far northern end of the jaguar's range. The habitat and jaguars found there were not essential to the animal's survival. But other experts disagreed.

"A peripheral animal does have biological importance," said Melanie Culver, the University of Arizona professor who led the study that discovered El Jefe. "In peripheral populations, you often get unique genetic variation and unique forms of genes. They're a little different than individuals at the center of the range." These animals are adapted to different habitats, Culver said, "particularly in the northern edge where the climate is more arid. They may be more adapted to drought and other conditions that could happen with future climate change. I would never understate the importance of a peripheral population, from a genetic adaptation standpoint."

In addition to its stance in favor of the mine, Arizona Game and Fish had a spotty history with jaguar recovery. In February 2009 the agency captured, sedated, radio-collared and released a jaguar named Macho B. Estimated at fifteen years old, Macho B went downhill quickly. Twelve days later he was recaptured and euthanized at the Phoenix Zoo. The episode led state and federal biologists on the U.S. side to avoid capturing and collaring the rare cats that appeared here, sticking to photographing them instead.

Arizona Game and Fish was just one of many agencies weighing in on the impact of the mine, and as was so often the case, different branches and jurisdictions and even people within these entities did not agree. The U.S Fish and Wildlife Service, for example, was divided on the question. In 1997 the service listed the jaguar as an endangered species after a lawsuit by the Center for Biological Diversity and other organizations. In 2014 another legal ruling resulted in the service designating 764,000 acres, including the mine site, as critical jaguar habitat. Its own scientists issued an opinion saying the mine would be detrimental to jaguar recovery. But in the service's final biological opinion on Rosemont in 2016, the conclusion was reportedly changed by higher-ups to say the mine would have no impact because only "lone wandering males" had been found on site.

There was no doubt the impact of the Rosemont Mine would be severe. Canadian-based Hudbay Minerals Inc. was building the $1.9 billion project. Plans called for a five-thousand-acre worksite with an open pit that would span one and one-quarter miles across and more than a half-mile deep into the ground. It was expected to extract 224 million pounds of copper annually for nineteen years.

In an op-ed in the *Arizona Daily Star*, Tucson conservationist Randy Serraglio described what would happen. "Hudbay Minerals, Inc. plans to blast a gaping hole in El Jefe's home turf," he wrote, "and then bury thousands of acres of surrounding public land under more than a billion tons of toxic mine waste. Along with brilliant lighting, daily blasting and huge trucks rumbling through the area every seven minutes, the rolling oak woodlands of the Rosemont Valley would be converted from prime jaguar habitat to a vast industrial wasteland." Mine opponents also expressed alarm about the project's impact on the mountains' watersheds, including the pumping and polluting of underground aquifers, which provided drinking water for Tucson and the surrounding region.

In 2017 key decisions by two agencies with the power to delay or stop the project went against the jaguar. The Arizona Department of Environmental Quality gave the mine the go-ahead, and, in a major blow to opponents, so did the U.S. Forest Service. The Forest Service decided that, under the 1872

Mining Act, it couldn't stop construction. Three Native American tribes, the Tohono O'odham, Pasqua Yaqui, and Hopi, filed suit in response in April 2018. They said the mine would destroy their sacred places and habitat for their sacred animal. Environmental groups also filed suit.

Aided by southern Arizona representative Raúl Grijalva, the tribes and environmentalists also took up the fight in Congress to reform the 1872 Mining Act. This outdated law allowed pretty much anyone, including foreign mining companies, unfettered license to extract minerals from U.S. public lands. Not surprisingly given its vintage, the law also failed to account for mining's serious and permanent environmental costs.

As the legal struggles unfolded, Hudbay Minerals continued to prepare the site. The company became a good corporate citizen in Tucson, donating money to schools and charities and receiving the backing of the local business community. In January 2018 its executives announced to investors at meetings in Toronto, Ontario, and Whistler, British Columbia, that the price of copper was high enough to start mining in 2022. Company officials said Rosemont would eventually be the third-largest copper mine in the United States and would generate about half of Hudbay's copper production in the Americas by the mid-2020s.

In March 2019 Rosemont cleared its last major regulatory hurdle when the U.S. Army Corps of Engineers issued it a Clean Water Permit. More lawsuits were filed in response, and though they had no power to stop construction, the Pima County Board of Supervisors voted again to oppose the mine. Politicians, Native nations, environmentalists, and others vowed to battle on, but the future of El Jefe's stomping grounds looked very much in doubt.

Then a miracle happened. In late July, on the evening before Hudbay Minerals was set to start filling in protected washes with debris (so it could claim the washes no longer existed to protect), a federal judge stopped the project. Ruling in the suit filed by the Tohono O'odham, Pasqua Yaqui, and Hopi nations, U.S. District Judge James Soto found that the Mining Act of 1872 gave Hudbay the right to do what it wanted with land that had proven mineral deposits, but the company did not have the right to do what it wanted—in this case dump millions of tons of waste rock and tailings—on adjacent land that did not have deposits. Claiming the decision was a threat to the entire mining industry, Hudbay, joined by the U.S. Justice Department, appealed Soto's ruling. Investors were told work would be delayed until 2023 at the earliest. But for the time being at least, El Jefe's home territory remained relatively unscathed.

Viviendo con Felinos

In May 2018 two photos of dead jaguars were presented at a conference in Tucson on the status of the endangered cats. One showed a large jaguar suspended from a rope that had been tied around its left rear paw and hoisted over a tree branch. The animal was sprawled out vertically, its muscled body almost filling the frame. The other photo showed a close-in image of a smaller dead jaguar rope-tied to a fancy western saddle on the back of a dark horse. Both images were said to have been captured in the mountains of southern Sonora or northern Sinaloa in 2017 and 2018.

The photos, which the Mexican conservation group Primero Conservation received from anonymous sources over WhatsApp, raised concern at the conference. Primero's research had shown a steep decline in jaguar sightings in a region some 110 miles south of the border, and Primero veterinarian Ivonne Cassaigne said she thought poaching was primarily responsible. The population had dropped 71 percent between 2009 and 2015. The group identified thirteen adult males, eleven adult females, and two cubs in 2014 and 2015, and even fewer in subsequent years. In one core area where ten jaguars were found in 2009–2011, none were found in 2017–2018.

The problem of poaching really hit home the following month, when another secretly taken photo of a dead jaguar was posted on Facebook. This one looked like a pelt on its way to becoming a jaguar-skin rug, split open and draped over a frame with the head still attached. Biologists in Mexico compared the image to photos of known jaguars, including several who'd been photographed in the United States. They then sent the photo to the Arizona Game and Fish Department, which also did a comparison. In the words of Assistant Wildlife Management Director Jim deVos, there was a "very high correlation" between the spot pattern of the pelt and one of the known jaguars.

Sadly, the spots exactly matched the coat of the jaguar who'd roamed southern Arizona's Huachuca Mountains in 2016 and 2017. It was the one who'd been named Yo'oko by the Pasqua Yaqui students.

"We're very upset that somebody killed that jaguar," preserve biologist Carmina Gutiérrez González said. "I just can't believe that. It's really sad for us."

"The real tragedy is having to explain to those kids at Hiaki High School that somebody killed their jaguar," Randy Serraglio said.

In late June a Nogales, Sonora, rancher who was involved with conservation said he'd heard Yo'oko was trapped and killed about six months prior in northern Sonora, somewhere between the Río Cocóspera Valley and the border. The Río Cocóspera ran through the rancher's land, which lay about twenty-five miles south of the line. The owner of the Rancho El Aribabi said the jaguar was apparently not intentionally killed but rather snared by a trap set for a mountain lion that had been killing calves.

Yo'oko joined Macho B as the two jaguars known to have been in the United States who were later confirmed dead.

Killing jaguars was illegal in Mexico, as it was in the States, but occurred with relative frequency. Some twenty-five jaguars were known to have been killed between 2010 and 2018, including at least six, two wearing radio collars, in a 170-square mile area in northern Sonora. One of the radio-collared kills was a female named Corazón ("Heart").

Corazón was an eight-year-old mother of three cubs. Biologists took some thirty-three photos of her, with and without her babies. In 2012 she was poisoned by a rancher. Her collar gave off the death signal. Lying next to Corazón were the remains of a javelina, also poisoned, and surrounding her were the footprints of her cub, who was never found. Her body had been burned but the collar left on.

The death of Yo'oko, and the ongoing evidence of poaching presented at the conference, showed the need for greater education and efforts to help Sonoran ranchers learn to live with cats. But the news wasn't all bad. Farther from the border, a healthy, breeding population appeared to be holding its own.

One hundred and twenty miles south of Douglas and Agua Prieta, in the foothills of the Sierra Madre, researchers using remote cameras had photographed hundreds of jaguars roaming a two-hundred-square mile survey area since the early 2000s. The area included the fifty-five-thousand-acre Northern Jaguar Reserve and fourteen surrounding cattle ranches. The reserve was run by the Northern Jaguar Project, a binational nonprofit founded by Arizona- and Sonora-based conservationists. In addition to maintaining the reserve, the project worked with local ranches, schools and government to cut down on poaching and help bolster the breeding population in Sonora.

Diana Hadley, one of the project's founders, grew up in Tucson and lived for many years on a ranch that fronted the border near Douglas. In 2003 she and her late husband, ecologist and writer Peter Warshall, helped arrange for the purchase of a ranch in prime jaguar habitat and "took the cows off it."

The reserve was located near the confluence of the Río Aros and the Río Bavispe in eastern Sonora. Its northern end formed a peninsula between the two rivers, both of which were forded easily by jaguars, including Corazón. In addition to rivers, the reserve featured mountains, canyons, cliffs, tropical deciduous forest, desert, thorn scrub, forest, and oak woodlands. Endangered and threatened animals living there included eagles, macaws, ocelots, badgers, desert tortoises, and otters.

"The program is called Living with Felines, or Viviendo con Felinos," Hadley said. "The ranchers sign contracts that they will not harm any of the four cats [jaguar, ocelot, mountain lion, and bobcat]. We gave them assistance with environmental projects like water tanks, outhouses, and gabions to stop erosion. We worked with local cowboys to help select camera sites, in pairs, on either side of an arroyo, because we want to see both sides of the animal.

"The project provides financial reward to the ranchers every time a cat is photographed on their land; 5,000 pesos [then about $320] for a jaguar, 1,500 for an ocelot, 1,000 for mountain lion and 500 for bobcat. One rancher said he loves having the cameras on his ranch so he can tell where predators are and can move cows away from them." Another rancher said he'd noticed there had been no predation by jaguars and very little by mountain lions after hunting was banned on his land. "Since they're not killing javelina and deer, they're not killing our cats. They are asking for 'No Hunting' signs on their ranches," Hadley said.

The research showing a jaguar population decline, Hadley noted, was conducted east of the Río Aros, north of the reserve and closer to the Chihuahua border, primarily between 2008 and 2014. But during the following four years, on the other side of the river and only a few miles southwest, the jaguar population showed some increase. The photos detected almost eighty individuals, including five cubs.

The jaguar population was increasing on the reserve and surrounding ranches because the prey population was increasing. "Ivonne's group imported javelina and vaccinated them for canine distemper and other diseases, so they are healthy and prospering and increasing too," Hadley said.

"A Surprising Eden"

The Sky Islands are a group of some forty mountain ranges stretching from the Sierra Madres in Mexico to the Mogollon Rim of Arizona and New Mexico. Encompassing hundreds of thousands of square miles of rocky cliffs, grasslands, pine forests, pure flowing streams, and impassable wilderness, they connect the Sonoran and Chihuahuan Deserts to both the Sierra Madres and the Southern Rockies. Like El Jefe himself, the Santa Rita Mountains are part of a single Sky Island bioregion, the Madrean Evergreen Woodland, which features oak, juniper and pine.

A May 2017 *Scientific American* article on the potential impact of the border wall called the Sky Islands "a surprising Eden." It said these mountains provided an essential refuge, passage, and water source for resident and migratory animals, many of which, like the jaguar, are threatened and endangered. The Coronado National Forest, which fronted fifty-three miles of border, encompassed most of Arizona's Sky Islands. It was extremely biodiverse, with some seven thousand identified species of plants and animals. Bird species were particularly diverse: although southeastern Arizona made up less than one percent of the land area of North America, more than four hundred species—almost half of all bird species in the U.S. and Canada combined—had been observed there. The region was an internationally known mecca for bird-watchers. The Coronado also contained the most at-risk species of any national forest, including key pollinators like bats, bees, and butterflies.

The U.S. Fish and Wildlife Service recognized the importance of the Sky Islands as migratory corridors when it put the jaguar on the Endangered Species List in 1997. Of the six formal units of critical habitat it designated for the jaguar, five crossed the border. In its 2017 recovery plan, the agency also addressed the impact of border barriers. It said the animals could pass through Normandy fencing used to prevent vehicle crossings, but "fences designed to prevent the passage of humans across the border also prevent passage of jaguars."

The jaguar was not the only animal threatened by border wall construction. The ocelot was another. About the size of a bobcat, with a coat pattern similar to a jaguar, the endangered feline was captured on camera several times in southern Arizona in the mid-2010s. Ocelots are extremely rare in the United States, and these were thought to have come over from Sonora. One was photographed in the Santa Ritas and two in the Huachuca Mountains. One of the Huachuca ocelots was also photographed by a private citizen in the town of Patagonia, meaning the cat traveled between the two mountain ranges. Twice during a twenty-four-hour period, a single camera captured all four native cats (jaguar, ocelot, mountain lion, and bobcat), making southern Arizona the only place in the United States where these creatures coexisted, and truly wildcat country.

Many other threatened or endangered species and subspecies lived in the border region, and some were already being affected by existing border security measures:

SONORAN PRONGHORN ANTELOPE: One of the original animals on the Endangered Species List in 1967, the Sonoran pronghorn has faced a variety of human-caused and environmental threats to its existence ever since. Almost all of the pronghorns' original range, from Nogales to Yuma, was lost to development and drought before the border buildup even began. Its range on the U.S. side of the border is now restricted to the Cabeza Prieta National Wildlife Refuge and part of the Barry Goldwater Bombing Range. After a severe drought in the early 2000s, the population dwindled to some thirty animals. A captive breeding program helped bolster its numbers, and by 2016 an estimated two hundred lived on the U.S. side and at least nine hundred on the Sonoran side. Watering holes were being provided for the pronghorns on the U.S. side, although as with leaving water in the desert for humans, the practice was controversial. Some experts said man-made waterholes attracted predators that killed pronghorn fawns and should only be used temporarily in the case of severe droughts. But other wildlife managers said they were only replacing water that had historically been available before humans drained the rivers dry.

Construction of border barriers across prime pronghorn habitat had made things worse. The two populations were cut off from each other by pedestrian walls along part of the border and Normandy fencing in others. Pronghorns could cross the Normandy barriers but usually didn't, biologists said. Migrant, smuggler, and border patrol activities also disturbed the shy and elusive animals.

BLACK BEARS: A study reported in 2011 in *Biological Conservation* magazine found that a subpopulation of black bears on the Arizona border was shrinking, possibly after being cut off from its main group in Sonora by border fencing. The study was done using bear DNA from hair snags collected by pieces of barbed wire set up near bait. The study also said roads and urban sprawl were affecting the bears, which were found to be more genetically similar to bears in Mexico than bears in other parts of Arizona.

CACTUS FERRUGINOUS PYGMY OWLS: This "desert gnome," as *Birds of Southeastern Arizona* calls it, sports rust-and-white streaked feathers and stands less than seven inches tall. It nests almost exclusively in saguaros, rarely flies more than five feet off the ground, and with its long talons is a crepuscular hunter of birds, rodents, scorpions, and lizards. Endangered in both the United States and Mexico, its migration patterns have already been disturbed by border wall construction. Habitat loss caused by population growth in southern Arizona is also a threat. A survey done in 2006 verified only twenty-six individuals in the state.

Additional animals threatened by the border barriers include the Mexican gray wolf, peninsular desert bighorn sheep, the Chiricahua leopard frog, as well as many types of turtles and fish. The U.S. Fish and Wildlife Service estimated that 111 endangered species and 108 migratory bird species could be harmed by border wall expansion.

Evidence of the wall's impact on wildlife also appeared in the form of photos or videos of animals interacting directly with, or being stopped by, border barriers. One photo showed a small herd of deer blocked by the border fence at dusk. Another showed a Sonoran Desert toad trapped up against a grate at the base of a wall. And one night in April 2015 two border patrol agents in Naco, Arizona, photographed ghostly images of a mountain lion straddling the top of the border fence. The cougar had somehow climbed the eighteen-foot-tall structure. The cat walked along the top of the fence for several yards before jumping off on the Mexican side. The photos went viral when posted on social media a month later by Arizona Game and Fish. Although the posting didn't say so, Diana Hadley told me she heard it was a mother whose cub had gone through the fence.

Despite the many hundreds of miles of walls and fences, a few places remained where animals could cross the border unimpeded. According to the conservationist group Sky Island Alliance, a total of forty-nine linear miles of Arizona border, mostly extremely rugged territory through the Baboquivari and Patagonia Mountains, had no barriers at all.

Groups like the Sky Island Alliance, the Sierra Club, the Wildlands Network, and others were fighting to protect these still-unbroken wildlife corridors. They worked with public and private organizations on both sides of the border to lessen the impact of border security on wildlife, prevent erosion and damage, and restore wetlands and riparian areas. Projects included:

SAN BERNARDINO NATIONAL WILDLIFE REFUGE: This 3.61-square-mile refuge lies along the border about twenty miles east of Douglas, Arizona. It was established in 1982 to protect the shrinking San Bernardino *cienega*, or wetlands, an essential migratory corridor through the Sky Islands. The refuge protects parts of the Upper Río Yaqui watershed as it flows across the border, and of the six native species found in the river—the Yaqui topminnow, the Yaqui chub, the Yaqui beautiful shiner, Yaqui catfish, Mexican longfin dace, and Mexican stoneroller—four are listed under the Endangered Species Act. The U.S. Fish and Wildlife Service operates a recovery program for the fish at the refuge. The service worked with a number of agencies and organizations, including the border patrol and the Sierra Club, to keep human activity away from the river and avoid fencing the Río Yaqui. The rest of the refuge had Normandy fencing.

CUENCA LOS OJOS FOUNDATION: This binational organization has had great success restoring wetlands in the San Bernardino Valley south of the wildlife refuge. Starting in the 1990s, it placed gabions—large galvanized wire cages filled with rocks—in and along arroyos dried out by years of drought and overgrazing. The gabions trapped the rainwater, and as the water table rose, more gabions were piled on—up to twenty-four feet high in Silver Creek. More than four thousand acres of wetlands were restored. The foundation was able to reintroduce a number of native plants, and the marshlands became overgrown with tall grasses buzzing with insects. The refuge also gave the foundation trees to plant in the washes, which help trap rainwater when the gabions broke or wore out. The border patrol reported the project also helped reduce smuggling in the area, since the ground was too wet to drive on.

On the Mexican side, residents of a downstream collective farm called the 18 de Agosto feared the gabions would collect all the water, but the opposite happened. "It doesn't rush by like before," Alberto Terán Figueroa, an 18 de Agosto resident who also worked for the Cuenca Los Ojos Foundation, told the *Arizona Republic*. "It doesn't dry up." The farm's well was replenished, and there was more surface water for the livestock.

BORDER BIOBLITZ: In March 2018 scientists from the Next Generation of Sonoran Desert Researchers, a binational organization of more than six hundred scientists across forty disciplines, began an annual, one-day citizen-science effort to record as many plant and animal species on the border as possible. The researchers surveyed eleven sites, ranging from the San Diego–Tijuana area to southeastern Arizona. Some 95 observers representing 16 organizations recorded 868 species during the event, which was held for a second time the following spring. N-Gen wanted to study the range of biodiversity in the border region to establish "what's out there, on the ground, when we're talking about a wall," director and cofounder Benjamin Wilder said. "We're trying to provide information and data to make informed land use decisions." Canceled in 2020 due to the COVID-19 pandemic, the BioBlitz resumed in the spring of 2021.

Other surveys of plant and animal life also took place regularly on the border; the Cuenca Los Ojos Foundation, for example, held an annual Christmas bird count. Among birds documented by a researcher at one watering hole in December 2017 were golden eagle, ferruginous hawk, red-tailed hawk, grasshopper sparrow, Sprague's pipit, chestnut-collared long-spur, northern harrier, horned lark, loggerhead shrike, vesper sparrow, eastern meadowlark, western meadowlark, and common raven. (According to my bird book, ravens are "bold and resourceful" and "widely considered the most intelligent of all birds." They are accorded the highest place in the origin stories of several Native American tribes, that of Creator Bird.)

MILKWEED AND AGAVES: In December 2019 volunteers with the Western Monarch Butterfly Conservation Plan planted milkweeds—the monarchs' only food—near the Whitewater Draw Conservation Area in McNeal, Arizona. Part of a multistate, fifty-year effort to slow the crash of monarch populations, the project aimed to put milkweeds all along the path of their annual migration from the Sierra Madre to Canada. Monarch conservation efforts were also underway in Mexico, where the butterflies' mountain homes were under siege from illegal logging, avocado farming, climate change and other threats. (In January 2020 two activists who'd worked to protect Mexico's largest monarch forest in Michoacán were found dead within the span of a week.)

Another multiyear, binational conservation effort centered on planting agaves. Volunteers with Bat Conservation International and other groups were planting a million agaves over ten years along the migration route of endangered bats between southern Arizona, New Mexico, and central Mexico. The Mexican long-nosed bat and lesser long-nosed bat are nocturnal feeders on agave flowers and fruit and pollinate many other native plants, including columnar cacti in Organ Pipe National Monument, along their way. Agave used to be abundant on the border, and it's been cultivated for millennia for uses including food, fiber, and tequila. But it grows slowly, and over-harvesting, development, climate change, and other factors led to its decline. This effort was already succeeding: in 2018 the lesser long-nosed bat—population two hundred thousand and rising—became the first bat ever to be removed from the Endangered Species List.

Nine

El Norte

On December 11, 2018, near the end of a hard year on the border, I was privileged to witness a religious ceremony that symbolized both the intermingling of Mexican and American cultures and hope for a better future the region represented.

The event was a mariachi Mass in honor of the Virgin of Guadalupe, held every year on the night before her feast day, at the Our Lady of Fátima Parish in southwest Tucson. The ceremony featured a reenactment of the Holy Mother's four appearances before humble peasant Juan Diego in December 1531, about ten years after the Spanish conquest. The apparitions occurred on a hillside called Tepeyac, near the Aztec capital of Tenochtitlán.

It had been a tumultuous year, and it wasn't over yet. Trump declared a national emergency on the border, and starting in the fall, ordered thousands of National Guard troops to the region. The soldiers strung thickets of razor wire along the tops and sides of fences in urban areas, and closed lanes at ports of entry for exercises, hurting trade and commerce. Border politicians decried the deployments. They said asylum-seeking Central American families then journeying to the border required a humanitarian, not a military, response. They called for the razor wire to be taken down and troops returned to the barracks as soon as possible. The Central American families,

Central American families camped at Nogales port of entry, hoping to apply for asylum. (Mary Whitehead)

meanwhile, who'd hoped to receive provisional entry into the United States, had arrived to find the ports were taking only few applicants a day. Upon learning they'd have to wait months just to be seen, people grew frustrated and desperate.

In late November several dozen migrants were arrested after trying to rush the border wall and port of entry at San Ysidro. Though no one got through, the port was closed briefly, and U.S. authorities faced condemnation when images appeared of women and children running and crying amid clouds of teargas and pepper spray. A former border patrol official defended the use of pepper spray on Fox and Friends, saying, "You could actually put it on your nachos and eat it." The year ended with the government shutting down over Trump's demand for $5 billion for a border wall, and more tear-gassing of migrants protesting in Tijuana on New Year's Day. (These episodes were a prelude to the police teargassing of Black Lives Matter protestors in front of the White House, and many other locations, during the pandemic summer of 2020.)

Some migrants made the decision to try to cross through the desert. Large groups of "quitters"—border patrol slang for migrants who crossed the border intending to surrender and possibly request asylum—were then being arrested and sent to overcrowded facilities. Taking that route meant getting into the country more quickly, but it also meant possible family separation, months in detention in miserable conditions, and either immediate or eventual expulsion. At the very least, it meant a permanent black mark on one's record, making one's chances for asylum even less likely. And it was very dangerous.

The danger of that route was made clear in December, with the deaths of two Guatemalan children in border patrol custody. The first one to die, seven-year-old Jakelin Caal Maquin, was in a group with her father and about 160 other parents and children who surrendered to agents on December 6 near the remote border crossing of Antelope Wells, New Mexico. It was about 9:15 p.m. The group was held overnight and boarded a bus for the Lordsburg station, ninety-four miles away, around 4:30 a.m. Jakelin began vomiting on the bus. When the bus arrived at 6:30, she had stopped breathing. She was airlifted to a hospital in El Paso, where she died at about 12:30 a.m. on December 8. An autopsy found she'd died of sepsis.

The other Guatemalan child who died in custody was eight-year-old Felipe Gómez Alonzo. He and his father traveled from their village in the impoverished and violent province of Huehuetenango to the border, where they planned to ask for asylum and go live with relatives in Tennessee. They were detained near El Paso on December 18, and bused to the Alamogordo station, about ninety miles away, the next day. After five days in detention, on December 24, Felipe was taken to the hospital in Alamogordo with flu-like symptoms. He was diagnosed with a cold and fever, given antibiotics and ibuprofen, and released after ninety minutes. His health continued to deteriorate and, vomiting and nauseous, he was returned to the hospital later that evening. He died there shortly before midnight.

After Felipe's Christmas Eve death, Homeland Security Secretary Kirst-jen Nielsen came to the border to vow changes. These included more training and supplies for border patrol in remote areas, improved communication with non-Spanish-speaking migrants (both Jakelin's and Felipe's parents spoke Indigenous languages), and better medical screening for migrant children in detention. Investigations were also launched into what occurred.

In between these two deaths, the Mass for Our Lady of Guadalupe took place. The event was a celebration of hope and faith amid hard times, and a demonstration of the true binational heart of border people.

El Grupo Guadalupano

Midcentury modern in design, the amphitheater-shaped sanctuary at Our Lady of Fátima church featured tall windows facing the mountains, and a stained-glass star of many hues at the center of a peaked, wood-beamed ceiling. Wooden pews surrounded the altar, and wide, carpeted steps led up to an elevated and open main floor, where stack chairs could be arranged in rows to accommodate large crowds. The Mass to welcome Guadalupe always occurred at night, and on this night, the building was warmly lit and full of people, from babes in arms to elderly in wheelchairs. Some wore their Sunday best, while others were dressed in jeans and T-shirts.

El Grupo Guadalupano, members of the congregation who'd been preparing all year for the celebration, wore red and sat in the pews up front. Those participating in the ceremony wore *folklórico* costumes: Colorful embroidery skirts and blouses for the women and girls and plain white tunic and pants for the men and boys. The altar and steps leading to it were adorned with more than two dozen poinsettias. A statue of Our Lady of Guadalupe stood to one side, on a throne surrounded by dozens more fresh red roses.

My son's mariachi group played the Mass, which took place entirely in Spanish. Led by Cameron on the trumpet, they began with a rousing song to accompany the processional, "Buenos Días Paloma Blanca":

Buenos días paloma blanca,
hoy te vengo a saludar,
saludando a tu belleza
en tu reino celestial.

[Good morning white dove,
today I come to greet you,
greeting your beauty
in your celestial reign.]

Eres madre del creador,
que a mi corazón encanta,
gracias te doy con amor
buenos días paloma blanca.

[You are mother of the creator,
Who enchants my heart,
I give you thanks with love
good morning white dove.]

The Mass followed the regular ritual, with the mariachis playing and singing most of the standard songs: "Señor Ten Piedad," "Alleluya," "Pescador de Hombres," "Santo," "Resusitó," "Amén," "Padre Nuestro," "Cordero de Díos," "Bendito," and "Ave María." But instead of a sermon, the play was acted out.

A female narrator read the story from the lectern while a man dressed in white peasant costume with a red bandanna around his neck took the part of Juan Diego. Recorded Spanish guitar music played as he trotted across the side aisle to the throne, where a dark-skinned teenage girl had appeared, dressed in the traditional dark green satin cape with gold trim and stars.

The narrator recounted that the first vision took place on December 9, 1531. Juan Diego was on his way to work when the familiar image appeared to him on Tepeyac Hill. Although evidently the mother of the God of the conquerors, she was a Native person like he was and spoke to him in his native language, Nahuatl.

Juan Diego fell to his knees in astonishment. Guadalupe told him she was "the mother of the very true deity" and directed him to tell the bishop that a church to her should be built on the site. (The place of these events, outside Mexico City, is now the site of the Basilica of Our Lady of Guadalupe, the most-visited center of Catholic veneration and third-most-visited holy place in the world. Juan Diego's *tilma* [cloak], with the image of Our Lady imprinted on it, is on display behind the altar.)

Spanish guitar music played as Juan Diego trotted across the front of the altar to where a man playing the bishop sat. On this night, the bishop was played by the recently retired bishop of Tucson, Gerald Kicanas, wearing a miter. Juan Diego told the bishop what he'd seen, but the bishop scoffed that Mary would have revealed herself to a lowly peasant. He told Juan Diego to go away and get back to work. The sequence was repeated, but still the bishop did not believe.

As the narrator next described, Juan Diego was supposed to go back to Tepeyac Hill to get proof. But his uncle, Juan Bernardino, fell ill. Believing his uncle was dying, Juan Diego went to Tlatelolco in the early morning of December 12 to find a priest to give his uncle last rites. He took a different route because he was embarrassed he hadn't shown up as promised. But the Holy Mother intercepted him on the road, and said her famous words:

Let not your heart be disturbed.
Do not fear any sickness or anguish.
Am I not here, I who am your mother?
Are you not under my protection?
Am I not your health?
Are you not happily within my fold?
What else do you wish?
Do not grieve or be disturbed by anything.

After chiding Juan Diego for not trusting in her, the Holy Mother assured him his uncle was recovered. Then she told him to go to Tepeyac Hill and gather the roses he would find there. Juan Diego danced across the room with his *tilma* folded in front of him. When he got before the bishop, he said, "Here are flowers in December." He opened the *tilma*, fresh roses fell out, and there was a sparkly embroidered image of the Our Lady of Guadalupe on the front.

The play concluded with a ceremony in which two lines of Guadalupanos formed and danced to Spanish guitar music across the side aisles toward each other. The women wore bright-colored headscarves and the girls wore flowers in their hair, and they both carried baskets of artificial flowers. The men danced with their hands clasped behind them. The two lines met at the center aisle and then danced to the altar to present the flowers to Guadalupe.

At the end of each line, a man carried a huge flag, one Mexican and one American. The men held the flags aloft as the two lines danced toward each other, and when they met, they waved and crossed the flags, again and again.

Afterward, everyone went to the church hall for hot chocolate and menudo (a spicy tripe soup).

In his book *Border People*, historian Oscar Martínez provided many insights into the different types who live on the border. He categorized the three major groups—Mexicans, Mexican Americans, and Anglo Americans—by their level of interaction with the other side. El Grupo Guadalupano, and other members of the Fátima parish, were what he would call "bicultural and transnational" Mexican Americans, "vast numbers" of whom "maintain substantial bonds with Mexico." These people were typically bilingual, had family on both sides, and traveled frequently back and forth (at least before the pandemic). The Guadalupe celebration was emblematic of their ability to integrate and take pride in both cultures. Most of the other parents of Cam's mariachi bandmates were also in this category. Because mariachi is such traditional Mexican music, some parents were relatively recent immigrants who spoke little or no English. Their children, however, all spoke English and were fully transnational.

Southern Arizona Democratic congressman Raúl Grijalva was also a bicultural and transnational Mexican American. He was born in 1948, on the Canoa Ranch south of Tucson, son of a *vaquero* (cowboy) who got citizenship under the Bracero program. A tireless crusader for the rights and interests of border people, Grijalva served on the Tucson Unified School District board and the Pima County Board of Supervisors before being elected to Congress in 2003. "Growing up on the border, having family in both Nogales, I've always seen this as a special place, unique in this country," he told me.

My friend Yolanda was another type of border person, the kind Martínez called "nationals." These were people who had little interaction with the other side. Even though she had a border-crossing card and came to visit me many times over the years, she spoke almost no English and remained an outsider to American culture.

Yolanda's children and grandchildren, however, were a different story. Her youngest daughter, Bobbi, married a U.S. Customs agent and moved to a big house in Sahuarita, south of Tucson. Bobbi's two daughters grew up bilingual and bicultural. Yoli's three other grandchildren by her older son also attained U.S. citizenship. In one generation, this family went from being national Mexicans who felt out of place in the States to being transnational Mexican Americans who were completely integrated into Mexican American society.

Martínez also divided the Anglos who lived on the border into several overlapping categories. Some were nationals whose interaction with the predominant culture was limited to, say, taking out-of-town guests to Mexican restaurants. (One on Tucson's south side, Mi Nidito ["My Little Nest"], was famous for a presidential plate commemorating a 1999 Bill Clinton visit, in which he ordered a prodigious amount of food.)

I still think of myself as a national, even though I've lived on the border almost my entire adult life. It's a multilayered phenomenon. In some ways, I'm an insider. My interest in border issues allows me to participate in the local culture more than most Anglos, and my friendship with Yolanda opened up a whole world I would otherwise never have been able to enter. But I grew up in Boston, and I'll always be an outsider to Mexican, Mexican American, and Native American societies. I miss cues and embarrass myself and others all the time. (Not to mention my Spanish is pretty sus, as Cam would say.) However, there's another level on which my whiteness makes me an insider. I'm able, for example, to get waved through checkpoints, while they are treated like outsiders in their own land. It's bound to cause resentment.

One native-born border Anglo who embraced the prevailing culture was Robert Francis "Beto" O'Rourke. A rising-star Democratic politician from El Paso, O'Rourke served as mayor and U.S. congressperson before running unsuccessfully against Ted Cruz for U.S. senator in 2018 and for president in 2019. Although a fourth-generation Irishman, O'Rourke grew up speaking Spanish and adopted the name Beto, short for Roberto, to signify his bicultural identification. He took on the issue of gun violence after a mass shooting at a Walmart in his hometown on August 3, 2019, ended the lives of twenty-two people, almost all Mexican or Mexican American. (The killer had driven nine hours from his hometown near Dallas to stop, as he wrote online, "a Hispanic invasion of Texas.") The most memorable moment of O'Rourke's presidential campaign occurred in response to this massacre, when he vowed during a debate, "Hell yes, we're going to take your AR-15!"

Yet, like a true border person, O'Rourke displayed divided political loyalties. He had big Republican support in El Paso, where his father-in-law was a real-estate developer, and he voted for many pro-corporate and pro-free-trade bills while in Congress. He was friends with African American Republican congressman Will Hurd, with whom he famously went on a live-streamed road trip from San Antonio to Washington, D.C., in 2017. (Hurd, who also represented a Texas border district, declined to run for reelection in 2020.) The 2020 presidential race was clearly not O'Rourke's time, as he was one of the first to drop out. Yet his participation in the race, along with that of former secretary of Housing and Urban Development and San Antonio mayor Julián Castro, meant that perspectives and values of border people were being increasingly represented on the national stage. (Castro's immigration plan is included in the epilogue.)

The Solar Wall

Ethnobotanist, nature writer, and sustainable agriculture advocate Gary Nabhan was another Mexican-identified, Anglo border person with a vision for the future. Founder of Native Seeds/SEARCH, Nabhan held the Kellogg Endowed Chair in Food and Water Security for the Borderlands at the University of Arizona Southwest Center. He lived with his wife, a nurse practitioner, on a quiet ranch nestled among the rolling hills outside Patagonia,

Arizona. I drove down from Tucson to interview him on a crystal-blue-sky winter morning in February 2018.

Nabhan met me at the highway in his Prius, and I followed him along a winding dirt road, past the Native Seed farm, with a sign that said "Nabhan" in Arabic (he is of Lebanese descent), then up a small hill to a comfortable, light-filled home. The living room overlooked the farm and had a sweeping view of the surrounding mountains. There we talked about the solar wall and other forward-thinking ideas for sustainable border development.

The idea for a solar wall was first proposed by Mexican poet, diplomat, and environmental activist Homero Aridjis in response to Trump's call to build a wall. A friend of Nabhan's, Aridjis was known for his innovative, problem-solving ideas. He'd founded an organization called the Group of 100 that, among other efforts, helped fight air pollution in Mexico City, create monarch butterfly sanctuaries in Michoacán, and save endangered whales, sea turtles, and vaquitas (tiny, nearly extinct porpoises) in the Gulf of California. In a December 2016 *Huffington Post* article, Aridjis and solar energy advocate James Ramey proposed, instead of a wall, an array of solar collectors on the border that would generate power, provide jobs, and be wildlife friendly and culturally sensitive.

The idea was later picked up in a *Wall Street Journal* op-ed written by Vasilis Fthenakis, director of the Center for Life Cycle Analysis at Columbia University, and Ken Zweibel, then director of the Solar Institute at George Washington University. They calculated that a string of solar panels built along on the Mexican side could generate two thousand gigawatts of electricity a year, enough to power the entire border region on both sides, while being far less costly and environmentally damaging than a wall.

In April 2017 Nabhan invited Aridjis, Ramey, and Fthenakis to Tucson to talk about the proposal. The discussion was held as part of an Earth Week forum at the University of Arizona. The panel explained that the project would not be a continuous wall of solar collectors. "No one involved in this idea wants a wall," Nabhan said. "We were upset when one of Trump's five finalists for the wall was fifty feet tall with a solar panel on top."

"We have to try to find a solution, because the wall exists already," Aridjis said. "We have to find a solution for the people and the environment and also the economy."

As Nabhan told me,

> We're talking about collectors in the valleys to create energy because both sides of many border communities are still off the grid. Statistics produced by Homero and his team found this area could produce with solar energy most of what the U.S and Mexico needed. We could create jobs, rebuild communities and legalize people being there. We could train people to be solar and potentially wind energy technicians, at twenty-five or thirty dollars an hour. Not just techs, but planners who could offer services in other communities on both sides of the border. We could break the glass ceiling out of menial jobs and end dependence on big power companies.

Nabhan would also like to see the solar wall address disparities in food security along the border in the form of an "agri-voltaic border cooperative." As he wrote in an op-ed in the *Arizona Daily Star*, "Heat sensitive food crops could be grown under the solar photovoltaic arrays, as they are now being done at three Tucson schools and at a demo project at Biosphere 2. Rainwater could be collected off the solar collectors to irrigate crops for use at nearby schools, clinics and homeless shelters in rural border communities."

Any discussion of a border wall, solar or otherwise, must include the Native peoples who live there, Nabhan noted. "A fifth of the land along the border belongs to Indigenous communities who also do not want a wall," he said. "The Tohono O'odham are interested in these projects, since they pay more for their energy than other users, but we don't make policy for them. None of us are solar missionaries. We respect the tribe's sovereignty. We will not get the border right if we think this is just a nation-to-nation negotiation."

Nabhan had a strong faith in what was possible on the border but was not unrealistic about the challenges. He cautioned that the U.S.-Mexico border has the greatest wealth disparity of any border on Earth, with poverty in Mexico resulting in poor diets, education, and health care, as well as a lack of access to clean water and sanitation. The economic disparity had also led to great exploitation of Mexican workers and natural resources by the United States and Canada, as well as the turning of Mexico into a narco state. There were persistent problems on the U.S. side as well, including lack of attention to crucial cross-border issues like water and wastewater flows.

"The entire border has been neglected for a long time," he said.

A more holistic approach was needed: "Rather than thinking the issue is about simply 'fixing things at the border,'" Nabhan said, "we need equity on both sides for how we treat people, particularly people who bring us our daily bread. The only way we'll get over border conflict is by reducing disparity and including the economic and social well-being of people on both sides."

Two and a half years after this interview, when the pandemic reached the border, the poverty and neglect Nabhan described exacted a huge price. For most of 2020, hospitals on the U.S. side were overwhelmed with people who'd contracted COVID-19. Many were relatively young, though already in poor health, or worked in low-paying jobs without proper safeguards. Those in Mexico also suffered greatly. Yolanda knew entire families who died, and migrants in Nogales lost a champion on December 18, 2020, when Juan Francisco Loureiro, the founder and director of Casa San Juan Bosco, died of COVID at age seventy-six. (His family said they would keep the shelter going.) Indigenous peoples on both sides were especially hard hit. The Navajo Nation, where poverty was so extreme many people lacked basic utilities, suffered one of the worst outbreaks in the United States. The nation responded with fortitude and self-reliance, however, and helped organize numerous public and private groups to provide water, food, health care, electricity, sanitation, and vaccines to the stricken communities.

As for idealistic notions like the agri-voltaic cooperative, they were put on hold throughout the Trump administration while environmentalists battled his walls (more on that in the epilogue). But the ideas were still viable; Nabhan was working on a demonstration project with Indigenous Seri and Comcaac people near El Desemboque, Sonora. During a visit in July 2020, he and other volunteers found these impoverished villages stricken by COVID-19 and terrorized by cartel violence in nearby Caborca and Puerto Libertad, but grateful they had not been forgotten by their American friends.

El Norte

On December 18, 2018—the same day eight-year-old Felipe Gómez Alonzo was apprehended by the border patrol—I attended a memorial service for all the migrants whose remains had been recovered in the Arizona desert the previous year. The late afternoon event was held annually, on International Migrants Day, at the potter's field behind Evergreen Cemetery in central Tucson. Although the weather was cold and blustery, several hundred showed up to pay their respects, including nuns, priests, border activists, lawyers, people in suits from the Mexican consulate and medical examiner's office, and families of those who'd died or gone missing in the desert. There were even a few homeless people.

A small platform had been set up for the speakers, and next to it hung a quilt representing the 123 human beings whose remains had been found or identified—including a number of *desconocidos*, or unknowns—in 2018. The names were embroidered on a quilt that also featured desert scenes and skulls and crosses and tombstones as well as an outline of the Arizona-Sonora border. It was made mostly from clothing and other artifacts abandoned by migrants in the desert. Debbi McCullough, a Green Valley Samaritan and artist whose work also featured objects left behind by migrants, described the scenes.

Tohono O'odham activist Mike Wilson and tribal leader David Garcia offered prayers. Then Álvaro Enciso, who headed the Tucson Samaritan project Where Dreams Die, was invited to plant a cross. Enciso had made and placed more than eight hundred crosses where migrants had died in the desert.

"These crosses are not just for the people here, but for the migrants who are dying all over the world to make a better life for their families," he said. "We honor the courage of people who left everything behind and came here to El Norte, looking for the American dream."

"This work will never end."

Enciso dug a hole beside the path around the pauper's field and planted a three-foot-tall, green wooden cross.

A man from the medical examiner's office wearing a three-piece suit spoke. After recounting the growth in the number of desert deaths over the previous twenty years, he said, "We wish it would slow down." He said this cemetery held the remains of about nine hundred unidentified migrants or those who had no family—the largest single location in the United States.

More prayers were spoken, and water sprinkled. The senior pastor of Catalina United Methodist Church, Dottie Escobedo-Frank, talked about Jesus and his family being migrants. John Fife, the retired pastor of Southside Presbyterian, spoke about solidarity with migrants dying in the Mediterranean and other places around the world. Five members of the church and altar society of the Yaqui Capilla Señor de los Milagros sang a mournful Native song, accompanied by a beating drum.

Robin Reineke, director of the Colibrí Center for Human Rights, introduced the family of a deceased border crosser who'd just been identified. Marco Antonio Ramírez Moreno's mother and sister carried pictures of a smiling young man, perhaps in his mid-twenties. Ramírez had tried to cross in 2013. His remains were found in 2016 and finally identified through a DNA match on November 20, 2018.

"We searched for him for five years. I couldn't sleep. I always had hope we'd find him alive," Ramírez's mother said in Spanish. His sister translated. "It was the first time he crossed. He thought it would be easy. He was coming to visit me. He was a good man, a good worker. He had three kids."

"He spent three years in the desert," Ramírez's mother said. Her voice trembled. "At last he can rest. Thank God for all those with good heart who helped me find him."

Afterwards, the names of the dead were called out, and the attendees each took a cross with the name, or the word *desconocido*, printed on it. Led by the Yaqui drummer, they processed slowly, in single file, around the potter's field. As the marchers reached the first corner, they passed between two columbaria—adobe, chest-high, wall-like structures built to hold cremains.

Each time the name or the word *desconocido* was spoken, the crowd responded "Presente!"

At the end of the recitation of names, the Guatemalan girl who died in border patrol custody was added.

"Jakelin Caal!"

"Presente!"

In *American Nations*, Colin Woodard wrote that one of the things that distinguished the people of El Norte from those of other regions was their democratic activism. The hundreds who showed up at this memorial service were an example. They were part of a larger, El Norte–based movement to defend and protect undocumented migrants that had grown up in response to the post-IRCA crackdown. This movement consisted of at least a dozen organized groups in southern Arizona alone. They included desert death, humanitarian aid, and search efforts such as Humane Borders, No More Deaths, the Samaritans, and the Colibrí Center; legal rights organizations such as Derechos Humanos and the Florence Immigrant and Refugee Rights Project; educational programs such as BorderLinks, which took church and student groups on border-study visits and tours; and umbrella groups such as the Border Action Network. Many similar and parallel organizations existed in Texas, New Mexico, California, Colorado, and other states, as well as on the Mexican side of the border.

The movement to defend and protect migrants was just the latest in a long line of political and social movements originating on the border. On the Mexican side, Woodard noted, many of the leaders of the Revolution came from Sonora. Among them were miners from Cananea, who in 1906 were the first to strike for better health and safety standards in mines (and were still fighting for their rights more than a hundred years later). The border was also the origin of political leaders who challenged the hegemony of Mexico's late twentieth-century ruling elite. Luis Donaldo Colosio, the martyred reform candidate assassinated in Tijuana in 1994, was from Magdalena, Sonora, where Padre Kino is buried.

On the U.S. side, the Chicano-rights movement naturally came out of El Norte. César Chávez and Dolores Huerta led the farmworkers movement in California, which became a powerful symbol of hope and resistance for those fighting nonviolently against overwhelming odds. The Raza Unida party, formed in Crystal City, Texas, in 1970, fought for bilingual education and organized Mexican Americans to vote.

Tucson began a tradition of welcoming refugees in the 1970s as well, with Chilean victims of the Pinochet regime and soon after, survivors of Central American civil wars, some of whom came through the sanctuary movement. Local Catholic, Jewish, Lutheran, and other resettlement organizations went on to help refugees from Africa, including the Lost Boys of Sudan and survivors of the Rwandan genocide. Groups that worked with refugees sprung up. Owl and Panther helped children recover from trauma through art and poetry. The Iskashitaa Refugee Network organized volunteers, primarily African and Middle Eastern refugees, to glean and distribute unsold produce from local farms and wholesalers. (*Iskashitaa* means "working together cooperatively" in Somali Bantu.) This group also helped distribute produce to refugees and asylum seekers stranded on the border after the Trump crackdown.

Other examples of social progress emanating from the border were described by Gary Nabhan in a November 2018 op-ed in the *Nogales International*:

> Arizona has been the nursery grounds for some of the most healing, culture-bridging social movements in American history. The right of any citizen to have access to clean drinking water was codified among our state's earliest legislative actions. The Collaborative Conservation Movement emerged from the Malpai Borderlands Group in southeastern Arizona and the Diablo Trust in northern Arizona into a respectful dialogue between ranchers and environmentalists throughout the West. And the Local Foods Movement demonstrated that both rural and urban dwellers could rally around the notion of environmentally-friendly food production practices which could create new jobs and even new businesses while bringing our families fresh, nourishing food.

Nabhan's examples pointed to another area in which border people were leaders, that of building coalitions and mediating conflict (even between northern and southern Arizona). On March 14, 2019, several Tucson conflict-mediation and peace-building groups got together to sponsor a symposium on nonviolent responses to the border crisis. The keynote speaker was Bernard Lafayette Jr., a seventy-eight-year-old civil rights icon who'd worked closely with Martin Luther King Jr.

Lafayette had been a Freedom Rider, led lunch-counter protests, and helped found the Southern Christian Leadership Conference and Student Nonviolent Coordinating Committee. His talk on "Kingian Nonviolence,

Border Justice and Immigrant Rights" at Pima Community College was sponsored by the Culture of Peace Alliance, the Center for Community Training and Dialogue, and other groups. He spoke on a panel with four locals: a teenage activist, a field biologist who studied small animals on the border, the head of the Border Action Network, and the head of the Culture of Peace Alliance, who also led a project to help Sikh teens in immigration detention. There were at least a hundred people in attendance, representing a variety of ages, races, genders, and ethnicities.

Lafayette began by praising Tucson. He said King got a lot of speaking invitations and had to be selective about which ones to accept. The requests he accepted were ones where he felt he could reach out to different groups and build coalitions. The variety of faces in the room and the diversity of organizations represented, Lafayette said, showed that Tucson was the kind of community King would have liked to encourage.

King in fact visited Tucson twice. The first time was in September 1959, when he visited the Tohono O'odham reservation and spoke to a Sunday Evening Forum at the University of Arizona. According to a *Star* story republished after his April 4, 1968, assassination, King told the group about having been denied a motel room in Phoenix the night before. He said: "Even though the vacancy signs were up, we were informed that they had just rented the last room. At one place, we watched and saw some white people check in. We had to sleep in our car all night. The next morning we went into a restaurant to get breakfast. They told us they didn't serve Negroes. They were very apologetic about it, but we couldn't get breakfast!"

The second time King came to Tucson was in March 1962. He spoke before the same forum and announced his plan to submit a "second Emancipation Proclamation" to President John F. Kennedy to end housing, education and employment discrimination. The *Star* article said he "hammered hard for 55 minutes on the thesis that integration was progressing, had a long way to go but would triumph eventually." The audience gave him a standing ovation.

Fifty-one years after King's assassination, Lafayette described to a similar Tucson audience the six principles of Kingian nonviolence. He said these principles were laid out in King's first book, *Stride Toward Freedom*, published in 1958, and were influenced by the teachings of Mahatma Gandhi and César Chávez. They were also influenced by Reverend James Lawson

Jr., who, through the interfaith Fellowship of Reconciliation, trained Lafayette, John Lewis, Diane Nash, and many more civil rights leaders in nonviolent protest. Lafayette, like fellow King associate Bayard Rustin, was also strongly influenced by Quakerism. He worked for the American Friends Service Committee in Chicago in 1963, organizing tenants living in dilapidated housing projects, teenagers facing gang violence, and families trying to integrate a public swimming pool. The principles are

- Nonviolence is a way of life for courageous people.
- The Beloved Community is the framework for the future.
- Attack forces of evil, not persons doing evil.
- Accept suffering without retaliation for the sake of the cause to achieve the goal.
- Avoid internal violence of the spirit, as well as external physical violence.
- The Universe is on the side of Justice.

Lafayette then outlined the six steps to nonviolent social change, derived from King's 1963 essay "Letter from a Birmingham Jail": information gathering, education, personal commitment, negotiations, direct action, and reconciliation. He talked about the importance of fighting structures of oppression rather than individuals; of listening to, without agreeing with, opponents; of being passively resistant, but still resistant; and of not abandoning principles or values to get agreement, yet seeking areas of shared values over which agreement can be forged.

After Lafayette spoke, the panelists talked about how they were applying these principles in their daily lives and work. The student activist described rising above internal injuries inflicted by teachers and other adults who'd discouraged him and let him down. The biologist described obstacles, physical and otherwise, to his cross-border studies of endangered snakes, lizards, and turtles, and how peaceful communication strategies had helped him, over thirty-five years in the field, to get along with border guards and local ranchers. (This peace-making scientist, Phil Rosen, died of cancer in September 2020.) The head of the Culture of Peace Alliance, who was named Sat Bir Kaur Khalsa and wore a white turban, explained how she practiced nonviolence in her work with teenage Sikh refugees from India and Pakistan, as well as with the staff at Southwest Key in Tucson and other shelters where they were detained.

Juanita Molina, head of the Border Action Network, spoke directly about the border crisis. Noting the thousands of desert deaths, she said, "The cumulative violence and death is leaving a generational footprint." The tragedy was compounded by the fact that most border patrol agents were Latinx or African American: "We are policing our own."

"The grief and militarization are polarizing," she said. Responding to the situation "requires radical acceptance. It requires listening to the grief and pain, listening to 'the enemy,' listening without agreeing, and challenging institutional violence, because we are fighting for the survival of our people."

Lafayette ended his talk with hope for the future. He told the group that, toward the end of his life, King had spoken about wanting to build an international community of love, peace, and justice. Lafayette had dedicated his life to bringing that vision into being.

"The beloved community is a global community," he said.

Border people were working to build this global community in many ways. In addition to the organizations and activities previously described, they were leading medical charities, businesses, art projects, sports, concerts, cultural events, and other programs that linked people binationally:

SAINT ANDREW'S CHILDREN'S CLINIC: This free clinic for low-income Mexican children with disabilities began operating out of Saint Andrews Episcopal Church in Nogales, Arizona, in 1972. Thousands of children with cerebral palsy, vision, hearing or speech impairments, amputations, and other conditions were helped by the all-volunteer medical and support staff. The nonprofit had a $4.5 million annual budget, all privately donated, 98 percent of which went to patient care. About 225 to 250 children were seen, mostly from Nogales, Sonora, but some from farther away, the first Thursday of every month except July. The clinic also arranged with Children's Surgery International and other organizations for fifty to sixty youngsters to receive cleft lip and cleft palate surgery in Hermosillo, Sonora, each October, and worked with Shriner's Hospitals so that children who needed surgical care in the States received it. The clinic paid for travel and other expenses for the children and families. The annual Christmas party was also an event, with volunteers and gifts coming from groups across southern Arizona.

CAFÉ JUSTO: This coffee roasting and exporting business in Agua Prieta, Sonora, linked a farmers' cooperative in southern Mexico to customers all over the United States and Canada. Inspired by a coffee farmer who migrated north to the border after Hurricane Mitch wiped out his livelihood in 1998, Café Justo (Just Coffee) began in 2002 with twenty-five families in the cooperative. It expected to sell 1,000 pounds of coffee its first year. It sold 13,000. By 2018 it was selling more than 56,000 pounds annually of organic arabica and robusta coffee, grown by more than a hundred families across four communities in the states of Chiapas, Veracruz, and Nayarit. The farmers controlled cultivating, roasting, packing, exporting, and set the price, while the cooperative provided health care, social security, emergency funds and potable water to the farms and nearby communities. It helped people stay in their hometowns and provide education for their children. In partnership with Frontera de Cristo, a binational ministry of the Presbyterian Church, Café Justo opened a coffee shop in Agua Prieta, called Café Justo y Más, in 2016. The coffee shop helped provide jobs for youth in drug rehab, a meeting place for local artists and activists, and a customer base for the coffee. Alonso López, one of the founders of Café Justo, said he's heard from people interested in starting similar enterprises in both Nogales and Ciudad Juárez.

BORDER YOUTH TENNIS EXCHANGE: Kids from the Casa Hogar Madre Conchita girls' shelter in Nogales, Sonora, and the Boys and Girls Club in Nogales, Arizona, received tennis lessons, played on courts at the University of Arizona, and shared photos, videos, and stories of their experiences. This ten-week program, which took place in 2017 and 2018, was modeled on Arthur Ashe's tennis programs for underprivileged youth. Although the exchange program was suspended during the 2020 pandemic, organizers continued to work with kids on the Mexican side. Father Sean at Kino Border Initiative told me they planned to use the enclosed driveway of KBI's new migrant center as a practice court.

HUGS NOT WALLS: In El Paso a group called the Border Network for Human Rights sponsored an event in which families separated by the border were allowed to meet in the middle of a concrete drainage channel near where the Rio Grande passes through downtown. U.S. authorities watched as people from both sides mingled for twenty minutes, and a Catholic Mass was held. For many, it was their once-a-year chance to embrace deported parents, children, or spouses. Some 240 families participated on Saturday, May 12, 2018, the sixth year for the event. In 2019, however, a big new fence was being built right where the families had met in the past and, organizers said, Customs and Border Protection and other agencies thwarted their every attempt to find an alternative location. They had no choice but to cancel.

"Today, in this America, led by this administration, a family hug and a fraternal embrace represent 'a threat to national security.' This is beyond irrational," Border Network leader Fernando Garcia said. Despite the obstacles, Garcia and others were able to hold the event in October and resume it again in 2021.

BORDER ART: A giant baby looming over the border wall was among the most memorable of dozens of artworks created in response to the crackdown. Built on scaffolding by the French artist JR, the sixty-five-foot-tall cutout of a boy appeared to be reaching over the fence from the Mexican town of Tecate, about forty miles east of San Ysidro, during the month of September 2017. Observers found the work delightful, and its existence all too brief.

A lot of border art was, by necessity, ephemeral. Bisbee, Arizona, artist Gretchen Baer ran Studio Mariposa, a cross-border art project that operated out of a colorfully painted house near the border crossing in Naco, Sonora. She brought in artists and musicians from all over the United States to work with local children. For eight years, Baer and her students painted a mural on the Mexican side of a mile-long stretch of border wall. In 2017 the painted section was torn down to make way for a new wall. Here and elsewhere on the border, some of the art-covered pieces of wall ended up in museums and galleries or incorporated into other artworks and installations.

In Nogales, fourteen-foot-tall metal sculptures of human figures pushing against the fence were allowed to stand for a while on the Mexican, but not the U.S., side. The figures were later moved to the University of Arizona mall. Other temporary art installations included twenty-eight tethered balloons, which looked like giant eyeballs, floating over a binational art walk in Douglas–Agua Prieta in 2015, and, in the spring of 2018, award-winning artwork from Tucson high school students projected on the border wall in Nogales, Arizona. The colorful images included children hugging,

Artwork of a giant baby looking over border wall near Tecate, California. (AP/Gregory Bull)

combined Mexican and American flags, and butterflies, symbols of freedom and migration.

BORDER MUSIC: Concert Without Borders was a binational music event that took place every year on both sides of the Raul Castro Port of Entry between Douglas and Agua Prieta. Started in 2013 by the Bisbee Binational Arts Institute, the concert received support from both cities, the Mexican consulate, Cochise College, and others and featured an international lineup of musicians, dancers, and entertainers. People played chess between the border fence poles while waiting for the music to start. Organizers said the concert was held in part to dispel myths about the border being a dangerous place.

World-renowned cellist Yo-Yo Ma also played music in the spirit of cross-border unity when he brought his Bach Project to Laredo and Nuevo Laredo on Saturday, April 13, 2019. Ma performed first on the U.S. side, with the Juárez-Lincoln International Bridge in the background. He then performed in Nuevo Laredo, where the mayor presented him with the key to the city. "In culture, we build bridges, not walls," Ma said. In response to Trump's telling refugees "our country is full," Ma said, "A country is not a hotel and it's not full."

These were just some of the positive happenings on the border.

For me personally, when I thought of good on the border, I thought of Yolanda and her family. It had been a long year since her brother's death, a year in which she'd faced some serious health problems. But she was still standing and her kids and grandkids were doing fine.

After Christmas, she came to visit. She said the lines to cross at the Deconcini Port of Entry were interminable, but she'd dressed for the wait in warm clothes. Her appearance reminded me of something she told me about a few years before, an encounter that showed human connection amid the dehumanization of the crackdown.

Yolanda had come to visit during a cold snap. She'd taken a shuttle van from Nogales, one of the many that ferry Mexicans back and forth to Tucson. The van was packed. When it stopped at the checkpoint, all passengers were required to get out and show their papers.

Yoli and the others got out and lined up, passports in hand. She and several others, shivering and stamping their feet, were bundled up against the cold, with scarves wrapped around their heads. The border patrolman took one look at them and said, "You guys look like Talibanes!"

They all laughed.

There's dark humor, yes, but even more than that, there's life, and the joy of new life, on the border. I'm thinking of the children and young adults I know—mine, their friends and bandmates, my friends' kids, Yolanda's grandkids—and the many more I don't. There are the children of immigrants, both recent and long term, documented and not. There are the children of border activists and border patrol agents, children waiting at the ports and crossing through the desert, children in prison, and children playing under the orange trees behind the monastery.

I have a lot of hope for these children of the border. I watch them playing on their phones, connected to each other and to all knowledge simultaneously. I like to imagine they'll be able to harness this technology in unforeseen ways, to end human suffering and death and environmental damage on the border at the same time as they lead global struggles against gun violence, police brutality, and climate change. I have hope that one day in the not-too-distant future, this generation will sit together under the tree of brotherhood—as Martin Luther King Jr. foresaw for his own children—and make lasting, transformative change in the way things are done. That they will usher in a new era, a Peaceable Kingdom, as in the passage from Isaiah 11:6: "The wolf also shall dwell with the lamb, and the leopard shall lie down with the kid; and the calf, and the young lion, and the fatling together: and a little child shall lead them."

In the meantime, we do what we can.

Epilogue

A Positive Vision for the U.S.-Mexico Region

In the summer of 2020, the world reeled from social unrest and economic devastation wrought by the pandemic and police killing of George Floyd. In Tucson, even the mountains were on fire. A lightning strike in early June set off a blaze that burned tens of thousands of acres in the Santa Catalinas overlooking the city. At night, the rivers of fire running down the ridges looked like a volcano. Towering columns of ash and smoke billowed into the air. The fire seemed symbolic of the wave of death occurring just then, as Tucson and Arizona had become hot spots for the pandemic. The fire also represented the process of purification and transformation that comes out of death and destruction—a process we were then passing through as a community, a nation, and a planet. It was as if the mountains themselves were pointing the way toward regeneration and rebirth.

But we weren't there yet. Besides being a hot spot for the virus, Tucson was in shock and sorrow over our own George Floyd. Body-cam video that was unbearable to watch had just been released of a local man dying in police custody on April 21. It showed twenty-seven-year-old Carlos Adrian Ingram-Lopez, face down and handcuffed on the floor of his family garage, crying for his grandmother while three uniformed officers stood by. They'd been called by the grandmother because Ingram-Lopez, high on cocaine, had been screaming and running around naked. The father of a two-year-old had begged for water and cried "nana, ayúdame" ("grandma, help me") numerous times over fourteen minutes before succumbing. The cops had put a spit hood on him, and he also could be heard saying the infamous words "I can't breathe."

Nearly two months passed before Ingram-Lopez's death was made public, during which time Police Chief Chris Magnus published an op-ed in response to the George Floyd murder bragging his department was a model of progressive policing. When the video finally came out, Tucsonans were outraged. They held protests in front of the police station, and vigils at the nearby El Tiradito shrine, wearing white T-shirts reading #NanaAyudame. (As it turned out, I knew Ingram-Lopez's family. His cousin, a talented violinist, played mariachi with Cam at Tucson High.) The three officers resigned, Magnus offered to resign, and reforms were promised. But former border patrol agent Francisco Cantú wrote in the *Arizona Daily Star* that the policemen's callous treatment of Ingram-Lopez reminded him of the "culture of militarized brotherhood" he witnessed during his years in the border patrol, and unless that was addressed, reforms were meaningless.

This death, the death of George Floyd, the deaths of others in police custody, and the disproportionate deaths of Black, Latinx, Asian, and Native peoples in the pandemic were a wake-up call for America. They revealed entrenched, structural inequities and attitudes that had allowed racism and injustice to flourish for far too long. On the border, we were well acquainted with these inequities and attitudes. We had seen the thousands of deaths that had resulted, and the official and public indifference to those deaths.

Eleven months before the murder of George Floyd, for example, millions worldwide viewed another unbearable image of death, this one captured on the bank of the Rio Grande. The photo sparked little protest, other than over whether it should be shown at all. But it crystalized the intentional infliction of pain and suffering on vulnerable people that was occurring on the border in the early twenty-first century.

The picture was taken on Monday, June 24, 2019, by Julia Le Duc, a photojournalist for the Matamoros newspaper *La Jornada*. It shows a thin man with short dark hair, wearing blue shorts and a black T-shirt, floating face down and barefoot in shallow water. He's surrounded by reeds, wedged against the shore. Tucked in the man's shirt, also face down, her head right beside his, is a child. She's got curly hair, and she's wearing a diaper, pink stretch pants, and shoes. Her little arm is draped around his neck.

They were, we soon learned, Óscar Alberto Martínez Ramírez, twenty-five, and his twenty-three-month-old daughter, Angie Valeria. Along with their wife and mother, Tania Vanessa Ávalos, twenty-one, they had journeyed to the border from their hometown in El Salvador, hoping to join relatives in the States. The family had arrived two days before at the Mexican side of the bridge between Matamoros and Brownsville. After finding out they would have to wait months just to get an appointment at the port, and even then were likely to fail the initial screening and be refused entry, the couple decided to take their chances with the river. The Rio Grande is not very wide in this area, maybe twenty to thirty yards, but runs deceptively fast and deep. Martínez managed to carry Valeria across, put her on the U.S. side, and went back for Ávalos. Valeria got scared and jumped in after him, he grabbed her, and as Ávalos watched in horror, father and daughter were swept away. Their bodies were found downstream on the Mexican side.

Both sides of the river, they died just the same.

Publication of this shocking image resulted in widespread backlash. Many felt the photo was traumatizing, desensitizing, and exploitative of the family's suffering for no good purpose. A few days after it appeared, I got an e-mail from the Colibrí Center for Human Rights. As an organization dedicated to upholding human dignity, the e-mail said, Colibrí would not be sharing the death photo. Instead, it would be distributing a photo of a joyful Óscar and Valeria in life. "Oscar y Angie, Presentes," read the subject line.

This book has described a lot of death and suffering. It's also attempted to portray another side of the border, a place where people like those at the Colibrí Center are responding to death and suffering with compassion and creativity. For decades now, border people have been on the front lines of some of the most difficult struggles we face as a nation. These include struggles against police militarization, both here and abroad; institutionalized racism and violence; the drug war; the proliferation of guns; criminalization of migrants; and environmental destruction. "We've been a voice crying in the wilderness for a long time," Congressman Raúl Grijalva said.

Grijalva was among a number of border leaders who'd put forth plans and ideas for how to address these problems. He repeatedly introduced legislation calling for, among other things, an end to police and border patrol militarization; an end to wall building and restoration, as much as possible, of damaged lands; compliance with environmental and cultural protection laws on the border; and expanded staffing and infrastructure at the ports. He also supported legislation on guns and farmworkers that will be discussed later in this essay. Nongovernmental organizations like the Southern Border Communities Coalition, a San Diego–based nonprofit representing more than sixty church, environmental, social justice, and human rights groups from Texas to California, issued vision statements and action plans as well. These plans, which called for welcoming migrants and an end to border militarization, generally dovetailed with the legislative agenda of progressive politicians like Grijalva.

Under Trump, the movement to welcome migrants spread far beyond the border. When ICE stepped up arrests of undocumented workers and families in 2018 and 2019, activists fought back. Jewish groups, sensitive to the images of internment camps, were leading a lot of the protests. A coalition called Never Again Action organized a demonstration of more than one thousand in front of ICE offices in Washington, D.C., on July 18, 2019. This group also coordinated nationwide with the immigrant-led coalition Movimiento Cosecha (Harvest Movement), as well as with dozens of others, including T'ruah: The Rabbinic Call for Human Rights in New York City, the Lutheran Immigration and Refugee Service in Baltimore, Keeping Families Together in Chicago, and Clergy and Laity United for Economic Justice in Los Angeles. In addition to protesting, these groups were conducting "know your rights" trainings and social media campaigns to inform people how to avoid being caught, and what to do if they were. Politicians were also taking a stand; Oakland, California, Mayor Libby Schaaf, for one, came under fire from both Trump and Attorney General Jeff Sessions when she warned undocumented residents of a pending ICE raid in February 2018.

Protests even occurred in deep-red Mississippi, after what was said to be the largest single-state workplace raid in history took place around Jackson on August 7, 2019. ICE conducted simultaneous sweeps of seven chicken processing plants and arrested 680 workers, mostly Guatemalan. The school superintendent and other local officials denounced the round-ups, which left dozens of children crying for mothers and fathers taken away during the first day of school. Church groups, many from African American congregations, organized to help provide food and other necessities for the families. The mayor of Jackson called the raids "dehumanizing and ineffective."

In the spring of 2020, when undocumented families were hit hard by the pandemic, their supporters responded as well. Organizations that had been fighting for migrants' civil and human rights took up the additional fight for their very health and lives. Groups like No More Deaths and Keep Tucson Together raised money to bond migrants out of ICE jails where the virus was rampant (more on this in the section on treating migrants humanely). And when undocumented families were excluded from the CARES Act and other emergency government benefit programs, progressive funders such as George Soros's Open Society Foundations gave tens of millions nationwide to public and private groups that assisted people regardless of legal status. The city of Tucson's We Are One | Somos Uno Resiliency Fund received $1.25 million from this foundation, and an anonymous donor, to aid all low-income residents who needed help paying for rent, utilities, and food during the pandemic.

In the wake of the police killing of George Floyd, the immigrant rights movement also joined with Indigenous-rights and other movements to support Black Lives Matter. Undocumented people and DACA recipients (those with temporary legal status under the Deferred Action for Childhood Arrivals program) risked arrest and deportation to protest police violence and brutality in cities including Phoenix, Tucson, and Albuquerque. At least four, including well-known DACA activist Máxima Guerrero, were arrested by Phoenix police during protests there in early June. The Phoenix police department cooperated with immigration authorities, and all four were turned over to ICE, though Guerrero was released the next day after pressure from supporters.

These acts of solidarity, and many others, were living fulfillment of another one of Jim Corbett's prophesies: "Individuals can and should resist injustice," he wrote, "but only in community can we do justice."

In 1988, two years after the Immigration Reform and Control Act set the nation on its quixotic quest to seal the Mexican border in response to undocumented migration and drug smuggling, a group of Quakers met in Philadelphia to form a position on borders. About a dozen representatives from the United States, Canada, and Mexico came together to grapple with the dilemmas international borders pose, such as the need for safety and security on one hand, and the free flow of people and goods on the other. The resulting document, "Borders and Quaker Values: Reflections of an AFSC Working Group," provides a framework for balancing these tensions. It calls not for "open borders" but for ordered and regulated borders where human, property, and environmental rights are respected.

In many ways the U.S.-Mexico border is already a model of Quaker values. It's a beehive of modern commerce, the busiest border on Earth, with more than 350 million legal crossings and $600 billion in trade annually. Despite the walls and fences, and even despite the great economic disparity of the two sides, its people remain friendly. Wall and fence construction so far hasn't prevented the border from remaining a single, interconnected, almost entirely rural bioregion. It's abundant with plant and animal life, like in the more than sixty paintings depicting the Peaceable Kingdom by nineteenth-century Quaker preacher Edward Hicks.

Of course, the Peaceable Kingdom is a utopian fantasy. On planet Earth, the lamb who lies down with the lion will almost certainly be its breakfast. If nothing else, I hope this book has shown how deeply complex and interwoven are the challenges faced by the border, Mexico, and Central America. History demonstrates these problems and tensions will never truly be resolved. At the same time, history points to some solutions.

The following five proposals are based on principles from "Borders and Quaker Values": peace and nonviolence, respect for the worth and dignity of all people, and good stewardship of natural and financial resources, among others. They're also based on analyses and policy ideas put forth by activists, academics, and politicians. These solutions are only a start, need much discussion, and may seem a little utopian. But America was built on utopian ideas, and sometimes, utopian ideas have a way of coming true. Besides—to finish Judge Earl Carroll's reference to Robert Browning during the sanctuary trial—what's a heaven for?

1. End Drug Prohibition.

In the opening scene of the 2015 documentary *Cartel Land*, a group of masked and armed young men mix vats of chemicals outdoors at night. They are making meth deep in the mountains of central Mexico, and as the chemicals react, one offers boastful and pointed commentary. He proclaims they are "the best meth cookers in Michoacán." Then he says to the film-maker, in response to why they make meth to sell to Americans: "We can't afford to have clean jobs like you."

I admired this scene, and not only because the filmmaker showed great guts obtaining it. I liked it because it revealed the meth cookers' humanity and interconnectedness with us. It made plain the border is not to blame for, and cannot solve, America's drug problem. Border enforcement only serves to protect domestic suppliers and drive their prices up. The masked, backwoods meth cookers featured on reality TV shows like *Drug Wars*—no doubt the best meth cookers in Arkansas—would love to see the meth cook-ers in Michoacán put out of business. Unless they're both working for the same cartel, which they probably are.

Since before the founding of the nation, people have been producing intoxicants, and trying to evade authorities who would prohibit, tax, and regulate their sale. *American Nations* describes eighteenth-century Appala-chian bootleggers doing things like piling up a four-foot wall of manure to keep Alexander Hamilton's revenuers out of their town. Today's cartels are very much like Prohibition-era gangsters: they are hugely powerful, global enterprises, and the difficulty of curtailing their murderous business is not to be underestimated. But the end of Prohibition showed it could be done. (Alcohol smuggling still goes on, albeit on a much smaller scale. At the mariachi conference a couple years ago, the other parents treated me to a backstage taste of *bacanora*, a homemade tequila distilled in the mountains of Sonora and Sinaloa and smuggled across the border, probably in a water bottle. It was delicious.)

Legalization of marijuana for recreational use was one sign the era of drug prohibition was slowly coming to an end in the United States. The process was proceeding in a patchwork fashion, resulting in unintended consequences and counterintuitive problems. Illegal production went up, not down, in Colorado after legalization in 2012, apparently because cartels began ramping up domestic production to supply states where pot was still illegal. Oversupply was also a problem in Oregon, another one of the first states to legalize in 2012. (In 2020 ever-forward-thinking Oregon became the first state to decriminalize possession of small amounts of hard drugs as well.) In California, taxes and regulation on recreational sales, and new restrictions on medical sales, were so burdensome that marijuana sales actually went down in 2018, the first year of legalization. These and other states also grappled with the social and racial justice aspects of legalization—such as how to keep big corporations from taking over the fast-growing industry, and how to compensate the many victims, primarily Black and brown, of marijuana prohibition.

Some of these problems, like the persistence of the illicit market, could be tied to the continued federal illegality of the drug. In early 2019 Senator Ron Wyden of Oregon introduced a bill to end federal banking restrictions and allow states to experiment with the legal cannabis market. The bill received support from dozens of politicians, judges, criminal justice reformers, and others. Although the Senate failed to act on it, a bipartisan majority in the U.S. House passed a bill similar to Wyden's that fall. A year later, with thirty-five states having legalized medical marijuana and fifteen recreational use, the House voted to legalize the drug nationwide. However, like the banking bill, the measure's future in the narrowly divided Senate remained uncertain, and incoming president Joe Biden's plan to decriminalize and reschedule cannabis at the federal level fell far short of what advocates wanted.

Canada's path to full legalization might serve as a model. Marijuana was treated pretty much like alcohol—available to adults in government or privately owned stores or by mail order. Different provinces and territories had different pricing schemes and rules on home growing, edibles, and other issues. Suppliers had to buy their pot from federally licensed growers. Taxes were less than in the States, and the Canadian government gave the provinces and territories 75 percent of the revenue. New Mexico became the first state to consider such a system in 2019, when a bill was introduced to the legislature establishing government-owned pot shops that would direct profits toward medical care for the poor.

In old Mexico, where drug prohibition had taken the heaviest toll, the government was moving to legalize both the use and cultivation of marijuana. But that was hardly going to do anything to curtail violence as long as pot remained prohibited in the United States. One prominent politician who advocated legal weed all across North America was former Mexican president and Coca-Cola executive Vicente Fox. As keynote speaker at the Southwest Cannabis Conference Expo in Phoenix in October 2017, he said his country was ready to supply America with 60 percent of its pot needs. He joined the board of *High Times* magazine and was lobbying for the plant's production and sale to be included in future trade agreements. He contended half the cartels' income would disappear if marijuana were legal in the States.

If seizures at the border were any indication, that was already happening. In addition to ramping up U.S. production, the cartels were responding to marijuana legalization by importing other drugs. Between 2011 and 2017, the amount of marijuana seized at the Mexican border declined 66 percent, from 2.53 million to about 861,000 pounds. Seizures of meth, heroin, and fentanyl, however, were way up. (During talks over the government shutdown in late 2018 and early 2019, many pointed out that, since 90 percent of hard-drug seizures were made at ports of entry, the best way to stop smuggling was to improve screening at the ports, not extend the wall.)

But the cartels' switch from pot to harder stuff only highlighted the impossibility of stopping drug smuggling as long as there were illegal profits to be had. (The flow of guns, also a huge part of the problem, will be addressed in the next section.) When speaking in Arizona, Vicente Fox advocated the ultimate legalization of all drugs. "Prohibitions don't work. They have never worked," he said.

The new president of Mexico, Andrés Manuel López Obrador, or AMLO as he was known, also appeared ready to surrender in the war on drugs. Acknowledging the heavy-handed approach of his two predecessors had been a dismal failure, he was elected in July 2018 in large part because he pledged to lead "a peaceful and orderly transition, but one that is deep and radical." One of his campaign slogans was *Abrazos, No Balazos* ("Hugs, Not Bullets").

"You cannot confront violence with violence," he said. "We won't forget, but we will forgive."

Soon after his election AMLO outlined his plans in a speech in Ciudad Juárez, where twenty-six people had been killed the previous week, and where six more were killed while he was speaking. He called the event a peace-building forum, one of many he intended to hold in the coming years. He promised to end the military's role in drug enforcement, tackle official corruption and impunity, and possibly offer amnesty to former cartel members. He also proposed funding for job training and alternatives to violence programs. (Another campaign slogan was *Becarios, No Sicarios*— "Scholarship Students, Not Cartel Hitmen.")

In early 2019 AMLO announced more plans, including economic development projects for drug-producing regions. He said a tree-planting campaign and forestry school in El Chapo's hometown of Badiraguato, Sinaloa, would bring twenty thousand permanent jobs to that part of the Sierra Madre. But as the year went on, it became clear Mexico's war on drugs was not going to end anytime soon. The United States rejected his proposal to direct Mérida Initiative money away from drug interdiction and toward development aid, and resolving the Central American migrant crisis to Trump's satisfaction took precedence over any attempts at reform. Over the summer, violence spiked again. Analysts said AMLO's peace overtures had only emboldened the cartels, which saw them as a sign of weakness.

Many atrocities took place, most of which were attributed to turf battles between the CJNG (the Jalisco New Generation Cartel) and various regional rivals. In August 2019, 9 half-naked bodies, 2 female, were found hanging from a bridge in Michoacán. Ten more were hacked up nearby. Later that month, a nightclub in Veracruz was torched with 28 trapped inside. The third week of October was particularly horrific. On Monday, 23 state policemen were massacred in a CJNG ambush outside El Aguaje, Michoacán. On Tuesday, another 15 people were killed in a cartel shootout near Iguala, Guerrero. Then, on Thursday, October 17, the Sinaloa cartel showed it was still relevant with a ferocious attack that lasted for hours and turned the streets of Culiacán into a war zone.

The assault began with the Mexican military's ill-advised capture of Ovidio Guzmán López, the twenty-eight-year-old son of cartel leader El Chapo Guzmán, who'd just been sentenced to life in prison in New York in July. With the family honor at stake, one of the drug lord's older sons launched a furious effort to free his little brother. He sent armored assault vehicles mounted with .50-caliber machine guns to take control of key intersections downtown. Buses and cars were set ablaze, windows shattered, and buildings peppered with explosions and gunfire during the siege. Thirteen people were killed, scores were injured, and some fifty prisoners escaped from a nearby jail (though most were later rounded up). The assault only ended when the soldiers agreed to release El Chapo's son in exchange for eight of their own being held hostage. AMLO praised the soldiers for backing down to prevent further bloodshed. He pleaded for more time for his peace plan to work. But the president's shifting explanations of what happened, his assignment of blame to the military, and the entire operation itself were widely condemned.

Not long after, another massacre took place that made big news in the States because the victims were U.S.-citizen women and children. On November 4, gunmen ambushed and killed nine members of a local Mormon farming community traveling in a caravan of SUVs outside La Mora, Sonora, about seventy miles south of Douglas. The murders of three women and six kids—eight other children survived—were said to be connected to a shootout in Agua Prieta earlier in the day and may or may not have been a case of mistaken identity. (The Mormons had battled cartels before.) The Mexican military reported U.S.-made ammunition was used in the massacre. By the end of the year, the official murder total in Mexico reached a new record high of 35,588.

Relentless, high-profile attacks continued in 2020. On July 1, twenty-six were killed at a rehab center in Guanajuato, a state lately engulfed in violence over control of the profitable stolen-fuel racket. This came just two weeks after a federal judge and his wife were murdered in Colima, and less than one week after a brazen attempt on the life of Mexico City's crusading police chief, Omar García Harfuch. At dawn on June 26, some two dozen men wielding .50-caliber rifles and grenades attempted to assassinate García, who was headed to work in a caravan of armored SUVs on a downtown avenue called the Paseo de la Reforma. Two members of his security staff and a woman driving by were killed. "I have three bullet wounds and various pieces of shrapnel," he tweeted from his hospital bed. Blaming the CJNG, he wrote, "Our nation has to continue standing up to cowardly organized crime. We will continue working."

Brave sentiments, but until drugs were treated like alcohol in the States, Mexican cemeteries would continue to be filled with brave ones.

2. End the Flow of Guns to Mexico.

This book has focused on violence by police in Mexico and by the U.S. Border Patrol, but the deaths of George Floyd and many others, as well as police attacks on journalists and people protesting police violence, have made clear this is a problem for U.S. domestic forces as well. Police violence and militarization are complex problems in both countries, rooted as they are in an underlying culture of violence. Cartel, gang, militia, vigilante, and family violence are also part of this culture, and, like police violence, they're fed by the proliferation of weapons. Chapter 3 described the ease with which guns and ammunition are obtained, legally and illegally, in the States and brought into Mexico to arm both sides in the war on drugs. Easy access to guns has also had severe consequences for the American police and public, including increased danger to, and justification of violence by, police; mass murders (there were several live shooter drills while Cam was at Tucson High, as well as one actual incident, in which students were cowering under their desks, sobbing and texting their parents goodbye); suicides; accidents; and kids killing each other in the streets of Chicago.

Although progress was slow, activists were working on this issue. On February 27 and 28, 2019, the U.S. House passed the most sweeping gun-control legislation in more than a decade. The measures, which required universal background checks for gun sales and transfers, would not yet become law, but they were a first step toward curtailing gun violence in America. The votes had been won by a coalition of groups, including one led by survivors of the February 14, 2018, massacre of seventeen students at a Parkland, Florida, high school, and another led by former southern Arizona congressperson Gabby Giffords and her husband, former astronaut and, as of 2020, U.S. senator for Arizona Mark Kelly. Giffords survived being shot in the head, and six others, including a federal judge and a nine-year-old girl, were killed in a mass shooting at a congressional meet-and-greet in front of a north-side Tucson Safeway on the morning of January 8, 2011.

On the evening of February 27, about twenty people gathered at the Global Justice Center in South Tucson to see a film on the making of the AFSC publication *Where the Guns Go*. The presenter, John Lindsay-Poland, coordinator of Global Exchange's Stop U.S. Arms to Mexico project, opened the event by noting the historic vote in Congress. He praised the work that had led to its passage and said, "Ending the flow of arms to Mexico needs to be part of the agenda of the gun-violence prevention movement."

Lindsay-Poland started the film on his laptop, and we watched it projected on a screen at the front of the room. The twenty-six-minute video showed places where people had been kidnapped or mass graves found, as well as interviews with some of the people quoted, including Maria Herrera, mother of the four men who'd been disappeared, and her surviving son Juan Carlos Trujillo, head of Familias en Búsqueda.

After the film was over, Lindsay-Poland called Trujillo over Skype. The connection was shaky, and though we could see a close-up view of his face on the screen, the audio was cutting in and out. He spoke in Spanish and I couldn't get all he was saying, so I concentrated on his face. He was perhaps around forty, studious looking, with short dark hair and beard. Every so often he would pause and look down. His eyes were indescribably sad.

Trujillo was talking about the disappearances of his brothers and about searching for their remains in mass graves. Massacre sites were being discovered all the time. He said President AMLO had expressed sympathy, and someone from the government had shown up to help with one recent search, so that was progress. He ended by thanking the small gathering and urged us to keep bringing the issue before the American public.

Where the Guns Go was a significant contribution to the research aspect of the movement to stop gun sales and trafficking to Mexico. Another was an August 2018 report by Lindsay-Poland sponsored by Global Exchange's Stop U.S. Arms to Mexico project, the Mexican Commission for the Defense and Promotion of Human Rights, and several other U.S. and Mexican governmental and nongovernmental organizations. *Gross Human Rights Abuses: The Legal and Illegal Gun Trade to Mexico* contained detailed research and information linking the growth in international arms sales and gun trafficking to the rise in bloodshed. Like *Where the Guns Go*, *Gross Human Rights*

Abuses offered recommendations on what the U.S. and Mexico could do to reduce gun violence and impunity:

To the United States Government:

1. Reduce legal firearms exports to Mexico to levels below their amount before the "war on drugs" was declared and the Mérida Initiative began in 2007.

2. Establish and implement criteria for end users of legally exported firearms that exclude exports to all police and military units for which there is credible information of members of those units having colluded with criminal organizations or committed gross human rights abuses.

3. Ensure that applications for gun export licenses correctly identify end users for exported weapons, including firearms and other equipment, and establish efficient mechanisms for tracing such weapons from producer to end users.

4. Until U.S. policy excludes firearms end users that are credibly alleged to have colluded with organized crime or committed human rights violations, and has implemented systems to identify end users, the United States should suspend firearms exports to the Mexican military and police, including the license for the Mexican Navy to conduct assembly of up to $265 million worth of military firearms parts produced by Sig Sauer, Inc.

5. Prohibit the sale of military-type assault weapons and high-capacity magazines, which are easily obtained by Mexican criminal organizations through retail purchases in the United States and trafficked over the border.

6. Continue to regulate export licenses for semi-automatic firearms (including designs for 3D printing of weapons) within the State Department, with Congressional oversight, rather than the Commerce Department.

To the Mexican Government:

1. As part of Mexico's overall change in security strategy, reduce legal firearms imports to levels below their amount before the "war on drugs" was declared and the Mérida Initiative began in 2007 (approximately $10 million annually).

2. Prioritize the enforcement of firearms prohibitions in national territory over drug enforcement, especially through performance incentives
   and resources, and applied analysis of firearms trafficking routes and
   modalities.
3. Increase transparency of legal weapons imports, in order to strengthen
   accountability and to counter weapons diversion.
4. Strengthen controls on the military's weapons transfers to Mexican police
   forces, especially regarding investigations of lost and stolen weapons.

In addition to research and education, nonprofits were organizing actions
and protests. A Change.org petition with more than seven thousand sig-
natures was submitted to the State Department in 2018 to end licensing of
firearm shipments to Mexican military and police. Demonstrations were
held over the State Department's licensing of $265 million in gun-part sales
by New Hampshire–based Sig Sauer to the Mexican navy, which was linked
to atrocities in Nuevo Laredo. (In October 2018 German authorities arrested
the CEO of Sig Sauer at the Frankfurt airport for allegedly selling thirty
thousand illegal pistols to Colombia.) And on November 16, more than three
hundred Tucsonans protested in front of Milkor USA, a local business that
made grenade multi-launchers sold to a Mexican army Special Forces Group
linked to the Zetas cartel.

A few lawmakers were starting to focus on the issue. In May 2018 Democratic U.S. Representatives Alan Lowenthal and Norma Torres from Southern California and Ruben Gallego from Phoenix held a briefing on Capitol
Hill on the issue of weapons smuggling to Mexico. Experts from the Violence
Policy Center, the Washington Office on Latin America, and other groups
testified on the southward flow of U.S. guns and murders connected to them.

The legislators called for federal authorities to do more to stop gun smuggling. They criticized them for backing off enforcement of cross-border trafficking after the Fast and Furious scandal broke in 2011. "I was deeply dis-
appointed the Obama administration did not do more," Gallego said. "They
were scared."

The issue of legal gun sales to Mexico also got attention from lawmakers in 2018. In June Representative Keith Ellison and eleven other members
of Congress wrote a letter to Secretary of State Mike Pompeo and Defense

Secretary James Mattis requesting "a full and public evaluation of the Mérida Initiative, U.S. security aid and arms sales to Mexico." Members of Congress also called for an examination of the Mérida Initiative by the GAO.

Many legislators spoke out against a Trump administration plan to shift oversight of foreign weapon sales and transfers from the State Department to the Commerce Department. Just a few days after Lindsay-Poland's talk in Tucson, Congressman Alan Lowenthal, Representative Raúl Grijalva, and twenty-two other members of Congress sent a letter to Secretary of State Pompeo opposing the proposal. The letter read in part: "We are concerned that your department's plan to aggressively promote American weapons exports without a proper tracking system for end users will continue to result in weapon transfers to Mexico that arm security forces with ties to criminal organizations or that have committed serious human rights violations."

As large groups of Central Americans arrived on the border in 2018 and 2019 and again in early 2021, questions also began to arise about U.S. weapon sales, training, and other assistance to Central American military and police forces. Gun-related violence, extortion, official corruption, and human rights abuses in Guatemala, Honduras, and El Salvador were apparently causing many people to flee their homes and come to the border and ask for asylum. These events showed the need to end the flow of weapons, equipment, and training to police and military forces in those countries as well.

3. Regularize the Status of Farmworkers.

From Carey McWilliams's groundbreaking 1939 study *Factories in the Field*—published the same year as John Steinbeck's *The Grapes of Wrath*—to Edward R. Murrow's 1960 TV special *Harvest of Shame*, to the 2013 book by Seth Holmes, *Fresh Fruit, Broken Bodies*, and many other works of journalism, art, and scholarship, the exploitation and abuse of American farmworkers has been thoroughly documented. A constant supply of cheap labor, mostly from Mexico except during the Depression, is the main reason conditions have remained in this sorry state for nearly a century. Those with papers have been pitted against those without. In one notorious case, the cousin of union organizer César Chávez set up a "wet line" outside Yuma in 1973, using United Farm Workers members to attack Mexican migrants, who were seen as strikebreakers, and torch their cars. Guest-worker programs haven't helped, as they've inevitably been structured to benefit growers. Document verification programs like E-Verify have also resulted in more abuse, giving rise to a fake-papers industry that allows employers to deny responsibility while at the same time adding another layer of potential criminality for the migrant.

Activists weren't surprised, for instance, that no owners or managers were charged after the massive August 2019 ICE raids on poultry-processing plants in Mississippi. Company officials, who helped organize the roundups, said they were shocked—shocked!—to learn their workers had been using fake IDs and Social Security numbers. (Some workers later reported having been hired while wearing ICE ankle monitors.) A few days later, one company held a job fair, offering the migrants' jobs to mostly African American locals, at eleven to twelve dollars an hour. Another company fired all the workers who'd remained after the raids.

Among the many societal fault lines exposed by COVID-19, a major one was how much our food supply depended on undocumented workers. An estimated 60 percent of the nation's 2.4 million farmworkers were undocumented, as were many workers, or family members of workers, in meat- and poultry-processing plants decimated by the virus. "A few months ago, they were the evil invaders. Now they're essential workers," Representative Grijalva said. Agricultural and food-supply workers were ordered to stay on the job, even though they weren't protected by their employers or the law. The close conditions under which they had to live, travel and toil contributed to many outbreaks among them, and lacking adequate health care, they died in disproportionate numbers. The pandemic showed how important it was, not only for their health and well-being but for ours, that those who provided and prepared our food have safe and sanitary homes and workplaces.

Grijalva, who was among those diagnosed with the virus, hoped the increased attention would result in passage of legislation that had languished for years. One such bill was the Children's Act for Responsible Employment, which outlawed child labor on farms. Cosponsored by Grijalva, it had been introduced by California Democratic Representative Lucille Roybal-Allard every year since 2001. These lawmakers, and advocates like the Washington,

D.C.–based group Farmworker Justice, supported additional proposals including:

AGRICULTURAL WORKER PROGRAM ACT: In early 2019 California Senator Dianne Feinstein and Representative Zoe Lofgren introduced farmworker protection legislation to both houses of Congress. Called the Agricultural Worker Program Act, the law would grant immediate blue card status, and eventual residency, to people who had been farmworkers for at least one hundred days over the previous two years. Among other provisions, Farmworker Justice said, the bill would help alleviate labor shortages by including "a future work requirement that addresses employer concerns about workforce stability" and that, "by enabling farmworkers to do their jobs without fear, the bill would help ensure compliance with labor, pesticide and food safety laws, improving the security of our entire food system."

H-2A REFORM: The H-2A guest-worker program, established in 1986 to replace a 1950s-era program, was, in the words of Farmworker Justice, "fundamentally flawed." H-2A workers could only work for the employer who hired them. If they tried to leave, they would be subject to arrest and deportation. As "seasonal and temporary" workers, they also had no path to permanent legal status. For some employers, this lack of rights made these workers preferable: the number of H-2A certified positions grew from 82,000 in 2008 to more than 240,000 in 2018, and employers were clamoring for more.

In December 2019 the U.S. House passed the Farm Workforce Modernization Act, which promised to fix some of the problems while also expanding the program. The bill set wage and workplace standards, offered a path to citizenship for longtime H-2A workers and their families, increased the number of visas, and made year-round jobs eligible for visas. Some two hundred agricultural businesses and lobbying groups backed the bill, which had yet to pass the Senate. Farmworker advocates, for their part, concluded it was better than nothing. But they noted the law would benefit only a relative handful of people at the same time as it continued to reinforce the documented/undocumented dichotomy. Felipe Guevara, who worked for the New Mexico Center on Law and Poverty, said farmworkers he knew considered the H-2A program unfair competition and wanted it abolished.

Further complicating the situation was the international nature of agribusiness. The morning after attending Bernard Lafayette's talk on "Kingian Nonviolence and the Border," I was preparing fruit for my family. The miniwatermelon and cantaloupe I'd just purchased at the Safeway were both labeled "Guatemala." The barcode stickers depicted a smiling sun wearing dark glasses. I marveled at the care and attention this fruit had received, to deliver it, a few days after being harvested, to a store less than a mile from my house, fresh, clean, unbruised, perfectly ripe, and at a cost of two dollars each. I wondered about the conditions under which it had been produced.

Conditions on foreign farms concerned a lot of border people. Thousands of livelihoods depended upon their successful operation. Mexico was the United States' top foreign produce supplier, and during the winter, Nogales was the nation's number one port of entry for fresh fruits and vegetables. (In the summer, it was Laredo and Hidalgo, Texas, with fruits and nuts.) More than 120,000 trucks carrying $2.5 billion in produce passed through the Mariposa Port of Entry in 2017, almost 60 percent of all produce eaten in the winter in the United States. The vast majority was grown in Mexico and included tomatoes, bell peppers, cucumbers, avocados, lettuce, and berries.

Naturally, Nogales was home to a multinational industry trade group called the Fresh Produce Association of the Americas (FPAA). Members included more than 120 businesses all along the supply chain, from growers to packers to truckers to brokers to warehouses to grocery stores. Its website touted their food safety practices, social responsibility toward workers, and environmental sustainability. Among other issues, the FPAA represented members in their support for the U.S.-Mexico-Canada Agreement—the NAFTA replacement passed in January 2020—and their ongoing battle with Florida over trade barriers to Mexican tomatoes. (As far as border people were concerned, tomatoes from Sonora and Sinaloa were better tasting, less expensive, and locally grown.) Many FPAA members also pitched in to fight hunger, donating millions of pounds of unsold produce to southern Arizona food banks and nonprofits each year. During the pandemic, these businesses volunteered transportation, cold storage, and labor to redirect produce originally intended for restaurants, schools, and hotels to organizations serving people in need.

"We're not trying to vilify vegetables produced in Mexico," ethnobotanist and sustainable agriculture proponent Gary Nabhan said. "We respect what the fresh produce industry is doing for food safety and worker health care and other assets." He cited two companies as proof the local food movement doesn't stop at the border:

WILSON PRODUCE: This three-generation, family-owned enterprise was headquartered in Nogales, Arizona, and had eight farms under cultivation in Sinaloa, Sonora, and Baja California. The company's website described the family's long relationship with the people of Bamoa, Sinaloa, building a church and school, "playing baseball with the village children and creating a sense of unity on the farm that could not be broken." Starting in the 1940s with tomatoes and peas, and later adding beans and melons, in 2020 Wilson Produce grew Roma and grape tomatoes, sweet mini peppers, jalapeños, squash, and eggplant. Its customers included major wholesalers and retailers like Walmart and Costco. The Wilsons also owned La Roca ("The Rock"), a restaurant in Nogales, Sonora, where they served dishes prepared with their homegrown vegetables.

WHOLESUM HARVEST: Also family owned and operated for three generations, this cross-border farm grew organic produce in both the U.S. and Mexico. The website described its three operations in detail. In Amado, forty miles south of Tucson, the company had eighteen acres of tomatoes. In Imuris, Sonora, thirty miles south of the border, it had nearly a hundred acres growing English cucumbers, eggplant, and squash, as well as three kinds of tomatoes. In Culiacán, Sinaloa, six hundred miles south of the border, it had another five hundred or so acres growing Roma, beefsteak, and on-the-vine tomatoes, eggplant, squash, and red bell peppers. The website said Wholesum Harvest met the highest standards for "certified organic growing, corporate responsibility and fair labor" practices, and described its Fair Trade support projects. (Fair Trade Certified is a California-based nonprofit that certifies sustainably produced goods.) In the spring of 2019, Wholesum Harvest worked with volunteers from partner businesses including Natural Grocers, Albert's Organics, City Market Co-op in Vermont, and Central Co-op in Seattle to build a community kitchen at a kindergarten in Los Janos, Sonora. The kitchen opened to serve local students nutritious meals at no cost.

These are just two examples of how cross-border, people-to-people farming could benefit workers and consumers in both countries.

4. Reform Immigration Laws to Treat Migrants Humanely.

Like farmworkers, migrants in detention were hit hard by COVID-19. At the La Palma Correctional Center in Eloy, Arizona, operated by CoreCivic, more than four hundred detainees had tested positive by October 2020. It was the highest number of positive tests of any facility in the U.S. immigration prison system. Advocates said detainees and staff at La Palma and other prisons were at great risk, due to inadequate testing and protection measures and a failure to quarantine infected individuals. Some detainees had tried to peacefully protest by holding a hunger strike, only to be met with tear gas and rubber bullets. Others said they were told if they didn't like it, they could take voluntary deportation.

Attorneys for detainees filed lawsuits against ICE for endangering their clients' lives and for not immediately releasing them. The agency did let go a few individuals who were pregnant, chronically ill, or otherwise high risk for contracting COVID-19. Groups like Keep Tucson Together and No More Deaths raised money to pay their bonds, usually five thousand dollars or more each. But as infections and deaths in ICE jails continued to mount—the Detention Watch Network found more people died in ICE custody in the first five months of 2020 than in all of 2019—a number of asylum seekers abandoned their cases and agreed to be deported. "I felt like it was more dangerous than back in my country," former detainee José Muñoz told Reuters after being returned to El Salvador. Deportees also died of COVID-19: transgender activist Durvi Martínez worked on a Vermont dairy farm for four years before being arrested for DUI and turned over to ICE in January 2020. Martínez, thirty-two, was held in deplorable conditions for three months, deported to Mexico despite a pending asylum claim, and died there of the virus on July 1.

Before the pandemic emerged, migrants and refugees had been very much in the news, and almost all the 2020 presidential candidates had put forth plans to address their plight. However, most of the proposals—like adding more judges and hearing officers to speed up asylum claims—were basically just ways to streamline, as it were, the same post-IRCA regime. Joe Biden's plan, for example, rolled back some of Trump's more extreme measures, such as making asylum seekers remain in Mexico or returning them to their home countries while their claims were decided. After his election, President Biden also proposed legislation giving DACA recipients and others with temporary legal status a path to citizenship. But many Republicans remained implacably opposed to amnesty for the undocumented, and faced with another wave of migrants early in his presidency, Biden largely returned to the policies of the Obama administration. As described in this book, these policies included Operation Streamline, constitutionally questionable checkpoints and roving patrols, continued expansion of border enforcement and militarization, use of private prisons, as well as ongoing conflicts with local landowners and jurisdictions over wall construction, sanctuary, police cooperation with ICE, and other immigration-related issues.

One 2020 candidate, former Housing and Urban Development secretary and San Antonio mayor Julián Castro, presented a far-reaching and innovative plan. Many of his ideas were later adopted by other progressive candidates, including Elizabeth Warren. Castro's plan has a lot of detail and some overlap, so I've shortened it a bit:

Reforming Our Immigration System:
- Establish an inclusive roadmap to citizenship for undocumented individuals who do not have a current pathway to legal status, but who live, work and raise families in communities throughout the United States.
- Provide a pathway to citizenship to Dreamers and those under Temporary Protected Status and Deferred Enforced Departure, through the Dream and Promise Act of 2019, and defend and expand DACA, TPS and DED protections, and re-institute the Deferred Action for Parents of Americans program during the legislative process.
- Revamp the visa system and strengthen family reunification through the Reuniting Families Act, reducing the number of people who are waiting to reunite with their families but are stuck in the bureaucratic backlog. . . .

- Terminate the three and ten year bars, which require undocumented individuals—who otherwise qualify for legal status—to leave the United States and their families behind for years before becoming citizens. . . .
- Increase refugee admissions, reversing cuts under Trump, and restoring our nation to its historic position as a moral leader providing a safe haven for those fleeing persecution, violence, disaster and despair. Adapt these programs to account for new global challenges like climate change.
- End agreements under Section 287(g) of the Immigration and Nationality Act and other such agreements between federal immigration enforcement agencies and state and local entities that erode trust between communities and local police and end ICE detainers.
- Allow all deported veterans who honorably served in the armed forces of the United States to return to the United States and end the practice of deporting such veterans.
- Strengthen labor protections for guest workers [addressed in the previous section].
- Protect victims of domestic violence, sexual assault and human trafficking, ensuring these individuals are not subject to detention, deportation or legal reprisal following their reporting these incidents.

Creating a Humane Border Policy:
- Repeal Section 1325 of Immigration and Nationality Act [Operation Streamline], which applies a criminal, rather than civil, violation to people apprehended when entering the United States. . . .
- Effectively end the use of detention in conducting immigration enforcement, except in serious cases. Utilize cost-effective and more humane alternatives to detention, which draw on the successes of prior efforts like the Family Case Management Program. Ensure all individuals have access to a bond hearing and that vulnerable populations, including children, pregnant women and members of the LGBTQ community are not placed in civil detention.
- Eliminate the for-profit immigration detention and prison industry, which monetizes the detention of migrants and children.
- End immigration raids at or near sensitive locations such as schools, hospitals, churches, and courthouses.

- Reconstitute the U.S. Immigration and Customs Enforcement (ICE), by splitting the agency in half and re-assigning enforcement functions within the Enforcement and Removal Operations to other agencies, including the Department of Justice. There must be a thorough investigation of ICE, Customs and Border Protection, and the Department of Justice's role in family separation policies instituted by the Trump administration.

- Reprioritize Customs and Border Protection (CBP) to focus its efforts on border-related activities including drug and human trafficking, rather than law enforcement activities in the interior of the United States. Extend Department of Justice civil rights jurisdiction to CBP, and adopt best practices employed in law enforcement, including body-worn cameras and strong accountability policies.

- End wasteful, ineffective and invasive border wall construction and consult with border communities about repairing environmental and other damage already done.

- End asylum "metering" and the "Remain in Mexico" policy, ensuring all asylum seekers are able to present their claims to U.S. officials. . . .

- Increase access to legal assistance for individuals and families presenting asylum claims, ensuring individuals understand their rights and are able to make an informed and accurate request for asylum. Guarantee counsel for all children in the immigration enforcement system.

- Protect victims of domestic and gang violence, by reversing guidance by [former] Attorney General Jeff Sessions that prohibited asylum claims on the basis of credible fear stemming from domestic or gang violence.

Speakers at an inspiring forum at the University of Arizona James E. Rogers College of Law in November 2019 advocated many of these same changes. More than a dozen lawyers, academics, and activists, mostly women and people of color, described traveling to detention centers in Eloy and elsewhere to represent migrants pro bono, documenting conditions, filing briefs and lawsuits, and educating and empowering people through community outreach and organizing. Groups represented at the Innovating Immigration Law and Policy: Visions for a Just Future conference included immigration and civil rights law clinics connected to both the University of Arizona and the University of California–Los Angeles; the Florence Immigrant and Refugee Rights Project; Casa Mariposa, which advocated for LGBTQ detainees; Keep Tucson Together, which offered free legal help every week at Pueblo High School; and the Southside Worker Center, which fought for worker rights at Southside Church.

Child migrant detention remained at the forefront of discussion throughout the day. The lawyers talked about their efforts to make sure every unaccompanied minor in custody had legal representation. They said this was already being mandated in New York state and elsewhere. They agreed all migrants and refugees, but especially children, should be given free psychological counseling in detention and after release. They talked about how hard it was to keep up with the shifting array of places where ICE was holding people. One lawyer described it as "an archipelago." (Around the same time as this conference, a United Nations Global Study on Children Deprived of Liberty reported the United States was holding more than one hundred thousand children in immigration detention—by far the most of any country for which reliable figures could be obtained.)

Roxie Bacon, a trailblazing attorney from Phoenix who'd founded the Bacon Immigration Law and Policy Program at the University of Arizona, gave the keynote address. She pointed out several instances in which federal judges were holding the line against violations of migrants' civil and human rights, such as stances against Operation Streamline, family separation, and forcing asylum applicants to remain in Mexico.

A significant instance of judicial resistance took place in June 2019, when a federal judge in Boston became the first in the nation to block ICE from making civil arrests at courthouses. Finding the arrests were having a chilling effect on the conduct of official business, U.S. District Judge Indira Talwani issued a temporary injunction blocking ICE "from civilly arresting parties, witnesses, and others attending Massachusetts courthouses on official business while they are going to, attending, or leaving the courthouses." Activists hoped the ruling would be a model for other states. The decision came at the same time as another Boston-area judge and a retired court officer faced obstruction of justice charges for allegedly letting an undocumented man escape out a back door. ICE officers had been waiting to arrest him in the hallway at Newton District

Court. In 2017 a Portland, Oregon, county judge was investigated and cleared of wrongdoing in a similar case.

Even the U.S. Supreme Court seemed to sympathize with migrants when, in June 2020, it let DACA protections stand and refused to hear a challenge to California's sanctuary law. Yet the following week, the same court decided 7–2 that Trump's policy of summarily deporting people who failed an initial asylum screening was acceptable. Other courts also weighed in on Trump's immigration policies, and while some decisions favored migrants and some did not, these rulings often contradicted each other, were made on procedural or technical grounds, and didn't really address the underlying intent or impact of the policies. The judicial confusion showed, as Roxie Bacon said in her talk, the ultimate answer lay with the legislative branch.

Bacon and others proposed several overarching principles to guide the updating of immigration law to reflect current realities. First, laws and regulations should be written to prioritize keeping families together and protecting people from harm, whatever the source. Second, laws should take into account the underlying causes of migration and address the reasons why people flee in the first place. And third, Bacon made the excellent suggestion that immigration laws should be subject to periodic review and adjusted as conditions evolve.

5. Repurpose Border Security Funds.

Last but not least, there stood the walls, both real and symbolic. Trump was determined to build them, no matter the cost.

Symbolic walls—real in their own way—went up in a few places. The ultimate in wall symbolism, the prototypes, stood like giant sculptures next to the border wall in Otay Mesa, south of San Diego, for sixteen months. The site was inaccessible from the U.S. side most of that time, so a makeshift tourist spot had grown up on the Mexican side. Reporters and thrill-seekers paid neighborhood kids to let them climb on a trash pile and peek through the fence at the seven sample walls, built at a cost of about a half-million dollars each. In February 2019 the prototypes were knocked down and hauled away to a landfill. Crews used a hydraulic jackhammer mounted on an excavator to reduce the concrete slabs, rebar, and other materials to rubble in about two hours. The Associated Press reporter who covered the demolition wrote that an owl flew out of a metal tube on the top of one, just before it collapsed in a cloud of dust.

The following year, another symbolic effort called We Build the Wall also collapsed under a cloud, this time one of suspicion. With former Trump advisor Steve Bannon in the lead, the group had set up a GoFundMe page, and raised a reported $25 million from half a million donors to build walls on private land near the border. We Build the Wall did manage to build about five miles of barriers in New Mexico and Texas, though the projects were mired in complaints and lawsuits related to lack of permits, shoddy construction and environmental damage. Those turned out to be the least of this group's problems. At a country-club fundraiser in Sahuarita in February 2019, Bannon had promised "100 percent" of donations would be spent on wall building and legal fees. But in August 2020 federal authorities arrested Bannon and three others for stealing We Build the Wall's donations. The indictment said they'd siphoned off more than $1 million for personal expenses including boat and car payments, travel, hotels, meals, clothing, jewelry, and plastic surgery. Anti-wall activists hoped to see Bannon face justice, but it was not to be. In one of his last official acts as president, Trump pardoned Bannon for his role in this scheme.

Although symbolic in their own way, real walls continued to do real damage. In early 2019, under orders from Trump, CBP announced plans to replace about sixty miles of vehicle fences in Arizona with thirty-foot-tall pedestrian fences. Most of these miles were in places where animals crossed, including Organ Pipe Cactus National Monument, Cabeza Prieta National Wildlife Refuge, the San Pedro Riparian National Conservation Area, and the San Bernardino Wildlife Refuge.

"It's the endgame for the jaguar if this goes through," said Chris Bugbee, senior scientist at Conservation CATalyst and one of the researchers who photographed El Jefe. Other wildlife experts agreed. The walls would be "a devastating blow" to many border species, including the endangered ocelot and Sonoran pronghorn antelope (discussed in chapter 8), said Myles Traphagen of the Wildlands Network. One of the massive structures would go right by Quitobaquito Springs, the desert oasis on the Camino del Diablo, where Padre Kino said Mass in 1698 or 1699. Activists were upset not only about damage caused by the wall itself, but that groundwater pumping to make concrete to anchor the poles would suck the spring dry. Native American and park officials also warned the construction would destroy valuable archeological sites and disturb ancient burial grounds.

On November 9 some three hundred people gathered at Quitobaquito Springs to pray and protest the wall. Gary Nabhan attended and wrote: "Among the many constituencies represented, I spotted the National Parks Conservation Association, the Center for Biological Diversity, International Sonoran Desert Alliance, Indivisible Tohono, Women Act Now, Grand Canyon Chapter of the Sierra Club, No More Deaths/No Mas Muertes, Episcopal Peace Fellowship, Friends of the Sonoran Desert, Deportados Unidos en La Lucha, the Jewish Voice for Peace Tucson, the Hia c-ed O'odham and Tohono O'odham Nations, Good Samaritans, Franciscan Action Network, the Raging Grannies and Univision Mexico." Nabhan said protestors called on the Army Corps of Engineers and Homeland Security to "use their budgets to begin efforts toward healing the wounds in the desert and re-sanctifying sacred sites."

Yet later that month, Homeland Security awarded hundreds of millions of dollars' worth of contracts to build the behemoth walls. Most of the money went to a subsidiary of construction giant Kiewit, but some also went to companies run by Trump associates and donors. One, North Dakota–based Fisher Sand and Gravel, was already under scrutiny for sloppy work on three miles of a We Build the Wall–funded barrier in Texas. Opponents charged in a lawsuit the wall's foundation was eroding just months after it was built a mere thirty-five feet from the riverbank, and part or all of it could slide into the Rio Grande. The Trump-appointed U.S. attorney for the Southern District of Texas, who was overseeing the lawsuit, said Fisher "didn't do any engineering beyond a PowerPoint slide." Nevertheless, after a lobbying campaign on Fox News, Breitbart, and other conservative outlets, Fisher received a CBP contract totaling $400 million to build thirty-one miles of wall in the Cabeza Prieta Wildlife Refuge. (This wasn't the first time border-wall contracts went to companies with dubious reputations. Among other cases, in 2006 the Golden State Fence Company was fined $5 million for hiring undocumented workers, some of whom helped build the border wall south of San Diego in the 1990s.)

Democratic members of Congress demanded an investigation into whether Fisher had won the contract due to improper political influence. Joined by environmental and other groups, they also filed for emergency injunctions to stop wall construction in sensitive areas before irreversible damage was done. They were upset Trump had done an end-run around their refusal to appropriate the money when he declared the wall essential to national security. Using a variety of emergency measures, Trump ended up taking a total of $18.4 billion in Pentagon funds for his wall, five times what Congress allocated for wall building in 2020. While these lawsuits were initially successful in stopping some projects, the delays turned out to be only temporary. Three times in 2019 and 2020, the Supreme Court overturned lower court decisions saying Trump had illegally transferred the funds and ruled the walls could proceed.

Construction got underway just as the pandemic hit. On April 15, 2020, Raúl Grijalva and eighty-nine other Democratic members of the House and Senate wrote a letter to the Army Corps of Engineers and Homeland Security demanding that wall building "halt immediately." They said the money should be used instead to help border towns prepare for the pandemic. Despite their efforts, and despite at least two construction workers who were living temporarily in Ajo testing positive, the building continued. It went on even as border communities, particularly Yuma and the Rio Grande Valley, were devastated by the virus. Trump, for his part, was triumphant when he visited Yuma three times over the summer of 2020. He declared the wall had been built as promised and called it a significant contribution to the fight against COVID-19.

But as summer dragged on, the extent of the damage became clear. Fisher Sand and Gravel received $1.28 billion—said to be one of the largest border-wall contracts ever—to build forty-two miles of thirty-foot walls over hilly terrain between Sasabe and Nogales. As soon as work began near Sasabe in July, there was an outcry from local residents. They said there had been no serious assessment work done, nor any consideration of aesthetic, environmental, or other impacts. Even people who generally supported the border patrol called the work "slapdash" and the wall a "monstrosity."

On the Fourth of July, the *Arizona Daily Star* reported the pond at Quitobaquito Springs had started to dry up. By mid-August, land managers at the San Bernardino Wildlife Refuge were warning groundwater pumping for wall building there was causing "a dire emergency." Myles Traphagen of the Wildlands Network said border cameras were revealing that many animals were facing "unprecedented" barriers. "Where sections of the new wall are in place, wildlife advocates already have seen javelina, bobcats and other animals spend hours struggling fruitlessly to find a way through the wall," reporter Curt Prendergast wrote in the *Star*. As construction proceeded into fall, one Cochise County rancher sued over damage caused by blasting in Guadalupe Canyon, and another rancher with land near the Cuenca Los Ojos project called for "emergency measures" to restore proper water flows before drought, floods, and other major problems occurred.

Protests over the wall near Quitobaquito Springs came to a head on October 12, Indigenous Peoples' Day. Tensions had risen in September, after two Tohono O'odham activists were arrested for interfering with construction workers—one had climbed in the bucket of a front-loader and refused to move—and Mexican and U.S. O'odham held a binational protest in which they'd met at the international fence. CBP had responded by ordering the National Park Service to shut down all roads to the site in the interests of "public safety." Then, around seven in the morning on October 12, several dozen O'odham activists blocked Highway 85 at the border patrol checkpoint thirty miles north of Lukeville. They prayed, sang, and shared information about the damage being done by wall building at the spring. About a half-hour later, state troopers showed up in riot gear and gave the protestors five minutes to disperse. When they didn't, the troopers fired smoke grenades, tear gas, and rubber bullets at them. One, David Manuel, was struck in the chest, thrown to the ground, and held down by several officers. Others were dragged from their cars parked by the side of the road. Twelve were arrested, including several parents who, supporters said, had their children taken by the border patrol. The remaining protestors went to the Pima County jail and held a ceremony out front, burning sage and singing songs, until those arrested were released. Tohono O'odham Nation Chairman Ned Norris Jr., among others, denounced the troopers' actions. Raúl Grijalva called for an investigation into "those responsible for this egregious display of excessive force."

Trump continued to wreak havoc on the border as his presidency lurched toward its violent culmination on January 6, 2021, when a riot by his supporters at the United States Capitol left five people, including a police officer, dead. During his final months in office, contractors raced to build as much wall as possible, and less than a week after the Capitol riot, Trump went to the Rio Grande Valley town of Alamo, Texas, to proclaim 450 miles had been built while he was president. Most of the new walls were thirty-foot-tall impenetrable barriers that replaced vehicle fencing in wildlife refuges. President Biden instituted a pause in the wall building when he took office, though he refused to say he'd tear down what Trump had built. Environmentalists insisted that not only must Trump's walls be removed, but the damaged lands restored as much as possible, perhaps by a border conservation corps-type program.

Like the border patrol, wall building was one of the few economic drivers in border towns, and local residents were reluctant to see the money withdrawn. They wanted it spent instead on actually needed projects and improvements. These proposals had bipartisan support:

WATER AND WASTEWATER: The long-standing problem of wastewater in the Nogales Wash reached critical proportions in the summer of 2017, when this channel that flows from south to north across the border was inundated with record-breaking rains. The storm overwhelmed a nearly seventy-year-old sewer pipe and caused it to break, spilling millions of gallons into the wash. Spills from this aging pipe, which carries wastewater from Nogales, Sonora, to a treatment plant nine miles north of the border, had been a threat to public health and sanitation for decades, and Arizona's entire congressional delegation had repeatedly tried to get the federal government to fix it. The feds, in turn, had tried to get Mexico to pay for repairs, since almost all the wastewater was theirs. But the Mexicans couldn't afford to pay, and even if they could, they would want the treated water— extremely valuable in this parched region—returned to them, rather than allowed to flow into the Santa Cruz River. That wasn't going to happen, so no progress was made. After the 2017 disaster, the House finally passed the Nogales Wastewater Fairness Act, which established that the International Boundary and Water Commission, and not the city or county, was responsible for the pipe. The bill directed $4 million of the commission's budget toward the pipe's operation and maintenance. It had yet to pass the Senate, however. In 2020 the commission also settled a long-standing lawsuit with the state of

Arizona by agreeing to spend $38.8 million to upgrade the pipe. Work was set to begin that fall.

In Naco, Sonora, heavy rains flooded the wastewater system in 2018 and 2019, resulting in cross-border sewage flows that prompted Cochise County health officials to offer immunizations against tetanus and hepatitis. Cross-border spills were also a constant problem in California. In March 2018 the cities of San Diego and Imperial Beach sued the federal government for failing to stop sewage flows from Tijuana that for many years had resulted in beach closures and other health hazards.

PORTS OF ENTRY AND STAFFING: Another thing border progressives and conservatives agreed on was the need to modernize and expand the ports and increase the number of inspectors. In Douglas–Agua Prieta, the Raul Hector Castro Port of Entry, built in 1933, was by 2018 overwhelmed with nearly 8 million pedestrian and 3.2 million vehicle annual northbound crossings. A partial expansion was completed in 2020, but additional work was required. In Nogales, where there were more than 7 million vehicle crossings annually, including 350,000 commercial trucks, the Mariposa port had undergone a $225 million expansion in 2014. But a flyover ramp was still needed to avoid the bottleneck getting on the freeway. This project got started in 2020 with a combination of $134 million in state and federal grants. A joint truck inspection program with Mexico had also been proven to speed traffic at the ports. The program was slowly being expanded to Arizona after successful implementation in California.

As for staffing shortages at the ports, this was a problem long before the spring of 2019, when lanes were closed and inspections slowed because customs agents were reassigned to cope with Central American migrants. A Cronkite News story written more than a year prior said the Nogales ports alone were three hundred people short of approved levels. And while Trump approved five thousand more border patrol agents (that agency was also having a lot of trouble hiring and retaining people, as described in chapter 6), he approved no more custom agents. This seemed shortsighted at best. A 2013 University of Southern California study found one additional inspector at the Mariposa port would boost the local economy by $2.3 million and the national economy by another $2 million. The same study also found hiring thirty-three more customs agents would lead to the creation of a thousand private sector jobs and ultimately result in a nearly $62 million increase in GDP.

Most border people also supported the idea of development aid for migrant sending regions, at least in principle. Problem was, since 1946 nearly $16 billion had been spent on foreign aid to Guatemala, Honduras and El Salvador—including a stepped-up program under Obama after the first wave of unaccompanied minors arrived in 2014—and there was precious little to show for it. Decades of U.S.-backed authoritarian governments and neoliberal economic policies had resulted in entrenched elites and deeply unequal, impoverished societies. A lot of what had passed for aid was, in fact, sweetheart deals between these elites and foreign-, mostly U.S.-, owned corporations (including agribusiness and weapons manufacturers). Aid in the form of trade agreements had also failed to end poverty and stem the flow of migrants.

There was some aid that was beneficial, to nongovernmental and inter-governmental organizations and the like, but that was reduced under Trump. He threatened to cut off aid entirely if those countries did not do more to stop migrants and take back more deported asylum seekers, which they did. But experts contended the United States should be doing much more to promote organizations working on reducing corruption and preventing violence, such as the Inter-American Foundation.

Some politicians called for a "Marshall Plan for Central America." The original Marshall Plan, named for the postwar secretary of state who proposed it, was a $13 billion aid and reconstruction package for Europe left in ruins by World War II. The historical analogy didn't quite fit, as the relationship between the United States and the three countries in the Northern Triangle was more like colonialism than economic partners and rivals. Aid primarily benefiting U.S. corporations was a big part of the Marshall Plan, and that had already been tried in Central America. What was needed was a plan that recognized the long history of exploitation and came to terms with the moral and legal obligations the United States had to these people and their land.

One aspect of the Marshall Plan that did fit the Central American context was food aid. William Lambers, author of a book on the original Marshall Plan, called for such a program in a July 2019 article in *USA*

Today. He quoted George Marshall saying, "Food is the very basis of all reconstruction."

Crop failure, brought on by climate change, deforestation, and other forces, evidently contributed to many migrants' decisions to head to El Norte in 2018 and 2019. Investigators working with Catholic Relief Services, Save the Children, and other agencies said Honduras was hard hit, as well as parts of Guatemala. In August 2019 the United Nations World Food Program (which went on to win the 2020 Nobel Peace Prize) announced it would be providing food aid to some 700,000 people in the drought-stricken regions of Guatemala, Honduras, El Salvador, and Nicaragua. That was up from 160,000 the already being helped.

The need for food aid to Central America became even more urgent in November 2020 when, amid the pandemic and persistent drought, two massive hurricanes hit the region. The Red Cross said some 4.3 million people were affected. Many of the migrants arriving on the border in early 2021 were fleeing these disasters.

Border people were working with Catholic Relief Services and similar agencies to distribute food, plant crops, provide medical care, and perform other acts of direct service to Central American communities. Several efforts were based in Tucson, including these three:

GUAMAP: The nonprofit Guatemala Acupuncture and Medical Aid Project was founded in 1994 by social activists Blake Gentry and Laurie Melrood. The married couple recruited volunteer professional acupuncturists to train rural health care workers in several communities in the Petén region of Guatemala. GUAMAP worked with local and regional health agencies, including the Asociación de Servicios Comunitarios de Salud (ASECSA), to train local health care *promotoras* and midwives. In Tucson GUAMAP conducted research into conditions in detention and, with the ongoing arrival of traumatized Guatemalan and other Central American refugees, held treatment clinics for migrants and aid workers.

IXIM ULEW: This organization of Guatemalan exiles was formed after Hurricane Stan sent people fleeing to the United States in 2005. Its full name means "Guatemalan Committee Land of Corn" in the Indigenous language Kaqchikel. (There were about 500 to 600 Guatemalans in Tucson, out of 15,000 in Arizona.) In the summer of 2018, Ixim Ulew mobilized to help survivors of another natural disaster in their native land, the June 3 eruption of the Volcán de Fuego. Guatemala's deadliest volcano eruption since 1929 killed more than 190 people, and displaced more than 13,000. Guillermina Xajab, a Tucson resident originally from the area, said her family was devastated. "They had just planted their crops and that's what they live off. The corn was just starting to grow, and it is now all yellow, it's dying." The UN said more than 1.7 million were affected by this disaster—many of whom, no doubt, wound up on the U.S.-Mexico border the following fall and winter.

Ixim Ulew donated the several thousand it raised to APRODE, an eco-tourism and adventure company based in the Acatenango region, which includes the Volcán de Fuego. APRODE was formed by deportees from the States who wanted to provide jobs and opportunities so people wouldn't have to migrate. In addition to guiding excursions to half a dozen volcanos, the group offered agriculture tours of the region. It promoted educational, environmental, and community development projects and was helping coordinate disaster relief.

GUAMAP also raised several thousand for volcano survivors. They sent the proceeds to their partner organization, the ASECSA, to purchase things like medical supplies, clean water, hygiene products, diapers, and baby formula. In addition, trauma specialists trained by GUAMAP helped survivors, especially children, deal with the tragedy. "Families have been lost in dramatically catastrophic ways," Laurie Melrood said. (In 2020 and 2021, GUAMAP continued its multinational efforts when it helped fund, train and equip twenty local health *promotoras* to deal with COVID-19 in Petén, Guatemala, and worked with the immigrants' rights group Paisanos Unidos to provide food boxes and other aid, including youth outdoor activities, to thirty-two needy families in Tucson.)

PANTANO ROTARY CLUB'S ECO FILTERS PROJECT: Partnering with other Rotary Clubs in Tucson and Guatemala, in 2018 and 2019 this eastside civic club raised more than ten thousand dollars to buy and install water filters for several hundred families and public buildings in Union Victoria, Guatemala, and another nearby village affected by the volcano eruption. Villagers went through training in how to use the filters, sanitation, and hygiene and committed to contributing five quetzals (sixty-five cents) a month to purchase a replacement filter every two years. The need for clean water in these regions is great, and the project hugely popular, Pantano Rotary Club Foundation President Eugene Medina said. In 2020 the pandemic made travel to remote villages difficult, so the club switched to installing filters in schools in villages closer to the city of Antigua, where the need is also great. The schools were introducing children to the filters and how they work. "The kids are going to lead the future to clean water and sanitation," Medina said. "This is just the beginning of our work in Guatemala."

The work that these and other border people were doing was the work of love in action, of building Martin Luther King Jr.'s beloved community as described by Bernard Lafayette. When Lafayette spoke in Tucson, he mentioned the beautiful mountains surrounding the city and, echoing King's last speech, said, "The mountaintop in Tucson is what King had in mind."

His reference to the mountaintop reminded me of my drive down to Patagonia to visit Gary Nabhan the previous February. The road had wound along the eastern flank of the Santa Rita Mountains, not yet spoiled by the Rosemont Mine. Several border patrol vehicles passed by going in both directions. The checkpoint on the opposite side of the road, heading north, was manned by a dozen or more agents. Then the big new border patrol station at the Sonoita crossroads came into view. U.S., Arizona, and border patrol flags flapped on three separate poles out front. Parked in the adjoining lot, and surrounded by a razor-wire-topped fence, were scores of brand new, bright white, dog-catcher-type SUVs. I slowed to count them. There were at least 150.

The sight was formidable. But as I looked south toward Mexico, the rows of vehicles were dwarfed by the Patagonia Mountains lining the horizon. The towering, jagged peaks put the enormity and futility of the border patrol's task into perspective.

The goal of a peaceful border, a border where so much death and suffering no longer occurred, loomed as great and mysterious and eternal as the mountains themselves. They filled my field of vision, yet as I approached, seemed to recede into the sky, as if containing a treasure forever out of reach. They were symbols of the Peaceable Kingdom, God's paradise, right here on Earth between the United States and Mexico.

Border Patrol SUV and southern Arizona mountains. (©iStock.com/phototreat)

Acknowledgments

This book was a labor of love, and I could not have written it without the help and encouragement of many people over many years.

I first want to thank everyone who allowed me to interview them, as well as all the people whose stories I've related secondhand. I've relied a lot on the work of other journalists, and I'm indebted to those cited in the notes for gathering so many great quotes, facts, and details. I'm particularly indebted to current and former *Arizona Daily Star* reporters Tim Steller, Tony Davis, Curt Prendergast, and Perla Trevizo. I also want to thank the Mexican reporters and photographers who continue to risk their lives, groups who are fighting for them like the Committee to Protect Journalists, and those who have died. I'm proud to have recorded some of their names.

Thanks also to the many artists, activists, and organizations, too many to name, who are fighting for the lives, land, rights, and dignity of all who live on the border. Keep up the good work.

Among professional colleagues and friends, a few deserve particular mention for their long-standing support: Gary Nabhan, Victor Braitberg and Lisa Soltani, Nancy Hernandez, Todd Miller, Isabel Garcia, and Ford Burkhart and Carolyn Niethammer.

I am grateful to the entire editorial, production, and marketing team at the University of Arizona Press, especially my wonderful editor, Kristen Buckles. I can't thank you enough for the work you have done to bring this book to fruition, especially in the midst of the pandemic.

Thanks as well to the teachers, parents, supporters, and members of the mariachi groups Las Aguilitas de Davis, Mariachi Milagro, Los Changuitos Feos, and the Tucson High Mariachi Rayos del Sol. It was an honor and privilege to attend so many special events such as weddings, quinceañeras, and feast days as a mariachi mom. I want to extend special thanks to the teachers, students, and other parents at Davis Bilingual Magnet School, notably the great youth mariachi instructor Alfredo Valenzuela and his family. The Valenzuelas are national treasures who've set countless kids, including mine, on paths to meaningful lives.

Friends from Pima Monthly Meeting have been hugely supportive over the years. Thank you for that, and for your work for peace and justice in the borderlands.

Members of the Community of Christ of the Desert have also been my spiritual guides and supporters for decades. They include Joanne and Chris Amoroso, Jeanette and Cliff Arnquist, Steve Baustian, Fran and David Buss, Rosa Camara, Barbara Clarihew, Jack Duncan and Ida Mae Cowart, Dorsett and Mimi and Eliza Edmunds, Ricardo Elford, Susan Gallegos, Rosemary and Bill Hallinan, Leslie Klusmire, George Mairs, Pat Manning, Lil Mattingly, Cindy and Leo Maturana-Callahan, Delle McCormick, Kathleen McLoughlin, Catherine Mullaugh, Marianna Neil, Ann Nichols, Tony and Veronica Nitko, Kathy Norgard, Laurie Olson, Kris Olson-Garewal, Kevin Serr, Philip Supina, and Mary and Michael Whitehead.

Personal friends who've helped me include Kate Davis, Ann Goethals, Ginny Pye, Mollie Sherry, Julia Lieblich, Vera Lander, and Deane Ford and Clark Rook. My deepest thanks also go to Yolanda and her family; my mother, Florence Davidson; and my family, Michael, Cameron, and Lee. Thanks for your love and care, and for the time and space to write this book. Special thanks to Lee for helping prepare the index.

Last but not least, I want to thank friends who've died, especially Florence and Ren Davis, Diana Lampsa, Nancy Mairs, Elizabeth Richards, Shawna Thompson, Ann and Trevor Weekes, and Mary Page Wilson. *Presentes!*

I also want to thank all those who've died trying to make it to the Promised Land. May your deaths not be in vain.

Miriam Davidson
Tucson, 2021

Notes

One. Mexico's Torment

Yolanda's story: Author notes from December 2018 conversation and research for *Lives on the Line*. Yolanda's surname has been omitted to protect her privacy. Mexican jokes about Navojoa: Author conversation with Nogales, Ariz., historian and activist Teresa Leal (1945–2016).

Arrest in Miroslava Breach murder: "Police Nab Suspect in Journalist's Killing," *Arizona Daily Star*, Dec. 26, 2017.

Mexico 2017 murder rate: Mark Stevenson, "Mexico Reports Highest Homicide Rate in Decades," *Arizona Daily Star*, Jan. 22, 2018; "Murders in Mexico Rise by a Third in 2018 to New Record," Reuters, Jan. 21, 2019 (updated 2017 figure from this article).

Netflix scout murder: "Location Scout for Netflix's 'Narcos' Shot Dead in Mexico," foxnews.com, Sept. 16, 2017.

California city official murder: "City Official Is Slain in Mexico Hotel Zone," *Arizona Daily Star*, Dec. 31, 2017.

From Paradise to Gangland

Mexican reporters' talk: Author notes from "Lens on Mexico's Mean Streets: Photojournalists Give Talk on Violence," presentation by Bernandino Hernández, Enric Martí, and Mort Rosenblum, University of Arizona Main Library, Feb. 13, 2018. Also Perla Trevizo, "For Journalists in Mexico, a Scramble for Survival," *Arizona Daily Star*, Feb. 11, 2018; José Antonio Rivera, "Armed Clashes Kill 11 in Mexico's Guerrero State," *Arizona Daily Star*, Jan. 8, 2018; Mark Stevenson, "Clash of Local Officials, Vigilantes Leaves 11 Dead," *Arizona Daily Star*, Mar. 2, 2018; author phone interview with CPJ Mexico City representative Jan-Albert Hootsen, Apr. 5, 2018.

No Excuse

Javier Valdez murder: Committee to Protect Journalists database; Monica Campbell, "Mourning Javier Valdez, the Mexican Journalist Who Said 'No to Silence,'" PRI.org, May 18, 2017; Carlos Lauría, "To Die Would Be to Stop Writing," *New York Times*, May 19, 2017; and Maria Verza, "Mexico Journalism Filled with Danger," *Arizona Daily Star*, Aug. 6, 2017. Valdez quotes from Campbell and Lauría articles.

FEADLE history and success rate, Miguel Díaz case: Committee to Protect Journalists, *No Excuse: Mexico Must Break Cycle of Impunity in Journalists' Murders*, report, New York, May 3, 2017. Los Piños event: "Mexican President Pledges to Prioritize Journalist Safety and Combat Impunity," CPJ news release, May 4, 2017.

Documented Border archive and Corchado quote: Author's notes of "Covering Mexico in Violent Times," talk by Corchado and fellow Mexican reporter Angela Kocherga, University of Arizona Special Collections Library, Nov. 18, 2014.

Ríodoce friends and enemies list: Verza, "Mexico Journalism Filled with Danger."

Ellerbeck quotes: Telephone interview with author, Apr. 2, 2018.

Journalist asylum cases: Mike O'Connor, "Family Murdered, Veracruz Journalist Seeks Asylum in US," CPJ blog, June 19, 2013; Gilbert Klein, "New Suit Beefs Up Effort to Free Mexican Journalist Emilio Gutierrez from Federal Detention," National Press Club news release, Mar. 6, 2018; and

Kate Linthicum, "U.S. Frees Asylum-Seeking Mexican Journalist Detained since Last Year," *Los Angeles Times*, July 27, 2018.

A Litany of Impunity

Monclova and Rosarito protests: "Mexican Police Attack Journalists Covering Protests," CPJ news release, Jan. 12, 2017.

Bernandino Hernández attack: Author notes from "Lens on Mexico's Mean Streets," University of Arizona Main Library, Feb. 13, 2018.

Cecilio Pineda Birto: "Mexican Journalist Shot Dead in Guerrero State," CPJ news release, Mar. 3, 2017.

Ricardo Monlui: "Mexican Journalist Ricardo Monlui Cabrera Murdered in Veracruz," CPJ news release, Mar. 20, 2017.

Miroslava Breach: "Mexican Journalist Shot Dead in Chihuahua," CPJ news release, Mar. 23, 2017.

Julio Omar Gomez and Armando Arrieta Granados: "Mexican Newspaper Editor Shot and Wounded in Veracruz," CPJ news release, Mar. 29, 2017; "Journalist Shot Outside His Home in Veracruz," *Arizona Daily Star*, Mar. 30, 2017.

Newspaper closes: Peter Orsi, "Mexican Newspaper Closes, Cites Insecurity for Journalists," *Arizona Daily Star*, Apr. 3, 2017; Kate Linthicum, "Mexico Newspaper Says 'Adios,' Citing Recent Violence," *Arizona Daily Star*, Apr. 5, 2017. Cantú quotes from Orsi article.

Maximino Rodríguez: "Police-Beat Reporter Shot, Killed in Baja," *Arizona Daily Star*, Apr. 15, 2017.

Javier Valdez: CPJ database.

Salvador Adame Pardo: CPJ database.

Carlos Barrios: "Reporter Threatened and Has Part of Ear Cut Off in Mexico's Quintana Roo State," CPJ news release, June 1, 2017.

Edgar Daniel Esqueda Castro: CPJ database.

Adolfo Lagos: "Televisa Official Killed by His Bodyguard," *Mexico News Daily*, Nov. 21, 2017. Attorney general's quote from this article.

Severed heads: "Icebox Containing Two Heads Found Outside Broadcaster in Mexico," CPJ news release, Nov. 29, 2017.

Gumaro Perez: "Journalist Killed at Child's School Party," *Arizona Daily Star*, Dec. 20, 2017.

Arrest in Breach murder: "Police Nab Suspect in Journalist's Killing."

Carlos Dominguez: "Mexican Journalist Killed in Tamaulipas," CPJ news release, Jan. 16, 2018; Kate Linthicum, "Mexican Journalist Is Stabbed 21 Times in Front of His Family," *Arizona Daily Star*, Jan. 17, 2018.

Pamika Montenegro: "Mexican Blogger and Satirist Killed in Guerrero State," CPJ news release, Feb. 8, 2018.

Leobardo Vásquez: "Mexican Reporter Killed in Veracruz State," CPJ news release, Mar. 23, 2018.

Sanchez murder convictions: "Two Mexican Policemen Convicted for Murder of Moisés Sánchez; Chief Suspects Still at Large," CPJ press release, Mar. 28, 2018.

Domínguez murder arrests: "Six Arrested in January Slaying of Journalist," *Arizona Daily Star*, Mar. 29, 2018; Ildefonso Ortiz and Brandon Darby, "Three Reporters, Mexican Border Politician's Relative Arrested for Columnist's Murder," Breitbart News, Mar. 30, 2018.

Valdez murder arrest and conviction: "Mexico Must Identify Mastermind in Murder of Javier Valdez Cárdenas," CPJ news release, Apr. 24, 2018; "CPJ Welcomes Conviction in Murder of Mexican Journalist Javier Valdez," CPJ news release, Feb. 28, 2020.

Juan Carlos Huerta: Kate Linthicum, "Gunman Ambush, Slay Mexico Radio Journalist," *Arizona Daily Star*, May 16, 2018.

Héctor González: "Mexican Journalist Found Dead in Tamaulipas State," CPJ press release, May 30, 2018.

José Chan Dzib: "Mexican Journalist Killed in Quintana Roo," CPJ press release, July 5, 2018.

Police commander suspended: "Journalist Hurt; Police Commander Suspended," *Arizona Daily Star*, July 9, 2018.

Rubén Pat Cauich: "Mexican Journalist and Media Owner Killed in Quintana Roo," CPJ press release, July 25, 2018.

Emilio Gutiérrez asylum case: Klein, "New Suit Beefs Up Effort to Free Mexican Journalist"; Linthicum, "U.S. Frees Asylum-Seeking Mexican Journalist"; and Niraj Warikoo, "Mexican Journalist Who Is a Fellow at University of Michigan Ordered Deported," *Detroit Free Press*, Mar. 14, 2019.

Javier Rodríguez Valladares: "Mexican Cameraman Killed in Quintana Roo," CPJ press release, Aug. 30, 2018.

Mario Gomez: "Alleged Lookout Nabbed in Murder of Reporter," *Arizona Daily Star*, Sept. 25, 2018.

Jesús Márquez: "Journalist Is Slain; Year's Total Rises to 10," *Arizona Daily Star*, Dec. 4, 2018.

Mexico most dangerous country in West in 2018, Rafael Murúa, and Martín Valtierra: "Mexican Reporter Assaulted with Baseball Bats in Baja California Sur," CPJ news release, Jan. 31, 2019.

Jesús Ramos: "Journalist Is Killed in Gulf Coast State," *Arizona Daily Star*, Feb. 10, 2019.

Santiago Barroso: "Mexico: Journalist Shot, Killed in Northern State of Sonora," *Arizona Daily Star*, Mar. 17, 2019; Tim Steller, "Officials: Sonoran Journalist Killed over Relationship, Not His Writings," *Arizona Daily Star*, Mar. 26, 2019.

Omar Camacho: "Mexican Reporter Omar Camacho Found Dead in Sinaloa State," CPJ news release, Apr. 2, 2019.

AMLO attitudes and actions toward press: Jan-Albert Hootsen, "Mexico's Press Question President's Commitment to Press Advertising Reform," CPJ, May 8, 2019; Jan-Albert Hootsen, "López Obrador's Anti-press Rhetoric Leaves Mexico's Journalists Feeling Exposed," CPJ, May 6, 2019.

Confrontation with Domínguez's son: "President Vows Justice in Journalists' Deaths," *Arizona Daily Star*, May 3, 2019.

Telésforo Enríquez: "Telésforo Enríquez, Founder of Mexican Community Radio Station, Shot Dead in Oaxaca," CPJ news release, May 6, 2019.

Summer 2019 violence: "Newspaper Stops Print Edition After Attack," *Arizona Daily Star*, Aug. 1, 2019; "Journalist Shot Dead Before He Can Testify," *Arizona Daily Star*, Aug. 4, 2019.

Year-end rating: "Syria, Mexico Deadliest Countries for Journalists in 2019," CPJ news release, Dec. 17, 2019.

Government spying: "Mexican Anti-corruption News Website MCCI Hit with Cyberattack," CPJ news release, May 10, 2019; "Widow of Slain Mexican Journalist Javier Valdez Targeted by Spyware," CPJ news release, Mar. 20, 2019.

Attacks on U.S. journalists: "Police Targeting Journalists Covering George Floyd Protests," CPJ news release, June 15, 2020; "In Rare Letter, CPJ Board Calls on U.S. Local Authorities to Halt Arrests, Assaults on Journalists,"

CPJ news release, June 5, 2020; and Paul Walsh, "Photographer amid Minneapolis Unrest Sues, Says Officers Blinded Her in Eye with Nonlethal Shot," *Minneapolis Star Tribune*, June 16, 2020.

Two. Prohibition Then and Now

Stills on both sides of the line: Author interview with Gary Nabhan, Patagonia, Ariz., Feb. 9, 2018. Nogales Prohibition-era history and mule story: Charles Fowler, "Nogales Rum Trail Mule-Run in 20's," *Nogales International*, c. 1976; and Charles Fowler, "Bootleggers '20's Customs' Target," *Nogales International*, Feb. 26, 1976. Customs agent deaths: Annerino, *Dead in Their Tracks*, 174. Kirpnick death: Davidson, *Lives on the Line*, 108.

The Border Then

Padre Kino saying Mass at Quitobaquito Springs: Gary Paul Nabhan, "Border Wall Construction: Imperiling Sacred Sites, Churches and Religious Freedom," *Acting Franciscan* (blog), Oct. 17, 2019.

Death of Melchior Díaz: Annerino, *Dead in Their Tracks*, 126.

Characterization of border people: Woodard, *American Nations*, 31 and 10.

Mexican-American War, Treaty of Guadalupe Hidalgo, Gadsden Purchase: Wikipedia. Number of Mexicans in U.S. in 1848: Fact sheet, Amistades, Inc., Feb. 2, 2016. Ongoing use of Spanish: Rosina Lozano, "Spanish Has Never Been a Foreign Language in the US," *Arizona Daily Star*, June 1, 2018.

Camp Grant massacre: Tom Beal, "Curing 'Amnesia' About State's Most Blood-Soaked Day," *Arizona Daily Star*, May 3, 2009. Number of Sonorans killed by Geronimo's band: *National Geographic* 182 (1992). Yaqui history, Santa Teresa Urrea: Wikipedia; Roscoe Willson, "The Witch of Nogales," Arizona Days and Ways, *Arizona Republic*, Jan 6, 1974. Sacred items stopped at border: Author's general knowledge.

Chinese Exclusion Act, anti-Chinese riot: Wikipedia; "The Chinese Exclusion Act," *American Experience*, PBS, May 29, 2018. Henry Flipper: Davidson, *Lives on the Line*, 6. Mingus: Wikipedia; Gerald Gay, "Charles Mingus Legacy," *Arizona Daily Star*, Apr. 17, 2014.

Mexican migration: Author notes, talk by historian Raquel Rubio-Goldsmith at And the Deaths, Disappearances and Deportations Continue . . . *No Vale Nada La Vida* symposium, Global Justice Center, South Tucson, Feb. 17, 2018; "Getting Up to Speed on Immigration Laws," timeline graphic, *Arizona Daily Star*, Jan. 29, 2017; Russell Contreras, "Before 'Abolish ICE,'" *Arizona Daily Star*, July 12, 2018.

Militia history, Porvenir massacre: Wikipedia; Russell Contreras, "Militias Have Long History Patrolling US Border," *Arizona Daily Star*, May 13, 2019.

"Deportee" lyrics: Woody Guthrie website. Reprinted with permission.

Nogales in 1950s and 1960s: Author's general knowledge and research for *Lives on the Line*. Baffert's brother's quote from NBC interview, June 9, 2018. Customs agents killed in 1974: Annerino, *Dead in Their Tracks*, 178; James Maish, "Somozas Part Legend, Part Terrifying Reality," *Arizona Daily Star*, May 24, 1987.

Tortilla Curtain, Mascareñas quote: Martínez, *Troublesome Border*, 134. Anti-immigrant activity: Miriam Davidson, "The Mexican Border War," *The Nation*, Nov. 12, 1990. IRCA: Author notes, talk by historian Raquel Rubio-Goldsmith at And the Deaths, Disappearances and Deportations Continue . . . *No Vale Nada La Vida* symposium, Global Justice Center, South Tucson, Feb. 17, 2018.

The Border Transformed

Nineteen-nineties border crackdown: American Friends Service Committee Immigration Law Enforcement Monitoring Project, *Operation Blockade: A City Divided*, report, July 1994; Davidson, *Lives on the Line* (Nogales border patrol agent quote, 87); "Ten Years of Death by Border Patrol," *In These Times*, Sept. 2019, 40.

NAFTA's impact on migration: Bacon, *The Right to Stay Home*.

Details on 1996 law: "Getting Up to Speed on Immigration Laws."

Esequiel Hernandez death: Wikipedia; Davidson, *Lives on the Line*, 110.

History of troops on border: Curt Prendergast, "Long Before Trump's Order, Guard Troops Were Helping on Arizona-Mexico Border," *Arizona Daily Star*, May 5, 2018; Perla Trevizo, "Troops Free Up Agents for Field by Performing a Variety of Duties," *Arizona Daily Star*, May 24, 2018.

Difficulty measuring border security: "Border Security Is an Elusive Goal," *Arizona Daily Star*, Feb. 25, 2013; Perla Trevizo, "Some See 'Border Surge' as Too Costly," *Arizona Daily Star*, June 28, 2013.

Migrant survey: Wayne Cornelius, "Border Enforcement and Immigration Reform," *New York Times*, Mar. 8, 2013; Wayne Cornelius, "Bandits, Not Costly Border Fences, Unnerve Potential Crossers," *Arizona Daily Star*, Aug. 12, 2015.

Cruzar la Cara de la Luna: Title song from a 2010 mariachi opera by José "Pepe" Martínez Jr.

Drug seizure figures: Curt Prendergast, "Most Hard Drugs Are Seized at Entry Ports, Records Show," *Arizona Daily Star*, May 7, 2017; Fowler, "Bootleggers '20's Customs' Target."

Tunnels and tunnel kids: Author's general knowledge and research for *Lives on the Line*; "US Border Patrol 'Tunnel Rats' Plug Underground Passages," Voice of America, Mar. 9, 2017 (DEA survey from this article).

Agua Prieta-Douglas supertunnel: Monte Reel, "Underworld," *New Yorker*, Aug. 3, 2015, p. 22; Caitlin Alexander, "El Chapo Guzman Has Ties to Southern Arizona," KVOA.com, Nov. 13, 2018.

Walls' impact on migration and costs: Damien Cave, "Long Border, Endless Struggle," *New York Times*, Mar. 2, 2013.

Rise in desert deaths: Brady McCombs, "Border-Crosser Deaths Reach a Low but Still, 182 People Died," *Arizona Daily Star*, Oct. 12, 2011; Tim Steller, "Border Deaths at Historic Highs even as Crossings Plunge," *Arizona Daily Star*, Aug. 19, 2012.

Post-9/11 border crackdown: "Getting Up to Speed on Immigration Laws"; and Mark Binelli, "Ten Shots Across the Border," *New York Times Magazine*, Mar. 3, 2016. Rep. King quote: "GOP Rep. Designs Electric Fence for Mexican Border: 'We Do This with Livestock All the Time,'" Truthdig. org, July 14, 2006.

Arizona fence construction: Stephanie Innes, "Trashing the Border," *Arizona Daily Star*, Sept. 27, 2006. Headline: "Migrants Called Threat to Bombing Range," *Arizona Daily Star*, Feb. 8, 2000.

Tohono O'odham position on wall and border security: Resolution No. 17-053 of the Tohono O'odham Legislative Council, "Border Security and Immigration Enforcement on the Tohono O'odham Nation," Feb. 7, 2017; Tyson

Hudson, "Tohono O'odham Nation Allows Surveillance Towers on Reservation, but No Wall," *Arizona Daily Star*, July 28, 2019; Todd Miller, "'The Most Militarized Community in the United States,'" *In These Times*, July 2019, 28; and J. Weston Phippen, "Like 'Building a 30-Foot Wall through Arlington Cemetery': Tribal Leaders in Arizona Are Worried Trump's Border Wall Will Decimate Sacred Sites and Leave Smugglers No Choice but to Cut Through Native Land," *Business Insider*, May 17, 2020.

Wall building in Rio Grande Valley: Seth Robbins, "Finishing Border Wall Would Be a Tall Task," *Arizona Daily Star*, Jan. 2, 2016; Matthew Daly and Alicia Caldwell, "Texas Wall Bumps into Geographical Realities," *Arizona Daily Star*, Mar. 30, 2017; Nomaan Merchant, "Border Wall Could Leave Some Americans on 'Mexican Side,'" *Arizona Daily Star*, Apr. 17, 2017; Lulu Garcia-Navarro, "Legal Battle over Border Wall Plays Out at Chapel in Mission, Texas," NPR, Feb. 10, 2019.

University involvement in surveillance tech: Tom Beal, "Tech Park Aims to Be Border Lab," *Arizona Daily Star*, Mar. 2, 2013; Jill Goetz, "Border Patrol Control," *Arizona Alumni Magazine*, fall 2017, 40–42.

Virtual fences: "High-Tech Border Towers' Launch Delayed," *Arizona Daily Star*, June 16, 2007; Brady McCombs, "Border-Security Plan Not Justified, GAO Says," *Arizona Daily Star*, Nov. 5, 2011 (GAO report cited in this article); and Perla Trevizo, "Border Patrol Pleased with New Tech Efforts," *Arizona Daily Star*, Dec. 27, 2015.

Zawada and Heid arrests: Brady McCombs, "2 Men Praying at Virtual-Fence Site Are Arrested," *Arizona Daily Star*, Aug. 7, 2009. Arivaca residents' objections: "High-Tech Border Towers' Launch Delayed."

Swartz case: Mark Binelli, "Ten Shots Across the Border," *New York Times Magazine*, Mar. 3, 2016.

The Border Now

Krentz murder: Wikipedia; Charles August, "Suspected Robert Krentz Killer Murdered in Agua Prieta," Bisbee Net News, Mar. 30, 2011.

Border crime rates: Ernesto Castañeda, "Is the Border Safe? Border Residents' Perceptions of Crime and Security," contexts.org, Sept. 5, 2016; and Will Weissert, "Crime Rate Doesn't Justify Bigger El Paso Wall, Foes Say," *Arizona Daily Star*, Feb. 11, 2019.

Smuggling methods: Author's general knowledge; interview with Gary Nabhan; Perla Trevizo, "Smugglers' Jeep Left atop Makeshift Ramp on Border Fence," *Arizona Daily Star*, Feb. 16, 2019.

Howard Buffett, vigilantes: Beau Hodai, "Howard Buffett's Border War: A Billionaire's Son Is Spending Millions in Cochise County," and "Border Cowboys: Howard Buffett Is a Perfect Fit with Cochise County's Legacy of Vigilantism," *Phoenix New Times*, Jan. 10, 2019. Rancher verdict: Susy Buchanan, "Border Vigilante Ordered to Pay Damages in SPLC-Sponsored Suit," Southern Poverty Law Center news release, Nov. 27, 2006. Crimes by militia members: Megan Cassidy, "Ex-Minuteman Chris Simcox Sentenced to 19.5 Years in Child Sex-Abuse Case," *Arizona Republic*, July 11, 2016; Eric Reidy, "Not in My Backyard," *Mother Jones*, May/June 2019, 50.

Border patrol declaring full operational control: Tim Vanderpool, "More Destruction," *Tucson Weekly*, Apr. 25–May 1, 2013. Cornelius quote: Letter to the editor, *New York Times*, Mar. 8, 2013. Massey quote: "Immigration from Mexico in Fast Retreat, Report Shows," *Arizona Daily Star*, Nov. 17, 2011.

Secure Communities, 287(g) program, deportation numbers: Serena Marshall, "Obama Has Deported More People than Any Other President," ABC News, Aug. 29, 2016; Curt Prendergast, "New Trump Border Orders Raise Questions for Sheriffs," *Arizona Daily Star*, Feb. 26, 2017.

Measuring border security: Astrid Galvan, "Data Lacking on Border Security, Study Says," *Arizona Daily Star*, Feb. 21, 2015; Elliot Spagat, "Watchdog: No Way to Judge Border-Wall Success," *Arizona Daily Star*, Feb. 17, 2017.

Central American migration: Perla Trevizo, "Apprehensions on SW Border Increasing for 2nd Straight Year," *Arizona Daily Star*, May 12, 2013; Seth Robbins and Alicia Caldwell, "Despite Rhetoric, Border Less Urgent Issue in 2015," *Arizona Daily Star*, Aug. 5, 2015.

Trump orders wall built: Julie Pace, "President Orders Wall to Be Built along Border," *Arizona Daily Star*, Jan. 26, 2017.

GAO report, damage costs: Curt Prendergast, "As Border Wall Planning Begins, GAO Reports on Current Fencing," *Arizona Daily Star*, Mar. 14, 2017; Spagat, "Watchdog: No Way to Judge Border-Wall Success"; Astrid Galvan, "Fixing Border Fence Cost US Gov't $730,000," *Arizona Daily Star*, Mar. 28, 2015; Howard Fischer, "Court: US Isn't Liable for Border-Fence Damages," *Arizona Daily Star*, Oct. 24, 2013.

Design contest: Elliot Spagat, "Construction Bids for Border Wall Include Solar Panels, Scenic Views," *Arizona Daily Star*, Apr. 5, 2017.

Lawsuits: Astrid Galvan, "Grijalva Files Lawsuit over Trump's Wall," *Arizona Daily Star*, Apr. 13, 2017; Elliot Spagat, "Judge Disparaged by Trump Rules Wall Can Proceed," *Arizona Daily Star*, Feb. 28, 2018.

Sessions in Nogales: Curt Prendergast, "Sessions: 'Trump Era' Means Greater Border Enforcement," *Arizona Daily Star*, Apr. 12, 2017.

Prototypes and protests: Greg Moran, "San Diego Paid $278K to Patrol Site Where Wall Prototypes Were Built," *Arizona Daily Star*, Jan. 7, 2018; Julie Watson and Kathleen Ronayne, "Trump to See Wall Prototypes as Protests Back, Oppose Plan," *Arizona Daily Star*, Mar. 13, 2018 (Gómez quote from this article).

Horses caught: "Police Say Man Used Horses to Ferry Drugs," *Arizona Daily Star*, Apr. 20, 2018.

Three. Where the Guns Go

Brian Terry killing: CBP website; Brian Terry Foundation website; Wikipedia; Tim Steller, "Wanted: US Seeking 4 Suspects in Slaying of Border Patrol Agent Brian Terry," *Arizona Daily Star*, July 10, 2012.

Fast and Furious

Prohibition, Waco, and timeline: ATF website and Wikipedia.

Fast and Furious: "ATF gunwalking scandal," Wikipedia (all quotes in this section from this article, except Jeff Sessions, from Curt Prendergast, "Man Suspected in Agent's Killing to be Arraigned in Tucson Today," *Arizona Daily Star*, Aug. 1, 2018.) Also Sari Horwitz, "Agent Who Started 'Fast and Furious' Defends Gun-Tracking Operation," *Washington Post*, June 27, 2012.

Brian Terry Foundation dinner: Joe Ferguson, "Political Strategist Steve Bannon Implores Tucson Crowd to Support Trump," *Arizona Daily Star*, Nov. 18, 2017.

Killers arrested and convicted: Tim Steller, "Coincidental Border Patrol Cases Test Justice System," *Arizona Daily Star*, Sept. 24, 2015; Ben Moffat, "Family of Slain Border Patrol Agent Seeks Details in Gun Probe," *Arizona Daily*

Star, June 10, 2017; Prendergast, "Man Suspected in Agent's Killing to be Arraigned in Tucson Today"; Curt Prendergast, "Suspect in Border Agent's Killing Pleads Not Guilty; Trial Set for September," *Arizona Daily Star*, Aug. 2, 2018; Curt Prendergast, "6th Suspect Guilty in Killing of Border Agent Terry; A 7th Awaits Extradition," *Arizona Daily Star*, Feb. 14, 2019; Astrid Galvan, "Gunman Is Sentenced to Life in Prison in 2010 Killing of Border Patrol Agent," *Arizona Daily Star*, Jan. 9, 2020; "Last of 7 Men Faces Trial in '10 Shooting Death of BP Agent," *Arizona Daily Star*, Feb. 6, 2020.

Where the Guns Go

Iguala teacher killings: J.C. Finley, "Mass Grave Discovered and 4 Arrested as Search for Missing Mexico Students Continues," UPI.com, Oct. 28, 2014; Wikipedia; and American Friends Service Committee, *Where the Guns Go: U.S. Arms and the Crisis of Violence in Mexico*, report, Philadelphia, Penn., 2016 (Colt Manufacturing quote: page 6. C4 quote, 7; Ramos quote, 3).

Jesús Murillo Karam press conference: "Mexican Officials Detail Horrific Scenario for Murdered Students," NBCnews.com, Nov. 8, 2014 (quotes from this article).

Second student identified: "Remains of One of Missing 43 Mexican College Students Are Identified," NBCnews.com, July 8, 2020.

Familias en Búsqueda quote: American Friends Service Committee, *Where the Guns Go*, 10.

Miguel Ángel Jiménez Blanco: Marlon Ramtahal, "Activist Who Led Search for Mexico's 43 Missing Students Killed," NBCnews.com, August 10, 2015.

Murillo Karam resigns: "'Enough': Mexican AG's Gaffe in Case of Missing Students Sparks Viral Fury," NBCnews.com, Nov. 9, 2014; Doug Ware, "Scandal-Tainted Mexican Attorney General Resigns," UPI.com, Feb. 27, 2015.

SEDENA: American Friends Service Committee, *Where the Guns Go*, 6.

Elbit Systems: American Friends Service Committee, *Where the Guns Go*, 7; David Wichner, "Surveillance Tower Builder Here Acquired by Mont. Firm," *Arizona Daily Star*, Jan. 18, 2019; Tyson Hudson, "Tohono O'odham Nation Allows Surveillance Towers on Reservation, but No Wall," *Arizona Daily Star*, July 28, 2019; Todd Miller, *Empire of Borders*, 77.

German response to Iguala killings: American Friends Service Committee, *Where the Guns Go*, 6.

Murphy's Guns, Milkor USA, and Dillon Aero: Gabriel Schivone and John Lindsay-Poland, "Arizona's Role in Weapons Exports to Mexico Must Be Eliminated," *Arizona Daily Star*, Dec. 17, 2018, and an expanded version of Schivone and Lindsay-Poland, "Ending Arizona's Role in Weapons Exports to Mexico," distributed at Global Justice Center film showing, South Tucson, Feb. 27, 2019 (quotes from this version). Also Mexican Commission for the Defense and Promotion of Human Rights and Global Exchange's Stop U.S. Arms to Mexico project, *Gross Human Rights Abuses: The Legal and Illegal Gun Trade to Mexico*, report, August 2018 (Tanhuato massacre quote, 16). María Herrera quote: American Friends Service Committee, *Where the Guns Go*, 9.

Profiteers Big and Small

Santana López case: Pablo López, "Affidavits: Exploding Bullets Halt Smugglers," *Arizona Daily Star*, Aug. 6, 2018 (Santana López quote from this article).

ATF estimate, number of smuggling cases filed: Curt Prendergast, "Easy Cash Drives Flow of US Guns Wielded by Cartels," *Arizona Daily Star*, Nov. 24, 2019.

Valles and Veninga cases: Curt Prendergast, "Agent: 'Every Family Member Had a .50 Cal' in Smuggling Plot," *Arizona Daily Star*, July 9, 2017 (agent quote from this article); Curt Prendergast, "Tucson Man Sentenced to 6½ Years in Gun-Buying Conspiracy for Cartels," *Arizona Daily Star*, Mar. 20, 2018.

Other cases: Curt Prendergast, "Traffickers Apparently Got Guns from Ex-DEA Agent," *Arizona Daily Star*, Aug. 15, 2018; Curt Prendergast, "Ex-DEA Agent Gets Probation for Selling Guns Without License," *Arizona Daily Star*, Jan. 8, 2019; Curt Prendergast, "Judge Laments Gun Smuggler's Punishment Can't Be Stiffer," *Arizona Daily Star*, Feb 24, 2018; and Jessica Suriano, "2 Tucsonans Sentenced in 'Straw Purchase' Gun Scheme," *Arizona Daily Star*, Oct. 14, 2017.

Money smuggling, Treasury Department estimate: Julianne Stanford, "Drug Cash Slips into Mexico as Border Seizures Plummet," *Arizona Daily Star*, Jan. 26, 2017.

Money laundering: Ed Vulliamy, "How a Big US Bank Laundered Billions from Mexico's Murderous Drug Gangs," *The Guardian*, Apr. 2, 2011; Zach

Carter, "Wall Street Is Laundering Drug Money and Getting Away with It," *Huffington Post*, July 14, 2010, updated May 25, 2011; author notes, talk by attorney and activist Isabel Garcia, Quaker Meeting House, Tucson, Nov. 19, 2017.

Chilling effect: Curt Prendergast, "Financial-Crimes Crackdown Puts a Chill on Border Banks," *Arizona Daily Star*, Mar. 25, 2018.

HSBC case: "HSBC Holdings Plc. and HSBC Bank USA N.A. Admit to Anti-Money Laundering and Sanctions Violations, Forfeit $1.256 Billion in Deferred Prosecution Agreement," U.S. Justice Department press release, Dec. 11, 2012.

NPR story and Javier Valdez quote: John Burnett, "Awash in Cash, Drug Cartels Rely on Big Banks to Launder Profits," All Things Considered, National Public Radio, Mar. 20, 2014.

Four. All They Will Call You

Streamline hearing: Author notes, DeConcini Federal Courthouse, Tucson, May 30, 2018.

Streamline impact and judges' reaction: Cindy Chang, "Immigrant Cases Now Dominate US Courts," *Arizona Daily Star*, May 23, 2013; Leslie Carlson and David Wolf, "Operation Streamline Effective on One Front: Helping CCA Profit," *Arizona Daily Star*, July 6, 2015 (OIG report mentioned in this article); Charles Sabalos, "Judges Should Stop Mass Immigration Plea Hearings," *Arizona Daily Star*, July 1, 2018; Elliot Spagat, "'Zero-Tolerance' Immigration Policy Scorned by Many Judges," *Arizona Daily Star*, Dec. 19, 2018.

Operation Streamline

Streamline hearings: Author notes, DeConcini Federal Courthouse, Tucson, May 30, 2018, and Sept. 25, 2018; Perla Trevizo and Curt Prendergast, "Tucson Judges Urge Reuniting Border-Crossing Parents, Kids After Release," *Arizona Daily Star*, June 3, 2018 (this article mentions Armando Ramírez Vásquez); Curt Prendergast, "Judge Asks Feds to Tell Migrants Where Their Children Are," *Arizona Daily Star*, June 7, 2018.

Streamline history: Author notes, talk by Tucson attorney Margo Cowan and fact sheet provided at And the Deaths, Disappearances and Deportations Continue . . . *No Vale Nada La Vida* symposium, Global Justice Center, South Tucson, Feb. 17, 2018; Alicia Caldwell, "Tough Immigration Court Serves as Model for Trump," *Arizona Daily Star*, Apr. 26, 2017; Curt Prendergast, "In Reversal, Crossers in US Court Here Face Criminal Charges on First Offense," *Arizona Daily Star*, June 29, 2017; Curt Prendergast, "Shackles Off Federal Defendants in Arizona," *Arizona Daily Star*, July 27, 2017. Also Gipe, *Operation Streamline.*

Protests: Perla Trevizo, "12 Immigration Protestors Convicted in Tucson Case," *Arizona Daily Star*, Apr. 14, 2015; Ernesto Portillo Jr., "Immigrant Activists Offered No Apologies," *Arizona Daily Star*, July 25, 2015; Dorothy Chao, "Streamline Bus-Stoppers Speak Out at Sentencing," No More Deaths newsletter, Fall 2015.

Changes under Trump: Elliot Spagat, "Sessions: 'Zero Tolerance' Policy for Border Crossers," *Arizona Daily Star*, Apr. 7, 2018; Curt Prendergast, "Prosecutions of First-Time Border Crossers Rise 71% Here under Sessions' Zero-Tolerance Policy," *Arizona Daily Star*, Apr. 22, 2018; Curt Prendergast, "In Busy Operation Streamline Proceedings, Dockets Often Full and Pleas Ordinarily Brief," *Arizona Daily Star*, June 24, 2018; Elliot Spagat, "Holdout California Adopts Mass Immigration Hearings," *Arizona Daily Star*, July 9, 2018.

Casa Alitas: Author interview with volunteer David Buss, Tucson, late December 2017.

Kids in Detention

Antar Davidson events and quotes: Author interview at Davidson's home, Tucson, Aug. 13, 2018.

Family separations: Curt Prendergast and Perla Trevizo, "Zero-Tolerance Border Policy Leaves Parents, Children Split," *Arizona Daily Star*, May 20, 2018; Trevizo and Prendergast, "Tucson Judges Urge Reuniting Border-Crossing Parents, Kids After Release"; Prendergast, "Judge Asks Feds to Tell Migrants Where Their Children Are"; Elliot Spagat and Morgan Lee, "US Retreats on 'Zero-Tolerance' Immigration Policy at Border," *Arizona*

Daily Star, June 26, 2018. *People* article: Sandra Sobieraj Westfall, "Migrant Crisis: Children in Limbo," *People*, July 9, 2018, p. 52.

Melania Trump: Leanne Italie, "First Lady's 'Don't Care' Jacket Sets Off Online Memer Frenzy," *Arizona Daily Star*, June 23, 2018; Curt Prendergast, "First Lady Tours Center, Visits with Tucson Border Officials," *Arizona Daily Star*, June 29, 2018; Laurie Kellman, "First Lady Seeing Lots, Saying Little at Migrant Centers," *Arizona Daily Star*, July 1, 2018.

Southwest Key: Southwest Key website; Craig Harris, "Housing Separated Children Is Big Business," *Arizona Daily Star*, June 25, 2018; and Nomaan Merchant, "CEO of Southwest Key, Which Houses Migrant Children, Exits amid Criticism," *Arizona Daily Star*, Mar. 12, 2019.

Casa Estrella del Norte: Author visit, fall 2015; Perla Trevizo, "3 Immigrant Teens Flee Shelter Facility Here," *Arizona Daily Star*, Oct. 17, 2015; Perla Trevizo, "Shelter for Unaccompanied Minors 'Homey,' Tour Reveals," *Arizona Daily Star*, Dec. 8, 2015. Also testimony by Nancy Hernandez, PhD, for the U.S. Office on Civil Rights. Dr. Hernandez served as a volunteer interpreter for investigators from the Center for Human Rights and Constitutional Law, who interviewed detainees at Casa Estrella del Norte over two days in August 2018. She helped lead the petition drive against Southwest Key and former CEO Juan Sanchez.

Abuses: Stephen Ceasar, "Arizonans Can Fight Against Immigrant Detention," *Arizona Daily Star*, Oct. 29, 2017; Nomaan Merchant, "Immigrants in Detention Facilities Face Sexual Abuse," *Arizona Daily Star*, Jan. 9, 2018; Mary Jo Pitzl, "Arizona Moves to Revoke Licenses from All Southwest Key Migrant Children Shelters," *Arizona Daily Star*, Sept. 20, 2018; Agnel Philip, "Arizona Southwest Key Shelter Was Closed Because Staff Abused Kids, Feds Say," *Arizona Republic*, Oct. 9, 2018; Nomaan Merchant, "Problems Escalate at Detention Centers for Migrant Children," *Arizona Daily Star*, Nov. 25, 2018; and Astrid Galvan, "Videos Show Migrant Children Dragged, Shoved at Phoenix Shelter," *Arizona Daily Star*, Jan. 1, 2019. Also David Dayen, "Below the Surface of ICE: The Corporations Profiting from Immigrant Detention," *In These Times*, Oct. 2018 ("baby jail" quote, 19; abuse allegations quote, 20.)

Lawsuit against CBP: Howard Fischer, "Appeals Court Says Border Patrol Must Provide Mats, Blankets in Holding Cells," *Arizona Daily Star*, Dec. 23,

2017. Lawyer arguing soap and toothbrushes not required: Video posted by Now This Politics on Facebook, June 21, 2019; Deanna Paul, "'The Taliban Gave Me Toothpaste': Former Captives Contrast U.S. Treatment of Child Migrants," *Washington Post*, June 25, 2019.

Conditions, deaths in ICE and BP facilities: Adriana Gomez Licon and Amy Taxin, "Motion: Migrant Kids Live in 'Prison-Like Conditions,'" *Arizona Daily Star*, June 2, 2019; Cedar Attanasio, Garance Burke, and Martha Mendoza, "Lawmakers Decry US Lockups of Migrant Kids," *Arizona Daily Star*, June 22, 2019; Caitlin Dickerson, "US Relocates Children from Migrant Site," *Boston Globe*, June 25, 2019. ACLU on family separations: Elliot Spagat and Astrid Galvan, "ACLU: 911 Children Split at Border Since 2018 Court Order," news.yahoo.com, July 30, 2019. Hysterectomy allegations: "Mexican Foreign Ministry Confirms Two Nonconsensual Procedures at ICE Facility, Hints at Class Action Suit," *International Business Times*, Oct 13, 2020; Jerry Lambe, "'Like an Experimental Concentration Camp': Whistleblower Complaint Alleges Mass Hysterectomies at ICE Detention Center," msn.com, Sept. 14, 2020.

Politicians tour shelters: Perla Trevizo, "Grijalva tours Tucson shelter for migrant kids," *Arizona Daily Star*, July 7, 2018; Emily Tillett, "Merkley Says Images of Migrant Processing Center Are 'Seared' in His Mind," CBS News, June 6, 2018 (quotes from these articles).

Anti-ICE protests: Dayen, "Below the Surface of ICE"; David Meyer, "McKinsey Ends Work with ICE after Contract Revelation," Fortune.com, July 10, 2018; Rachel Sandler, "Amazon, Microsoft, Wayfair: Employees Stage Internal Protests against Working with ICE," Forbes.com, July 19, 2019; Janelle Nanos, "Wayfair Faces Walkout over Sales to Border Detention Camp," *Boston Globe*, June 26, 2019.

Airlines and hotels refuse cooperation with ICE, Motel 6: Dee-Ann Durbin, "US Hotels Caught Up in Raucous Debate on Migrants," *Arizona Daily Star*, July 22, 2019; Tiffany Hsu, "Motel 6, Which Gave Guest Data to ICE Agents, Will Pay $12 Million," *New York Times*, Apr. 5, 2019; and Terry Tang, "Accord Called Near in Lawsuit Saying Motel 6 Workers Shared Info with Agents," *Arizona Daily Star*, June 4, 2019 (numbers from this article).

Migrants held in hotels during pandemic: Catherine Shoichet and Geneva Sands, "Hundreds of Migrant Children Were Detained in Hotels as the

Pandemic Flared in the US," CNN, Sept. 3, 2020; "Tucson to House Asylum Seekers, Migrants at City Hotels," AP, Apr. 13, 2021.

Illinois bans private immigration prisons: Sophia Tareen, "Advocates Hope Illinois Private Detention Ban Sparks Change," *Arizona Daily Star*, July 14, 2019 (Pritzker quote from this article). California: Louis Casiano, "California Bans Private Prisons and Immigrant Detention Centers," Foxnews.com, Oct. 11, 2019.

Deportees

Kino Border Initiative: Author's notes of Mar. 19, 2018, visit to comedor. Grupo Beta and Casa San Juan Bosco: Author's notes of visits during border-study tour led by University of Arizona professor Victor Braitberg, Apr. 23, 2017.

Cartel threats to migrants: Author's notes of "Deported to Death: Removal and Asylum from Obama to Trump," talk by Jeremy Slack, University of Arizona Latin American Studies Department, Oct. 11, 2019.

Remain in Mexico policy, Mexico crackdown: Alfredo Corchado, "Trump Policy That Returns Asylum Seekers to Mexico Is Expected to Expand to Arizona," *Arizona Daily Star*, Mar. 2, 2019; Elliot Spagat and Nomaan Merchant, "13,000 Asylum Seekers Waiting in 8 Mexican Cities Along Border," *Arizona Daily Star*, May 10, 2019; Azam Ahmed and Kirk Semple, "Mexico Is Carrying Out Trump's Agenda Along Much of the Border," *New York Times*, Mar. 1, 2019; Sonia Perez D., "Mexico Detains Hundreds of C. American Migrants," *Arizona Daily Star*, Apr. 23, 2019; Peter Orsi, "Mexico Buses Asylum Seekers Back to Their Home Countries," *Arizona Daily Star*, July 3, 2019.

Violence against migrants and shelter workers: Cedar Attanasio, "Migrants Face Violence as US Makes Them Wait in Mexico," *Arizona Daily Star*, June 28, 2019; María Verza and Nomaan Merchant, "US-Mexico Asylum Program Widens to Reject All Migrants," *Arizona Daily Star*, Aug. 29, 2019 (Méndez quotes from this article); and "Mexican Pastor and Priest Murdered at Their Churches," *Christianity Today*, Aug. 30, 2019.

COVID-19 impact: "Migration, the U.S.-Mexico Border, and Covid-19," webinar hosted by University of California at Berkeley's Center for Latin American Studies, May 29, 2020.

Pope donation and new KBI building: "Pope Francis Donates $500K to Help Migrants in Mexico," *Arizona Daily Star*, Apr. 29, 2019; author notes of

Dec. 11, 2019, tour; and phone interview with Reverend Sean Carroll, June 2, 2020.

Sasabe shelters, desert deaths: Ryan Devereaux, "Border Patrol Leaves Migrants in Remote Town as Deaths Rise," *The Intercept*, Oct. 13, 2020.

Five. Death in the Desert

Man in the road story: Author notes of conversations with Mary Whitehead, May 2017, and June 2020.

The Man in the Road

Byrd Baylor story and quote: Debbie Weingarten, "When a Cactus Blooms," *Edible Baja Arizona*, July/Aug. 2017, 78.

History of Humane Borders, Samaritans, and No More Deaths: Author's general knowledge; María Jiménez, *Humanitarian Crisis: Migrant Deaths at the U.S.-Mexico Border*, ACLU of San Diego and Imperial Counties and Mexico's National Commission of Human Rights, Oct. 1, 2009, pp. 40–43. John Hunter and All-American Canal: Jiménez, *Humanitarian Crisis*, 39–40; "It's Time to Stop Drownings in the All American Canal," ACLU of San Diego and Imperial Counties news release, Nov. 10, 2009; Bob Price, "Two Migrants Rescued from California Border Canal—One Found Dead," Breitbart News, Feb. 21, 2019.

Ángeles del Desierto: Jiménez, *Humanitarian Crisis*, 37–38; Águilas del Desierto and Armadillos de la Frontera: Perla Trevizo, "Center Helps Families Locate, ID Missing Border Crossers," *Arizona Daily Star*, July 29, 2018; Austin Westfall, "Bringing Closure: Volunteer Group Searches for Migrant Remains near the Southern Border," *Tucson Weekly*, May 9, 2019.

Brooks County: Molly Hennessy-Fiske, "Migrant Border Crossings Are Down, but in Texas the Bodies Keep Showing Up," *Los Angeles Times*, Jan. 17, 2019.

Border patrol on water stations, Passement quote: Molly Hennessy-Fiske, "The Border Patrol Chooses a New Target: A Volunteer Helping Migrants," *Los Angeles Times*, Jan. 25, 2018.

Official rejection of water stations: Alex Devoid, "Aid Workers, US at Odds in Bombing Range, Wildlife Refuge," *Arizona Daily Star*, Jan. 2, 2018; Robin

Hoover, "Border Aid Groups Don't Appreciate Banishment Threats in SW Arizona," *Arizona Daily Star*, Jan. 3, 2018. Sabotage: Alexis Huicochea, "Tire Slasher Hits Vehicles of Humane Borders Group," *Arizona Daily Star*, Aug. 12, 2008.

Water station locations and usage: *Desert Fountain*, Humane Borders newsletter, Sept.–Oct. 2008.

Tohono O'odham on water stations: Jiménez, *Humanitarian Crisis*, 44; Brady McCombs, "Reservation Ban of Water for Migrants Is Reported," *Arizona Daily Star*, Sept. 3, 2008.

Arrests and convictions of aid workers: Perla Trevizo, "Aid Volunteer Arrested After Agent Shown Kicking Over Water Jugs," *Arizona Daily Star*, Jan. 23, 2018; Curt Prendergast, "No More Deaths Member Charged with Illegally Aiding Migrants," *Arizona Daily Star*, Feb. 21, 2018; Devoid, "Aid Workers, US at Odds in Bombing Range, Wildlife Refuge"; "10 Years of Death by Border Patrol," *In These Times*, Sept. 2019, 40.

Byrd Camp arrests: Carmen Duarte, "4 Mexican 'Patients' Arrested at Aid Camp," *Arizona Daily Star*, June 16, 2017; Curt Prendergast, "Border Patrol Says Arrests at Aid Camp Not Policy Shift," *Arizona Daily Star*, June 17, 2017.

More aid workers convicted: Curt Prendergast, "US Judge Convicts 4 Border-Aid Volunteers," *Arizona Daily Star*, Jan. 19, 2019.

Water Poured Out

Video of border patrol agents dumping water: Posted on No More Deaths website and YouTube, Jan. 18, 2018.

Warren arrest: Trevizo, "Aid Volunteer Arrested After Agents Shown Kicking Over Water Jugs"; Curt Prendergast, "No More Deaths Member Charged with Illegally Aiding Migrants," *Arizona Daily Star*, Feb. 21, 2018.

No More Deaths report: Rory Carroll, "US Border Patrol Routinely Sabotages Water Left for Migrants, Report Says," *The Guardian*, Jan. 17, 2018; and Curt Prendergast, "Agents Destroyed Water Jugs Left for Illegal Crossers, Aid Group Alleges," *Arizona Daily Star*, Jan. 18, 2018.

"Toncs" texts: Curt Prendergast, "'Toncs at the Barn': Texts in Court Filings Shed Light on Ajo Arrest of Border-Aid Worker," *Arizona Daily Star*, May 6, 2018.

Bowen case: Curt Prendergast, "Grand Jury: Border Patrol Agent in Nogales Struck Crosser with Truck," *Arizona Daily Star*, June 6, 2018; Curt Prendergast, "Border Agent Calls Migrants 'Subhuman,' 'Savages' in Text Messages," *Arizona Daily Star*, May 19, 2019 (Chapman quotes from this article); Tim Steller, "Callousness, Caring Are Both Part of Border Patrol's Culture," *Arizona Daily Star*, May 22, 2019.

Facebook group: Cedar Attanasio and Colleen Long, "Border Patrol Chief Says Sexist Facebook Posts 'Inappropriate,'" *Arizona Daily Star*, July 2, 2019. Other Border Patrol misbehavior: Cantú, *The Line Becomes a River*, passim.

Agents saving lives: Steller, "Callousness, Caring Are Both Part of Border Patrol's Culture"; Silvia Foster-Frau and Bob Owen (photographer), "Migrants Rescued from Raging Rio Grande," *San Antonio Express-News*, May 10, 2019; Manny Fernandez, Caitlin Dickerson, and Simon Romero, "Infant Dies, Three Migrants Feared Dead in Raft Tragedy on Rio Grande," *New York Times*, May 2, 2019; Price, "Two Migrants Rescued from California Border Canal—One Found Dead."

Pilot shaken: "Lorraine Rivera Tours the Border Patrol Yuma Sector by Helicopter and Boat," *Arizona 360*, Season 1, episode 133, Arizona Public Media, Aug. 17, 2018.

BORSTAR rescues, light towers: Perla Trevizo, "Light Towers Guide Crossers, Send Signals to BP Rescuers," *Arizona Daily Star*, May 1, 2014; Devoid, "Aid Workers, US at Odds in Bombing Range, Wildlife Refuge" (Jackson quote from this article).

Warren trial: Curt Prendergast, "Lawyer: Smuggling Trial for Aid Worker Hinges on 'Intent,'" *Arizona Daily Star*, May 30, 2019; Curt Prendergast, "Scott Warren Testifies to Aid, Not Smuggling, of Migrants," *Arizona Daily Star*, June 7, 2019; Curt Prendergast, "Medical Care Is 'Cover Story' in Aid-Worker Trial, Prosecutor Says," *Arizona Daily Star*, June 8, 2019; Curt Prendergast, "Hung Jury Prompts Mistrial in Case of Border Aid Worker," *Arizona Daily Star*, June 12, 2019; Tim Steller, "In Warren Case, Government Puts Aid Groups on Trial, Fails," *Arizona Daily Star*, June 12, 2019.

Warren and Bowen outcomes: Stephanie Casanova, "Border Officer Gets Probation for Using Truck to Hit Migrant," *Arizona Daily Star*, Nov. 21,

2019; Henry Brean, "Border Aid Volunteer Warren Found Not Guilty of Harboring," *Arizona Daily Star*, Nov. 21, 2019.

Convictions overturned, Warren case dropped: "Judge Absolves 4 Border Activists, Saying Religious Beliefs Guided Them," *Arizona Daily Star*, Feb. 5, 2020; Curt Prendergast, "Border Aid Case Ends as Feds Drop Last Complaint," *Arizona Daily Star*, Feb. 28, 2020 (Marquez quote from this article).

Byrd Camp raids: Curt Prendergast, "Aid Group: Border Patrol Grabs 30-Plus Migrants in Raid," *Arizona Daily Star*, Aug. 2, 2020; Astrid Galvan, "Border Aid Group's Camp near Arivaca Raided by BP for 2nd Time Since July," Oct. 9, 2020; "Border Agents on Horseback Surround No More Deaths Camp Just Before Christmas," *Tucson Sentinel*, Dec. 24, 2020.

Naming the Dead

Number of dead migrants, extra cooler, medical examiner office procedures: Brady McCombs, "Nearly 1,700 Bodies, Each One a Mystery," *Arizona Daily Star*, Aug. 24, 2010; Perla Trevizo, "Center Helps Families Locate, ID Missing Border Crossers," *Arizona Daily Star*, July 29, 2018; author interview with Robin Reineke at Colibrí Center office, Tucson, Mar. 13, 2018. All Reineke quotes from this interview except as noted.

Border deaths report, Binational Migration Institute study: Jiménez, *Humanitarian Crisis*, 24 and 28. Pima County ME figures: Trevizo, "Center Helps Families Locate, ID Missing Border Crossers."

FBI database: Juan Lozano, "FBI, Groups at Odds over Efforts to Identify Immigrant Remains," *Arizona Daily Star*, July 4, 2017. Colibrí database, $1 million grant: author notes of Reineke interview.

Nancy Ganoza: Author interview and notes from Reineke's talk at And the Deaths, Disappearances and Deportations Continue . . . *No Vale Nada La Vida* symposium, Global Justice Center, South Tucson, Feb. 17, 2018. Ganoza's memorial service: Trevizo, "Center Helps Families Locate, ID Missing Border Crossers" ("Nancy facts" from this article).

Boulder conference: James Anderson, "Groups Seek Help in Getting IDs for Vast Store of Migrant Remains," *Arizona Daily Star*, Oct. 6, 2018 (Irma Carrillo quotes from this article).

Migrant deaths in 2020: Curt Prendergast, "Known Migrant Deaths Hit Record Last Year in S. Arizona," *Arizona Daily Star*, Jan. 6, 2021.

Six. Under Color of Law

José Antonio Elena Rodríguez shooting: Author notes of Swartz trial closing statements, including photos and videos shown in court, Apr. 16, 2018, and visit to scene, Apr. 23, 2017.

New York Times article: Mark Binelli, "Ten Shots Across the Border," *New York Times Magazine*, Mar. 3, 2016.

Border Agents on Trial

Swartz trial closing statements: Author notes of Swartz trial closing statements, including photos and videos shown in court, Apr. 16, 2018, and visit to scene, Apr. 23, 2017. Verdict and reaction: Perla Trevizo, "Protests Erupt as Jury Acquits Border Agent in Killing of Teen," *Arizona Daily Star*, Apr. 24, 2018. Juror quotes: Perla Trevizo, "Jurors of Different Minds in Border Shooting Trial," *Arizona Daily Star*, Apr. 29, 2018.

Second acquittal, Boren arrest: Perla Trevizo, "Agent in Fatal Cross-Border Shooting Is Acquitted on Manslaughter Charge," *Arizona Daily Star*, Nov. 22, 2018. Also Paul Ingram, "Feds Won't Pursue 3rd Trial of BP Agent in Cross-Border Shooting," *Tucson Sentinel*, Dec. 6, 2018.

Previous border patrol shootings, outcomes, comparisons to Swartz case: Davidson, *Lives on the Line*, 80-117; Binelli, "Ten Shots Across the Border"; Perla Trevizo, "Shooting Details Emerge in Civil Trials," *Arizona Daily Star*, Aug. 1, 2015; Trevizo, "Protests Erupt as Jury Acquits Border Agent in Killing of Teen." Elmer lawyer's quote: Davidson, *Lives on the Line*, 113.

Swartz going AWOL: Howard Fischer, "Attorney Seeks to Bar Border Agent's Military Records," *Arizona Daily Star*, Jan. 18, 2018. "Immaturity" quote: Howard Fischer, "Defense: Let Jury in Border Agent's Murder Trial Visit Site of Shooting," *Arizona Daily Star*, Feb. 5, 2018.

Video, admission of rock throwing: Curt Prendergast, "Video of BP Shooting Played at Hearing," *Arizona Daily Star*, June 20, 2017; and Howard Fischer, "Agent Shot Nogales Boy Throwing Rocks," *Arizona Daily Star*, June 30, 2017.

Hernández case, Supreme Court rulings: Howard Fischer, "Ruling Could Aid Mom Suing Border Agent," *Arizona Daily Star*, June 27, 2017; Howard Fischer, "Court OKs Lawsuit in Killing of Teen by US Agent," *Arizona*

Daily Star, Aug. 8, 2018; Howard Fischer, "Justices Take Case on Lawsuits in Cross-border Shooting Deaths," *Arizona Daily Star*, May 29, 2019; and Howard Fischer, "Ruling Brings Tears to Mexican Family," *Arizona Daily Star*, Feb. 26, 2020 (RBG quote from this article).

Montoya article: Chris Montoya, "Is Our Border with Mexico Really Such a Dangerous Place?" *Arizona Daily Star*, Dec. 2, 2018.

Agents under threat: Curt Prendergast, "Gov't Taking a Harder Line on Attacks of Border Feds," *Arizona Daily Star*, Oct. 22, 2017.

Van Horn deaths: Claudia Lauer and David Warren, "Border Agent's Death in Texas Culvert Being Treated by FBI as Result of 'Potential Assault,'" *Arizona Daily Star*, Nov. 22, 2017; "Border Agent Whose Death Is Unexplained Is Saluted at Texas Funeral," *Arizona Daily Star*, Nov. 26, 2017; Tim Steller, "For Border Alarmists, an Inconvenient Reckoning," *Arizona Daily Star*, Feb. 11, 2018.

Assaults exaggerated: Debbie Nathan, "How Border Patrol Faked Statistics Showing a 73% Rise in Assaults Against Agents," *The Intercept*, Apr. 23, 2018 (quote from this article); Tim Steller, "As Border Agent Acquitted, Assault Exaggerations Exposed," *Arizona Daily Star*, Apr. 25, 2018. Cato study: Alex Nowrasteh, "Border Patrol Agent Deaths in the Line of Duty," Cato Institute report, Nov. 27, 2017.

DHS report, recommendations rejected: Elliot Spagat, "Border Patrol to Keep Shooting at Rock-Throwers," *Arizona Daily Star*, Nov. 6, 2013; Perla Trevizo, "Jurors Take On Issue of Lethal Force vs. Border Rock Hurlers," *Arizona Daily Star*, Mar. 25, 2018; Colleen Long, "Despite Tear Gas Use, Border Force by US Is on the Decline," *Arizona Daily Star*, Nov. 29, 2018.

Checkpoints

Tadeo case, quotes, description of video: Tim Steller, "Worrying Signals That Agents Distort Border Dangers," *Arizona Daily Star*, Dec. 10, 2017. Stats on assaults by U.S. citizens: Prendergast, "Gov't Taking a Harder Line on Attacks of Border Feds."

CBP/ICE jurisdictional reach and overlap: Miller, *Border Patrol Nation*, map, 10; Melissa del Bosque, "Checkpoint Nation," *Harper's Magazine*, Oct. 2018. Legality of racial profiling, quote on CBP complexion chart: del Bosque, "Checkpoint Nation."

Raúl Castro: Tim Steller, "Border Patrol Detains Former Arizona Gov. Castro After Radiation Alarm Is Tripped," *Arizona Daily Star*, June 23, 2012.

Arivaca checkpoint: Howard Fischer, "In 'Papers Please' Move, Activists Want Police to Keep Info on Stops," *Arizona Daily Star*, Sept. 9, 2015; Howard Fischer, "ACLU Sues for Info on Border Agent Checks," *Arizona Daily Star*, Apr. 29, 2014; Howard Fischer, "Report Finds Border Patrol Checkpoint Abuses," *Arizona Daily Star*, Oct. 16, 2015; Howard Fischer, "Judges Question Border Patrol's Observer Limits," *Arizona Daily Star*, Dec. 6, 2017; Howard Fischer, "Court Restores Arivaca Residents' Lawsuit Against Border Patrol," *Arizona Daily Star*, Feb. 14, 2018; and Howard Fischer, "Magistrate Criticizes Info Lack in Checkpoint Legal Action," *Arizona Daily Star*, Jan. 31, 2017 (Velasco quotes from this article).

Waste, Fraud, and Abuse

CBP growth and arrest rates: Melissa del Bosque, "A Group of Agents Rose Through the Ranks to Lead the Border Patrol. They're Leaving It in Crisis," ProPublica, Feb. 10, 2020; Binelli, "Ten Shots Across the Border"; Ron Nixon, "U.S. Border Agency Says Hundreds of Employees Have Been Arrested over 2 Years," *New York Times*, Oct. 13, 2018; Justin Rohrlich and Zoë Schlanger, "Border Officers Are Arrested 5 Times More Often than Other US Law Enforcement," Quartz, July 16, 2019.

Houses in Ajo: Brenna Goth, "US Spent $13M on 21 Homes in Ajo," *Arizona Republic*, Aug. 13, 2013; Luis Carrasco, "Feds: Ajo Housing Project for Border Agents Mismanaged, Too Costly," *Arizona Daily Star*, Sept. 11, 2014.

Accenture: Greg Moran, "CBP Has to Hire 5,000 New Border Patrol Agents. It's Paying a Private Company $297 Million to Help," *San Diego Union-Tribune*, Dec. 12, 2017. Treasury union objections: Jessie Bur, "CBP Ends Its Controversial Hiring Contract with Accenture," *Federal Times*, Apr. 8, 2019. Employee petition, quote: Josh Eidelson, "Accenture Workers Petition to End $297 Million Border Patrol Contract," Bloomberg.com, Nov. 15, 2018. Cancelation, costs, number of hires: Stef Kight, "DHS Blames 'Political and Economic Environment' for Border Patrol Hiring Crisis," Axios.com, Apr. 4, 2019 (quote from this article); Nicole Ogrysko, "CBP Ends Accenture Hiring Contract 'for Convenience,'" Federal News Network, Apr. 5, 2019.

CBP attrition stats, Associated Press on polygraphs, plan to exempt law enforcement: Moran, "CBP Has to Hire 5,000 New Border Patrol Agents. It's Paying a Private Company $297 Million to Help" ("changing generational values" quote from this article).

Stonegarden: Perla Trevizo, "Pima County Supervisors Turn Down Federal Grant Tied to Border Security," *Arizona Daily Star*, Feb. 8, 2018 (OIG report from this article and from Richard Elías, "Operation Stonegarden Not Good for Pima County," *Arizona Daily Star*, Feb. 18, 2018); Murphy Woodhouse, "Pima Does a U-turn on Border Funding," *Arizona Daily Star*, Feb. 21, 2018; Caitlin Schmidt, "Border Policy Worries Spur New Look at County Grant," *Arizona Daily Star*, Sept. 3, 2018; Joe Ferguson, "Supervisors, on 3–1 vote, Reject $1.4M Border Grant," *Arizona Daily Star*, Sept. 5, 2018; Mark Napier, "Board's Rejection of Grant Makes Life Easier for Drug and Human Traffickers," *Arizona Daily Star*, Sept. 9, 2018; Terry Bressi, "Stonegarden Was Hardly a Benefit to Public Safety," *Arizona Daily Star*, Sept. 16, 2018; "Pima County Supes Explain Opposing Votes on Stonegarden," Arizona 360, Arizona Public Media, Sept. 17, 2018 (Valadez quote from this interview); Caitlin Schmidt, "Pima Sheriff Taking Steps to Resurrect Stonegarden Border Funds," *Arizona Daily Star*, Mar. 19, 2019; Danyelle Khmara, "Pima County to Resume Use of Controversial Federal Border Security Grant," *Arizona Daily Star*, May 8, 2019.

Casa Alitas, monastery, move to juvenile jail: Steve Kozachik, "Migrants' Mass Release Is Political, and They Need Our Help," *Arizona Daily Star*, Oct. 13, 2018; David Fitzsimmons, "Monastery-Turned-Sanctuary Truly Extraordinary," *Arizona Daily Star*, Feb. 16, 2019; Joe Ferguson, "Supervisors OK Deal to House Migrants at County's Juvenile Detention Facility," *Arizona Daily Star*, July 23, 2019. Also: Justin Sayers, "Feds Deny Reallocation of Funds to Shelter for Migrants," *Arizona Daily Star*, Dec. 28, 2019; Justin Sayers, "TPD to Stop Accepting Funds from Nat'l Border Safety Grant," *Arizona Daily Star*, Jan. 19, 2020; and Jasmine Demers, "Pima Board Votes 3–2 to Turn Away $1.8M Border Safety Grant," *Arizona Daily Star*, Feb. 5, 2020.

Sawmill Fire: Tony Davis, "Video Shows Explosion and Fire at Agent's Gender-Reveal Party," *Arizona Daily Star*, Nov. 27, 2018; Tony Davis, "Longer Video Shows Missed Shots Before Target Was Hit, Sparking Fire," *Arizona Daily Star*, Dec. 8, 2018.

Sexual assaults: Laura Gottesdiener, Malav Kanuga, and Cinthya Santos Briones, "Violated at the Border," *The Nation*, June 4–11, 2018; Curt Prendergast, "Tucson BP Agent Facing Charges of Sexual, Aggravated Assault," *Arizona Daily Star*, May 23, 2019; Manny Fernandez and Mitchell Ferman, "Senior Border Patrol Agent Faces Charges of Sexually Assaulting Colleague," *New York Times*, Oct. 5, 2019 (author helped research this story); Curt Prendergast, "Tucson Sector BP Agent Arrested on Charges of Lewd Acts with Minor," *Arizona Daily Star*, Oct. 13, 2017.

Murder: Simon Romero and Manny Fernandez, "Border Patrol Agent Arrested in Connection with Murders of 4 Women," *New York Times*, Sept. 15, 2018; Tim Acosta and Eleanor Dearman, "Border Patrol Agent's Arrest for 'Serial Killer' Murders Rocks Laredo," *Corpus Christi Caller-Times*, Sept. 16, 2018; Susan Montoya Bryan and Matt Sedensky, "Police: Border Agent Targeted Victims for Vulnerability," *Arizona Daily Star*, Sept. 18, 2018; Nomaan Merchant, "Arrest of Border Agent in Women's Deaths Puts Focus on Agency's Hiring Challenges," *Arizona Daily Star*, Sept. 19, 2018; and Susan Montoya Bryan, "Agent Accused in Serial Killings Lived Quiet Suburban Life," *Arizona Daily Star*, Sept. 21, 2018.

Numbers of agents vs. apprehensions: Tim Steller, "Steep Drop in Crossings Undermines Case for a Wall," *Arizona Daily Star*, Sept. 3, 2017 (Tucson Sector figures); Southern Border Communities Coalition Border Reality Check webpage, Nov. 2018 (nationwide apprehension figures and quote); John Gramlich and Luis Noe-Bustamante, "What's Happening at the U.S.-Mexico Border in 5 Charts," Pew Research Center, Nov. 1, 2019 (2019 arrests).

Seven. The Triumph of Sanctuary

Sanctuary declaration: Davidson, *Convictions of the Heart*, 68–73 (Corbett's statement, 69; photo of event, after 84). Also author phone interview with John Fife, Tucson, June 2018. "Sanctuary in its broadest sense" quote: Davidson, *Convictions of the Heart*, 158.

Sanctuary Established

History of 1980s movement, Corbett's involvement, and background: Davidson, *Convictions of the Heart*, passim (Fife quote, 65; Juana story, 118–22;

border-crossing photo, after 84; Elder and Merkt cases, 87 and 89). Deme-tria Martínez case: Wikipedia. Jury selection quotes, judge's bias, MLK comment: Davidson, *Convictions of the Heart*, 106–107. "Man's reach" exchange: Author's notes from trial. "Ears and eyes" quote: Davidson, *Convictions of the Heart*, 123. Juror quote: Davidson, *Convictions of the Heart*, 152. Corbett's death: Author's "Corbett Offered Sanctuary to Refugees," *National Catholic Reporter*, Sept. 14, 2001.

Sanctuary Revived

Rebirth of sanctuary after 2008: Author's general knowledge; Luis Carrasco, "Another Tucson Church Shields Immigrant from Deportation," *Arizona Daily Star*, Sept. 25, 2014; Puck Lo, "Inside the New Sanctuary Movement That's Protecting Immigrants from ICE," *The Nation*, May 6, 2015.

Tucson, university declarations: Raúl Alcaraz Ochoa and Stephanie Quintana, "Tucson Has a Colossal Civil-Rights Crisis," *Arizona Daily Star*, Oct. 21, 2013; Perla Trevizo, "Petition Seeks to Make Tucson a Sanctuary City," *Arizona Daily Star*, Jan. 12, 2019; "Tucson: Voters in Liberal US City Reject Sanctuary City Status," BBC News, Nov. 6, 2019; Yoohyun Jung, "Arizona's 3 Public Universities Shy Away from 'Sanctuary' Label," *Arizona Daily Star*, Feb. 12, 2017.

Daniel Neyoy Ruiz: Luis Carrasco, "Illegal Immigrant Sheltered at Church Gets Deportation Stay," *Arizona Daily Star*, June 10, 2014.

Rosa Robles: Author's general knowledge; "Migrant Woman Leaves Sanctuary of Arizona Church After 15 Months," *The Guardian*, Nov. 11, 2015; Carmen Duarte, "S. Arizona Churches Pledge to Shield Those Here Illegally," *Arizona Daily Star*, Jan. 19, 2017.

Francisco Pérez Córdova: Carrasco, "Another Tucson Church Shields Immigrant from Deportation."

Arturo Hernández García: Elaine McArdle, "Immigrant Finds Sanctuary in Denver Unitarian Church," *UU World*, Nov. 10, 2014.

Sanctuary Everywhere

Sheriff Sally Hernandez: Claudia Lauer, "Immigrants Find Sanctuary in Austin Church Network," *Arizona Daily Star*, Mar. 26, 2017; Paul Weber, "Court Rules in Favor of 'Sanctuary Cities' Law," *Arizona Daily Star*, Sept. 26, 2017.

Trump's anti-sanctuary policies, Kelly memo: Jacques Billeaud and Amy Taxin, "Immigrant Crackdown to Again Use Local Cops," *Arizona Daily Star*, Jan. 30, 2017; Andrew Selsky, "Trump's 'Sanctuary City' Action Widens Divide Among States," *Arizona Daily Star*, Feb. 3, 2017; Prendergast, "New Trump Border Orders Raise Questions for Sheriffs."

Sessions threatens sanctuary cities: Sadie Gurman, "Sessions Warns 'Sanctuary Cities' May Be Risking Federal Funding," *Arizona Daily Star*, Mar. 28, 2017; Sadie Gurman, "Sanctuary Areas Say They Won't Fold to Justice Dept. Fund Threats," *Arizona Daily Star*, Apr. 22, 2017.

Hernández arrested: "Mexican Who Took Refuge in Church Is Detained," *Arizona Daily Star*, Apr. 27, 2017. ICE arrests in sensitive locations: Lo, "Inside the New Sanctuary Movement That's Protecting Immigrants from ICE."

Cities respond to letters: Sadie Gurman and Russell Contreras, "Cities Baffled by Sessions Letter on Immigration," *Arizona Daily Star*, Aug. 4, 2017; Prendergast, "New Trump Border Orders Raise Questions for Sheriffs."

Flash mob traffic stop: Ochoa and Quintana, "Tucson Has a Colossal Civil-Rights Crisis"; Carli Brosseau, "Pair Whose Traffic Stop Prompted Immigration Protest Released," *Arizona Daily Star*, Oct. 16, 2013.

Magnus op-ed: Chris Magnus, "Tucson's Police Chief: Session's Anti-Immigrant Policies Will Make Cities More Dangerous," *New York Times*, Dec. 6, 2017.

ICE in Pima County jail: Caitlin Schmidt, "Sheriff Removes ICE from Pima Jail" *Arizona Daily Star*, Oct. 19, 2018.

Total grants in 2016, Orrick injunction: Gurman, "Sessions Warns 'Sanctuary Cities' May Be Risking Federal Funding"; Sudhin Thanawala, "Judge Blocks Trump Threat to Deny 'Sanctuary City' Funds," *Arizona Daily Star*, Apr. 26, 2017; Sudhin Thanawala, "Judge Permanently Blocks Trump Sanctuary Cities Order," *Arizona Daily Star*, Nov. 22, 2017.

Chicago: Michael Tarm and Sophia Tareen, "Chicago Sues Over Sanctuary City Funds Threat; Sessions Fires Back," *Arizona Daily Star*, Aug. 8, 2017; Sophia Tareen, "Sanctuary City Threat Prompts More Suits," *Arizona Daily Star*, Aug. 15, 2017; Don Babwin, "Judge: Sanctuary Cities Can Get Grant Money," *Arizona Daily Star*, Sept. 16, 2017 (Sessions quote from this article).

Texas: Paul Weber, "TX Governor Signs Ban on 'Sanctuary Cities,'" *Arizona Daily Star*, May 8, 2017; James Barragan, "Suit Seeks Hearing on Texas'

New Ban on Sanctuary Cities," *Arizona Daily Star*, June 6, 2017; Kevin McGill, "Texas Asks Court to Allow 'Sanctuary Cities' Ban," *Arizona Daily Star*, Sept. 23, 2017; Weber, "Court Rules in Favor of 'Sanctuary Cities' Law."

California: Jazmine Ulloa, "California Legislature Approves Bill to Create a 'Sanctuary State,'" *Arizona Daily Star*, Sept. 17, 2017; Jonathan Cooper and Kathleen Ronayne, "California's New Sanctuary Law Limits Local Police Cooperation," *Arizona Daily Star*, Oct. 5, 2017 (Brown quote from this article).

Supreme Court on SB 1070: Dylan Smith, "Supreme Court Strikes Down Most SB 1070 Provisions," *Tucson Sentinel*, June 25, 2012.

Orange County: Amy Taxin, "Orange County Votes to Join Trump's 'Sanctuary' Lawsuit," *Arizona Daily Star*, Mar. 28, 2018; Amy Taxin, "More Cities Vote to Oppose California's Sanctuary Law," *Arizona Daily Star*, Apr. 16, 2018.

Federal cases won: Claudia Lauer, "In 'Sanctuary City' Case, Judge Sides with Philadelphia," *Arizona Daily Star*, June 7, 2018; Sudhin Thanawala, "Court Strikes Down Trump Push to Cut 'Sanctuary City' Funds," *Arizona Daily Star*, Aug. 2, 2018; Sophie Tatum, "Judge Rules Against Administration in 'Sanctuary Cities' Case," CNN, Dec. 1, 2018; Wilson Ring, "Sanctuary Cities Receiving Their Grants Despite Threats," *Arizona Daily Star*, Mar. 3, 2019.

Calif. after sanctuary, García deaths: Michael Greenberg, "In the Valley of Fear," *New York Review of Books*, Dec. 20, 2018.

ICE arrests at courthouses: Alanna Durkin Richer, "Ex-judges to ICE: Courthouse Arrests Have Effect of Closing Courtrooms, Should End," *Arizona Daily Star*, Dec. 13, 2018.

Oliver-Bruno arrest, deportation: Nicole Chavez and Janet DiGiacomo, "Undocumented Man Is Arrested After Leaving Sanctuary Church. His Supporters Were Detained Too," CNN, Nov. 24, 2018; Annie Rose Ramos, "Woman Who Sought Sanctuary in Church in 2017 Is Still There," msn.com, Mar. 3, 2019.

Dutch service: Kate Shellnutt, "Dutch Asylum Service Concludes with Its Final 'Amen,'" *Christianity Today*, Dec. 5, 2018, updated Feb. 1, 2019.

Monastery: Perla Trevizo, "Border Patrol Frees Hundreds; Volunteers in Tucson Step Up," *Arizona Daily Star*, Oct. 9, 2018; Curt Prendergast, "Faith Groups, Tucson City Officials Ask for Help Housing Migrant Families," *Arizona Daily Star*, May 4, 2019; Fitzsimmons, "Monastery-Turned-Sanctuary Truly Extraordinary."

Eight. The Jaguar

El Jefe video: "New Video Shows America's Only Known Wild Jaguar," Center for Biological Diversity press release, Feb. 3, 2016. Also on YouTube.

Rosemont Mine: Tony Davis, "Arizona Jaguar 'Biologically Insignificant,' Wildlife Manager Says," *Arizona Daily Star*, June 12, 2016; Tony Davis, "Jaguar Video Sparked Controversy That Rages Six Months Later," *Arizona Daily Star*, Aug. 15, 2016; Tony Davis, "Corps Gives Rosemont Mine Final Permit for Construction," *Arizona Daily Star*, Mar. 9, 2019.

El Jefe

El Jefe: "New Video Shows America's Only Known Wild Jaguar," Center for Biological Diversity press release, Feb. 3, 2016; Tony Davis, "Nation's Wild-Cat Hot Spot in S. AZ," *Arizona Daily Star*, June 12, 2016; Davis, "Jaguar Video Sparked Controversy."

Cat lounge, mural: Gabriela Rico, "'Big City' Venue Comes to Tucson: A Cat Lounge," *Arizona Daily Star*, Oct. 26, 2019; and Cally Carswell, "Trump's Wall May Threaten Thousands of Plant and Animal Species on the U.S.-Mexico Border," *Scientific American*, May 10, 2017.

Sombra, Yo'oko: Tony Davis, "New Jaguar in Huachuca Mountains, Photo Shows," *Arizona Daily Star*, Dec. 8, 2016; Tony Davis, "Video of Chiricahua Jaguar Released by Enviro Group," *Arizona Daily Star*, Sept. 15, 2017.

Jaguar facts and mythology: Wikipedia; Chip Brown, "The Shrinking Kingdom of the Jaguar," *National Geographic*, Dec. 2017, 70; and Jason Mark, "Walled Off: How Trump's Border Wall Threatens the Desert Wilderness," *Sierra*, Sept.–Oct. 2017. Alebrijes: Wikipedia.

"Spotted one" quote: Tony Davis, "Tribes Sue over Rosemont Mine, Citing 'Irreversible' Damage to Sites," *Arizona Daily Star*, Apr. 15, 2018.

Jaguar sightings in Arizona, deVos quote: Davis, "Arizona Jaguar 'Biologically Insignificant,' Wildlife Manager Says."

Reintroduction: Tony Davis, "Environmental Groups Say More Research Is Needed on Reintroducing Jaguars to Southwest," *Arizona Daily Star*, Mar. 21, 2017. Diana Hadley: Author interview at Hadley's home, Tucson, May 29, 2018.

Culver quote: Davis, "Nation's Wild-Cat Hot Spot in S. AZ."

Macho B: Dennis Wagner, "Macho B: Cover-Up amid Celebrations," *Arizona Republic*, Dec. 10, 2012.

Rosemont: Tony Davis, "Feds Sending Mixed Signals on Jaguar Protections," *Arizona Daily Star*, Mar. 31, 2017; Randy Serraglio, "El Jefe, Jaguars Before Him Came of Age at Tucson's Doorstep," *Arizona Daily Star*, June 5, 2016 (his quotes from this article); Tony Davis, "Rosemont Mine Ready to Build in '19 if Final Permit Goes Through," *Arizona Daily Star*, Jan. 27, 2018; Davis, "Tribes Sue Over Rosemont Mine, Citing 'Irreversible' Damage to Sites"; Tony Davis, "Rosemont Mine Opponents Sue to Overturn Water Permit," *Arizona Daily Star*, Mar. 28, 2019; Tony Davis, "3 Tribes Sue to Block Rosemont Mine Permit," *Arizona Daily Star*, Apr. 11, 2019; Joe Ferguson, "Supervisors Vote 3–2 for Resolution Opposing Rosemont," *Arizona Daily Star*, Apr. 17, 2019.

Tribes win lawsuit: Tony Davis, "Ruling by Federal Judge Bars Rosemont Mine Construction," *Arizona Daily Star*, Aug 1, 2019. Hudbay and Justice Department appeal, work delayed: Tony Davis, "Feds: Valid Claim Not Needed for Rosemont Mine OK," *Arizona Daily Star*, June 28, 2020; Tony Davis, "Hudbay: Work at Rosemont Delayed Until '23 at Earliest," *Arizona Daily Star*, Nov. 13, 2019.

Viviendo con Felinos

Jaguar conference and poaching: Tony Davis, "Research Suggests Jaguars Declining in Sonora," *Arizona Daily Star*, May 20, 2018. Yo'oko killed: Tony Davis, "Experts: Jaguar Seen in Arizona Has Died," Arizona Daily Star, June 22, 2018; Tony Davis, "Mountain Lion Hunter Trapped Jaguar That Was Killed, Mexican Rancher Told," *Arizona Daily Star*, June 28, 2018; Randy Serraglio, Louise Misztal, and Diana Hadley, "Death of Yo'oko a Call to Secure Safe Spaces for Jaguars," *Arizona Daily Star*, July 8, 2018.

Corazón, Northern Jaguar Project, Viviendo con Felinos: Author interview with Diana Hadley at Hadley's home, Tucson, May 29, 2018 (all quotes from this interview); Northern Jaguar Project website and brochure.

"A Surprising Eden"

Sky Islands, animals endangered by wall: Carswell, "Trump's Wall May Threaten Thousands of Plant and Animal Species on the U.S.-Mexico Border"; Mark, "Walled Off: How Trump's Border Wall Threatens the Desert Wilderness." One percent of land and nearly half the bird species: Taylor, *Birds of Southeastern Arizona*, 1.

Ocelots: Davis, "Nation's Wild-Cat Hot Spot in S. AZ"; Mark, "Walled Off: How Trump's Border Wall Threatens the Desert Wilderness"; and Cybele Knowles, "5 Animals Threatened by the Border Wall," Center for Biological Diversity, Medium.com, Feb. 22, 2017.

Pronghorns: Alex Devoid, "Back from the Brink, Sonoran Pronghorn Roam an Increasingly Political Landscape," *Arizona Daily Star*, Apr. 8, 2018.

Bears: Marc Lacey, "Border Fence Blocks Bears in Migration, Study Finds," *New York Times*, Dec. 21, 2011.

Cactus pygmy owls: Mark, "Walled Off: How Trump's Border Wall Threatens the Desert Wilderness"; Taylor, *Birds of Southeastern Arizona*, 169.

Animals blocked by fence, peninsular desert bighorn sheep: Knowles, "5 Animals Threatened by the Border Wall." Cougar on Naco fence: Norma Coile, "Mountain Lion Balancing on the Border Fence," *Arizona Daily Star*, May 9, 2015. Sky Island Alliance, unfenced miles: Carswell, "Trump's Wall May Threaten Thousands of Plant and Animal Species on the U.S.-Mexico Border."

San Bernardino Wildlife Refuge, Cuenca Los Ojos: Foundation websites; Todd Miller, "A Tale of Two Walls," *Edible Baja Arizona*, Jan./Feb. 2017, 94–111; Miller, *Storming the Wall*, 229–33; Alex Devoid, "Border Wall Is Seen as Threat to Land Restoration," *Arizona Daily Star*, Dec. 24, 2017 (Alberto Terán Figueroa quotes from this article).

Border BioBlitz: Mikayla Mace, "Public Invited to Participate in Survey of Border Species," *Arizona Daily Star*, Mar. 2, 2018; N-Gen 2018 Border BioBlitz report, Next Generation Sonoran Desert Researchers, 2018; and

Mikayla Mace, "2nd Effort to ID Species at Border Is This Weekend," *Arizona Daily Star*, Feb. 28, 2019.

Christmas bird count: Cuenca Los Ojos Foundation website; Raven quote: Taylor, *Birds of Southeastern Arizona*, 257.

Milkweeds: James Carr, "Ariz. Volunteers Plant Milkweed Hoping to Boost Butterfly Visits," *Arizona Daily Star*, Dec. 23, 2019; Kevin Sieff, "Second Man with Ties to Mexico's Largest Monarch Butterfly Reserve Found Dead," *Washington Post*, Feb. 2, 2020.

Agaves: Gary Paul Nabhan, "Agaves Are Us," *Tucson Weekly*, Apr. 25, 2019, p. 10; Johanna Willett, "130 Agaves Are Planted Around Tucson as Part of Project to Aid Migratory Bats," *Arizona Daily Star*, May 16, 2019; Susan Montoya Bryan, "Bat That's Key to Tequila Trade Removed from Endangered List," *Arizona Daily Star*, Apr. 17, 2018.

Nine. El Norte

Guadalupe Mass, apparition: Author's notes of event at Our Lady of Fátima Parish, Dec. 11, 2018, and Wikipedia.

Troops, razor wire, local objections: Perla Trevizo, "Razor Wire near AZ Ports of Entry Needed to Prevent Rush on Border, US Officials Say," *Arizona Daily Star*, Nov. 10, 2018; Curt Prendergast, "Troops, Razor Wire, Blocked Lanes Raise Concerns at Nogales Border," *Arizona Daily Star*, Nov. 16, 2018; "Nogales Tells Federal Gov't to Take Down Razor Wire or Face Lawsuit," *Arizona Daily Star*, Feb. 7, 2019.

Migrants tear-gassed: "US Agents Fire Tear Gas as Some Migrants Try to Breach Fence," msn.com, Nov. 26, 2018; Owen Daugherty, "Former Border Patrol Deputy Chief Defends Using Pepper Spray: You Could 'Put It on Your Nachos and Eat It,'" msn.com, Nov. 26, 2018; "US: Tijuana Rock Throwers Were Targets of Gas, Not Wall Climbers," *Arizona Daily Star*, Jan. 2, 2019.

Mass arrests: "Nearly 200 Migrants Detained near Lukeville," *Arizona Daily Star*, Sept. 20, 2018; Anita Snow, "Border Officials Alarmed by Number of Migrants Abandoned in AZ Desert," *Arizona Daily Star*, Oct. 12, 2018; and Nick Miroff and Josh Dawsey, "Record Number of Families Crossing

U.S. Border as Trump Threatens New Crackdown," *Washington Post*, Oct. 17, 2018.

Jakelin Caal and Felipe Gómez: Colleen Long and Elliot Spagat, "Girl, 7, Was Healthy, Border Agents Said; Hours Later She Died," *Arizona Daily Star*, Dec. 15, 2018; Nomaan Merchant, "Second Guatemalan Child Dies in US Immigration Custody," *Arizona Daily Star*, Dec. 26, 2018; "DHS Chief Nielsen Visits El Paso after Second Child's Death," *Arizona Daily Star*, Dec. 29, 2018; Sonia Perez D., "2nd Child Dead in US Custody Mourned in Guatemala Village," *Arizona Daily Star*, Dec. 31, 2018.

El Grupo Guadalupano

Guadalupe Mass, basilica site of veneration: Author's notes of event at Our Lady of Fátima Parish, Dec. 11, 2018, and Wikipedia. Mary's words from Catholic liturgy in English.

Border types: Martínez, *Border People*, passim (quotes p. 60).

Raúl Grijalva: Author's notes from phone interview with Grijalva, June 16, 2020, and his website, www.grijalva.house.gov.

Beto O'Rourke: Norman Solomon, "Beto O'Rourke Owes His Career to the GOP," Truthdig, Mar. 21, 2019; Kevin Diaz, "Beto O'Rourke and Will Hurd Road Trip Wins Them 'Civility in Public Life' Award," *Houston Chronicle*, July 17, 2018; Robert Moore and Mark Berman, "El Paso Suspect Said He Was Targeting 'Mexicans,' Told Officers He Was the Shooter, Police Say," *Washington Post*, Aug. 9, 2019; Matt Pearce, "Beto O'Rourke: 'Hell, Yes, We're Going to Take Your AR-15,'" *Los Angeles Times*, Sept. 12, 2019.

The Solar Wall

Gary Nabhan, solar wall: Author's notes of interview with Nabhan at his home, Feb. 9, 2018 (all Nabhan quotes from this interview except as noted); Tom Beal, "Poet: Build Solar 'Wall' in Mexico, Sell Power to US Customers," *Arizona Daily Star*, Mar. 30, 2017 (Aridjis quote from this article); Gary Nabhan, "Solar Idea Is a Viable, Job-Creating Option to Border Wall," *Arizona Daily Star*, Apr. 16, 2017; and Jill Colvin, "Solar Wall at U.S.-Mexico Border Could Create Energy, Pay for Itself," *Arizona Daily Star*, June 23, 2017.

COVID-19 impact on border and Native people: Stephanie Innes, "The Number of Patients Hospitalized for Covid-19 Has Tripled in Yuma," azcentral. com, May 27, 2020; Paul Weber, "'We Are No Less American': Virus Deaths Piling Up in Poor Border Region of Texas," *Arizona Daily Star*, Aug. 6, 2020; Rafael Carranza, "Longtime Nogales Migrant Shelter Director Juan Francisco Loureiro Dies from COVID," *Arizona Daily Star*, Jan, 1, 2021; Rosie Nguyen, "How Navajo Nation Curbed One of the Worst COVID-19 Outbreaks in the Country," ABC4 News, Aug. 10, 2020; Kate Groetzinger, "Navajo Homes Getting Electricty with CARES Act Funds," *Arizona Daily Star*, Nov. 28, 2020; and Moira McCarthy, "How the COVID-19 Vaccines Are Providing Hope to a Hard-Hit Navajo Nation," healthline.com, Jan. 4, 2021.

Seri project: Gary Paul Nabhan, "Report from Seriland: Care, Hope and Healing in a Time of Covid," unpublished paper, July 10, 2020.

El Norte

Migrant memorial: Author notes and program from International Migrants Day Tucson Candlelight Vigil, Evergreen Cemetery, Tucson, Dec. 18, 2018. Also Mark Pratt, "Quilts Made from Discarded Clothes Honor Dead Migrants," *Arizona Daily Star*, May 7, 2018.

Mexican revolutionaries, Cananea mine: Woodard, *American Nations*, 31; David Bacon, "Immigrant Workers' Resistance and Survival," online seminar hosted by Salt of the Earth Labor College, Tucson, Sept. 12, 2020.

Border organizations, Tucson's history with refugees: Author's general knowledge. Iskashitaa Refugee Network: Organization website, www.iskashitaa. org, and presentation by Saudi refugee Sami Al Sharif at Innovating Immigration Law and Policy: Visions for a Just Future, University of Arizona James E. Rogers College of Law, Tucson, Nov. 15, 2019.

Nabhan quote: Gary Paul Nabhan, "Guest Opinion: Heal Arizona's Chasms," *Nogales International*, Nov. 23, 2018.

Bernard Lafayette Jr.: Author notes from "Kingian Nonviolence, Border Justice and Immigrant Rights" talk and panel discussion, Pima Community College Downtown Campus, Tucson, Mar. 14, 2019, cosponsored by the Culture of Peace Alliance, Our Family Services Center, Pima Community College, and the University of Arizona Mexican-American Studies

Department. "Six Principles of Kingian Nonviolence and Six Steps to Non-violent Social Change": Fact sheets provided at event.

Also: Loni Nannini, "Hear Civil-Rights Pioneer at Our Family Event," *Arizona Daily Star*, Mar. 5, 2019; Ronna Bolante, "AFSC Alumni: Bernard Lafayette, Nonviolent Activist and Civil Rights Leader," *Quaker Action*, spring 2019, 13.

Martin Luther King in Tucson: "King Visited Tucson Twice," Apr. 5, 1968, reprinted in "50 Years Ago: Tucson Mourned with Nation After Assassination of Martin Luther King Jr.," *Arizona Daily Star*, Apr. 4, 2018 (King quotes from this article).

Saint Andrew's Clinic: Friends of Saint Andrew's Children's Clinic website, including spring 2018 newsletter and FY 2017 fact sheet; Danyelle Khmara, "Nogales Clinic Helps Children in Need," *Arizona Daily Star*, Aug. 14, 2016.

Café Justo: Perla Trevizo, "Coffee Co-op with Clients All Over US Keeps Mexican Farmers' Families Intact," *Arizona Daily Star*, Nov. 25, 2018.

Tennis: Curt Prendergast, "Tennis Program Brings Children from Both Sides of the Border Together," *Arizona Daily Star*, Apr. 15, 2017; author phone interview with Fr. Sean Carroll, June 2020.

Hugs Not Walls: Julio-César Chávez, "Families Reunited in 'Hugs Not Walls' Event at US-Mexico Border," Reuters, May 12, 2018; Patrick Timmons, "El Paso Border Wall Rises at Place Once Marked by Unity," UPI, Oct. 2, 2018; and "'Hugs Not Walls' Mexico Border Reunions Cancelled as US Refuses Permits," afp.com, May 9, 2019 (Garcia quote from this article).

Art: "Giant Portrait of Toddler Peers over U.S.-Mexico Border Wall," *The Guardian*, Sept. 8, 2017; Adriana De Alba, "In Naco, Bisbee Artist Unites American Musicians, Mexican Kids," *Arizona Daily Star*, Jan. 29, 2018; Julieta Gonzalez, "'Border Dynamics' Sculpture Begins National Tour on UA Mall," University of Arizona News Service, July 21, 2003; Perla Trevizo, "Border Art Installation Features Floating Giant Eyeball Balloons," *Arizona Daily Star*, Oct. 8, 2015; and "Project Shines Student Art onto Nogales Border Fence," *Arizona Daily Star*, Apr. 23, 2018.

Music: Sarah Jarvis, "Concert at Douglas-Agua Prieta Border About Unity, Not Politics," *Arizona Daily Star*, May 7, 2017; Aaliyah Montoya, "Sister Cities Continue Concert Without Borders," *Douglas Dispatch*, June 4, 2018; Amanda Jackson, "Cellist Yo-Yo Ma Plays a Concert at a US-Mexico Border Crossing to Make a Point," CNN, Apr. 14, 2019.

Talibanes story: Originally in Miriam Davidson, "More Walls Won't Work in My Neighborhood," New America Media, June 20, 2007.

Epilogue: A Positive Vision for the U.S.-Mexico Region

Carlos Adrian Ingram-Lopez: Stephanie Casanova, "Hundreds Gather to Remember Local Man Who Died in Custody," *Arizona Daily Star*, June 27, 2020; Tim Steller, "TPD's Long Delay in Reporting Death Leaves Lingering Feeling of Deception," *Arizona Daily Star*, June 28, 2020; Chris Magnus, "TPD Chief Magnus: What Happened to George Floyd in Minnesota Is Indefensible," *Arizona Daily Star*, May 31, 2020; Francisco Cantú, "Mayor, Council Must Move to Limit TPD," *Arizona Daily Star*, June 26, 2020.

Drowned dad and daughter photo: Peter Orsi and Amy Guthrie, "A Harrowing Image of Crossing's Peril," *Boston Globe*, June 26, 2019; Marcos Alemán and Peter Orsi, "Drowned Migrant's Mother: I Told Him Not to Go," *Arizona Daily Star*, June 27, 2019; Christopher Sherman and Marcos Alemán, "'Going There Is Risking Everything,'" *Boston Globe*, June 28, 2019; Colibrí Center for Human Rights e-mail, "Oscar y Angie, Presentes," June 26, 2019.

Grijalva quote, border plans: Author notes from phone interview with Grijalva, June 16, 2020; his website, www.grijalva.house.gov; Vision Plan on Southern Border Communities Coalition website, www.southernborder.org.

Groups organize, politicians speak out: Sophia Tareen, "Activists Increase Trainings amid Trump Deportation Threats," *Arizona Daily Star*, June 23, 2019; David Crary and Hannah Grabenstein, "US Clergy Mobilize to Support Vulnerable Migrants in the Face of Anticipated Sweeps," *Arizona Daily Star*, July 19, 2019; Hana Sarfan, "US Jews on Trump's Camps: 'Never Again,'" *Arizona Daily Star*, Aug. 9, 2019; Stephanie Russell-Kraft, "Jews to Trump: 'Close the Camps,'" *In These Times*, Sept. 2019, 6–7; Amy Held, "Oakland Mayor Stands by 'Fair Warning' of Impending ICE Operation," npr.org, Mar. 1, 2018.

Mississippi raids: Rogelio Solis and Jeff Amy, "Immigration Raids Target 7 Food Plants in Mississippi; 680 Workers Arrested," *Arizona Daily Star*, Aug 8, 2019; "ICE Raids: 300 People Released amid Outrage over Mississippi

Arrests," bbc.com, Aug. 9, 2019 (Jackson mayor quote from this article); Jeff Amy and Rogelio Solis, "Immigrant Community Rallies Around Families After Large Miss. Raids," *Arizona Daily Star*, Aug. 9, 2019.

COVID-19, Black Lives Matter response: Margo Cowan, "Facing Death in Detention," No More Deaths newsletter, Summer, 2020; "Open Society Foundations Commit Emergency Support to Address the Impact of COVID-19 in New York City," Open Society Foundations press release, Apr. 16, 2020; Jasmine Demers, "$1.25M Donated for Immigrants Here Hit by Virus," *Arizona Daily Star*, Aug. 20, 2020; Astrid Galvan, "Immigrants Risk Arrest as They Rally with Black Lives Matter," *Arizona Daily Star*, June 13, 2020.

Jim Corbett quote: Davidson, *Convictions of the Heart*, 97.

Borders and Quaker Values: "Borders and Quaker Values: Reflections of an AFSC Working Group," American Friends Service Committee, Philadelphia, Apr. 1989.

Border crossings, value of trade: "U.S.-Mexico Border," Wikipedia; Jeffry Bartash, "How Mexico Tariffs Could Hurt $600 Billion in Cross-Border Trade—and the U.S. Economy," MarketWatch, May 31, 2019.

End Drug Prohibition.

Opening scene from *Cartel Land*, documentary directed by Matthew Heineman, 2015.

Appalachians evading alcohol taxation: Woodard, *American Nations*, 159–61.

Marijuana legalization: "The Green Rush," PBS News Hour series on marijuana industry, July 9–18, 2019; Andrew Selsky, "Oregon, Awash in Marijuana, Aims to Curb Production," *Arizona Daily Star*, June 3, 2019; Jeff Daniels, "California Proposes Slashing Pot Taxes to Help Regulated Industry Compete with Black Market," cnbc.com, Jan. 28, 2019; Michael Blood, "Proposed Bill Would Give States Free Hand to Allow Pot Markets," *Arizona Daily Star*, Feb. 9, 2019; Brooke Staggs, "U.S. House of Representatives Passes Historic Marijuana Banking Bill," *Mercury News*, Sept. 26, 2019; Nicholas Kristof, "Republicans and Democrats Agree: End the War on Drugs," *New York Times*, Nov. 7, 2020; Matthew Daly, "House Votes to Decriminalize Marijuana at the Federal Level," *Arizona Daily Star*, Dec. 5, 2020; Gene Johnson, "Weed Rollout Different than US," *Arizona Daily*

Star, June 24, 2018; Morgan Lee, "NM Bill Would Open 1st State-Run Pot Shops, Subsidize Poor," *Arizona Daily Star*, Mar. 13, 2019; and Juan Montes, "Mexico Set to Become World's Largest Legal Cannabis Market," *Wall Street Journal*, Dec. 29, 2020.

Vicente Fox, seizure figures: Jason Pohl, "At Phoenix Cannabis Expo, Vicente Fox Talks Marijuana Legalization, Donald Trump," *Arizona Republic*, Oct. 14, 2017 (his quote from this article); Michael Blood, "Former Mexico President Fox Joins High Times Directors Board," *Arizona Daily Star*, June 19, 2018; Curt Prendergast, "Most Hard Drugs Are Seized at Entry Ports, Records Show," *Arizona Daily Star*, May 7, 2017; and Kate Irby, "New Pot Policy Could Aid Cartels, Increase Violence," *Arizona Daily Star*, Jan. 13, 2018 (2011–2017 seizure figures from this article).

AMLO: Mark Stevenson, "Mexico's Lopez Obrador Pledges $7.5 Billion for Youths, Elderly," *Arizona Daily Star*, July 5, 2018; Christopher Sherman and Maria Verza, "Mexico Gets Leftist Leader Vowing 'Deep, Radical' Shift," *Arizona Daily Star*, Dec. 2, 2018; Daniela Guzman, "Lopez Obrador Changes Course on Mexican Security," *Arizona Daily Star*, Aug. 12, 2018 (AMLO talk in Juárez, "we will forgive" quote); "Drug War Is Over, AMLO Says: Drug Lords No Longer a Target," *Mexico News Daily*, Jan. 31, 2019; "AMLO Announces Plans for Badiraguato, El Chapo's Hometown," *Mexico News Daily*, Feb. 14, 2019; "Mexico Wants to Re-invent US Merida Aid Program," ABC News, May 7, 2019.

Analysts: Irby, "New Pot Policy Could Aid Cartels, Increase Violence"; and Mark Stevenson, "In Many Parts of Mexico, Government Long Ago Relinquished Control to Cartels," *Arizona Daily Star*, Oct. 20, 2019.

Violence continues: "Grisly Gang Feud Leaves 19 Bodies in Michoacan," *Arizona Daily Star*, Aug. 9, 2019; Mark Stevenson, "Mexico's New Drug War Shaping Up to Be Its Bloodiest and Most Ruthless," *Arizona Daily Star*, Aug. 31, 2019; Azam Ahmed, "The Stunning Escape of El Chapo's Son: It's Like 'a Bad Netflix Show,'" *The New York Times*, Oct. 18, 2019; Christopher Sherman, "Doubts About Mexican Security Strategy Raised By Failed Mission," *Arizona Daily Star*, Nov. 2, 2019; Mark Stevenson, "9 US Citizens Living in Mexico Killed in Cartel Ambush; 8 Youths Found Alive," *Arizona Daily Star*, Nov. 6, 2019; Anita Snow, "Incidents Heighten Travelers' Concerns," *Arizona Daily Star*, Nov. 8, 2019; Curt Prendergast,

"Easy Cash Drives Flow of US Guns Wielded by Cartels," *Arizona Daily Star*, Nov. 24, 2019 (U.S. ammo used in attack); Bradford Betz, "Mexico's Homicide Rate Hits New Record High in 2019," Fox News, Jan. 21, 2020; Eduardo Verdugo, "Death Toll Rises to 26 in Mexican Drug Rehab Center Attack," Yahoo News, July 1, 2020; "Murders in Mexico Rise by a Third in 2018 to New Record," Reuters, Jan. 21, 2019 (Guanajuato violence); "Federal Judge and Wife Killed in Colima, Mexico," *Yucatan Times*, June 17, 2020; Christopher Sherman and E. Eduardo Castillo, "Gunmen Wound Mexico City Police Chief; 3 Dead," AP News, June 27, 2020 (Garcia tweets from this article).

End the Flow of Guns to Mexico.

John Lindsay-Poland film showing and talk: Author notes from event at Global Justice Center, South Tucson, Feb. 27, 2019. Also Lisa Mascaro, "House Passage of Gun Safety Bills Reflects Political Shift," *Arizona Daily Star*, Mar. 1, 2019.

Recommendations: Mexican Commission for the Defense and Promotion of Human Rights and Global Exchange's Stop U.S. Arms to Mexico project, *Gross Human Rights Abuses*, 28.

Petition, Sig Sauer, Milkor protest: "@StateDept: Stop Licensing Gun Sales to Mexican Military and Police," petition, www.change.org; Mexican Commission for the Defense and Promotion of Human Rights and Global Exchange's Stop U.S. Arms to Mexico project, *Gross Human Rights Abuses*, 19; "CEO of Gun Company Sig Sauer Arrested in Germany," www.stopusarmstomexico.org press release, Nov. 23, 2018; Gabriel Schivone and John Lindsay-Poland, "Arizona's Role in Weapons Exports to Mexico Must Be Eliminated," *Arizona Daily Star*, Dec. 17, 2018; and expanded version of Schivone and Lindsay-Poland article distributed at film showing.

Lawmakers protest: "American Guns Are Fueling Record Homicides in Mexico. Experts Urge the White House to Take Action," The Trace, May 25, 2018 (Gallego quote from this article); Mexican Commission for the Defense and Promotion of Human Rights and Global Exchange's Stop U.S. Arms to Mexico project, *Gross Human Rights Abuses*, 6 (Ellison letter); Travis Waldron and Nick Wing, "Trump Opens Door for U.S. Gun Industry to Sell More Firearms Abroad," *Huffington Post*, May 24, 2018; "Congressmen

Lowenthal and Grijalva Lead Congressional Letter on U.S. Firearms Sales to Mexico," www.lowenthal.house.gov news release, Mar. 7, 2019.

Regularize the Status of Farmworkers.

Farmworker history, "wet line": Author's general knowledge; Cindy Carcamo, "Farms Deal with Shrinking Immigrant Labor Pool," *Arizona Daily Star*, Jan. 21, 2018; Russell Contreras, "Militias Have Long History Patrolling US Border," *Arizona Daily Star*, May 13, 2019.

Employers not charged: Jeff Amy, "Days After ICE Raids, Mississippi Chicken Plant Hosts Job Fair," *Arizona Daily Star*, Aug. 14, 2019; "Mississippi Plant Fires Undocumented Workers, Denies Pay After ICE Raid," moneyandmarkets.com, Aug. 16, 2019; Nomaan Merchant, "ICE Raids Raise Question: What About the Employers?" *Arizona Daily Star*, Aug. 19, 2019.

Number of undocumented farmworkers: Pew Research Center, cited on Farmworker Justice website (www.farmworkerjustice.org).

COVID-19 impact on migrant workers: Author notes from phone interview with Grijalva, June 16, 2020 (his quote); Stephen Groves and Sophia Tareen, "Migrant-Heavy Meatpacking Industry Hit by Concerns over Worker Shortages," *Arizona Daily Star*, June 27, 2020; Helena Bottemiller Evich, Ximena Bustillo, and Liz Crampton, "Harvest of Shame: Farmworkers Face Coronavirus Disaster," Politico, Sept. 8, 2020.

CARE Act: "Rep. Roybal-Allard Introduces CARE Act to Protect Child Farmworkers," www.roybal-allard.house.gov news release, June 12, 2017.

Agricultural Worker Program Act, H-2A reform: "Immigration Reform and Agriculture," position paper on Farmworker Justice website, Mar. 2019 ("fundamentally flawed" quote and number of H-2A visas from this paper); Marco della Cava and Ricardo Lopez, "A Blight in the Fields," *USA Today*, Feb. 8–10, 2019; Megan Boyanton, "New Proposal Seeks to Expand Immigrant Workforce in Ariz.," *Arizona Daily Star*, Nov. 5, 2019; "Farmworker Justice Statement on the Passage in the House of Representatives of the Farm Workforce Modernization Act, HR 5038," Farmworker Justice news release, Dec. 11, 2019. Felipe Guevara spoke at Innovating Immigration Law and Policy: Visions for a Just Future, James E. Rogers College of Law, University of Arizona, Nov. 15, 2019.

Value of produce industry, FPAA, tomato trade war: Kate Duguid, "Avocado Shortages, Virgin Margaritas: Border Shutdown Would Hit American Palates," msn.com, Apr. 1, 2019; Philip Athey, "Temporary Rotations Being Used to Staff Nogales Ports of Entry," *Arizona Daily Star*, Feb. 6, 2018; Fresh Produce Association of the Americas website, www.freshfrommexico.com; Rafael Carranza, "Produce Growers in Southern AZ Fighting USDA over Safety Risk from Inspections," *Arizona Daily Star*, May 3, 2020; Gabriela Rico, "Surplus Produce from Mexico Directed to S. Ariz. Food Banks," *Arizona Daily Star*, Apr. 26, 2020.

Gary Nabhan quote: Notes from author interview, Patagonia, Ariz., Feb. 9, 2018.

Wilson Produce, Wholesum Harvest, Fair Trade project: Wilson Produce website, www.wilsonproduce.com; Wholesum Harvest website, www.wh.farm.

Reform Immigration Laws to Treat Migrants Humanely.

COVID-19 in ICE jails: Spencer Hardenbergh, "Detention Center in Eloy Has Most COVID-19 Cases of Any ICE Facility," *Arizona Daily Star*, Oct. 10, 2020; Tim Steller, "At Eloy Detention Center, Inmates Must Fight Poor Conditions Along with Virus," *Arizona Daily Star*, May 31, 2020; "Free Migrants from Eloy Center's Terrible Conditions," op-ed by Tucson clergy members, *Arizona Daily Star*, July 12, 2020 (Detention Watch Network stat from this article); Margo Cowan, "Facing Death in Detention," No More Deaths newsletter, summer 2020; Laura Gottesdiener, "Die in Detention or at Home? U.S. Pandemic Forces Cruel Choice on Asylum Seekers," msn.com, July 6, 2020 (Muñoz quote from this article). Durvi Martínez: "Durvi Martinez, Presente!" www.migrantjustice.net, July 7, 2020; and Arvind Dilawar, "Deported to Death," *In These Times*, Oct. 2020, 6–7.

Biden immigration plans: Alexandra Jaffe, "Biden: Reversing Trump Immigration Policies to Take Time," *Arizona Daily Star*, Dec. 23, 2020, and Adrian Carrasquillo, "Exclusive: Advocacy Groups Say Biden's 'Disappointing' Immigration Policies Don't Go Far Enough," newsweek.com, Feb. 4, 2021. Julián Castro immigration plan: Castro's website, www.juliancastro.com. Also Doyle McManus, "It's Time for Democrats to Tell What They'd Do About Asylum Seeker Crisis," *Arizona Daily Star*, Apr. 11, 2019.

Immigration law forum: Author's notes and program from "Innovating Immigration Law and Policy: Visions for a Just Future," James E. Rogers College of Law, University of Arizona, Nov. 15, 2019. UN report: "Expert: 100,000 Kids in Detention in US," *Arizona Daily Star*, Nov. 19, 2019.

Judge blocks ICE arrests, Newton and Portland cases: Danny McDonald, "Judge Limits ICE Arrests at Courts," *Boston Globe*, June 21, 2019 (quote from this article); Andrea Estes and Maria Cramer, "ICE Agent Was in Courthouse. Did Judge and Others Help Man Flee?" *Boston Globe*, Dec. 2, 2018 (updated to include Apr. 25, 2019, filing of obstruction of justice charges against the judge and court officer); Aimee Green, "Judge Didn't Violate Rules in Letting Immigrant Leave Through Back Door, Review Finds," *The Oregonian*, June 19, 2017.

Supreme Court, other rulings: Mark Sherman, "DACA Safe for Now as High Court Rejects Bid to Annul It," *Arizona Daily Star*, June 19, 2020; "Justices Dismiss Bid Against Sanctuary Law," *Arizona Daily Star*, June 16, 2020; Mark Sherman, "High Court: Asylum Seekers Who Fail First Screening Can Be Deported Expeditiously," *Arizona Daily Star*, June 26, 2020; Elliot Spagat, "Judge Overturns 'Third Country' Asylum Rule on Procedural Grounds," *Arizona Daily Star*, July 2, 2020.

Repurpose Border Security Funds.

Prototypes torn down: Elliot Spagat, "Border Wall Prototypes Fall After 16 Months of Spectacle," *Arizona Daily Star*, Feb. 28, 2019.

We Build The Wall: Curt Prendergast and Joe Ferguson, "Bannon, Others Tout Proposal for Privately Built Border Wall," *Arizona Daily Star*, Feb. 9, 2019; Alan Feuer, William Rashbaum, and Maggie Haberman, "Steve Bannon Is Charged with Fraud in We Build the Wall Campaign," *New York Times*, Aug. 20, 2020; Curt Prendergast, "Former Trump Strategist Bannon Charged with Fraud in Border Wall Funding Scheme," *Arizona Daily Star*, Aug. 21, 2020; Ryan Lucas and Ayesha Rascoe, "Trump Pardons Steve Bannon, Lil Wayne in Final Clemency Flurry," npr.org, Jan. 20, 2021.

Wall plans: Curt Prendergast, "New Fencing in Organ Pipe, Cabeza Prieta in Wall Plans," *Arizona Daily Star*, May 12, 2019 ("endgame" and "devastating blow" quotes from this article); Tony Davis, "New Wall Sections Would

Spell End for Ariz. Jaguars, Environmentalists and Ex-Official Say," *Arizona Daily Star*, Apr. 19, 2020.

Quitobaquito Springs: Myles Traphagen, "Sonora Desert Gem's Destruction Is Ensured with Border Wall Plan," *Arizona Daily Star*, Sept. 1, 2019; Curt Prendergast, "Ancient Watering Hole at Risk from Border Wall Construction," *Arizona Daily Star*, Sept. 8, 2019; Rocky Baier, "Hohokam Sites in Organ Pipe at Risk, Park Service Warns," *Arizona Daily Star*, Sept. 29, 2019; Gary Paul Nabhan, "Healing the Desert Wounds that Trump's Wall Is Opening," progressive.org, Nov. 11, 2019 (quotes from this article).

Wall contracts, corruption: Curt Prendergast, "Legislators Want Review of AZ Border Wall Contract with ND Firm," *Arizona Daily Star*, Dec. 8, 2019; Curt Prendergast, "Company Making Steel for Ariz. Wall Donated $1.7M to Pro-Trump PAC," *Arizona Daily Star*, Feb. 16, 2020; Curt Prendergast, "CBP Seeks 'Private Entities' Who Have Interest in Building Wall near Tucson," *Arizona Daily Star*, June 11, 2020; Nomaan Merchant, "Trump Rips Texas Border Wall Privately Built by Supporters," *Arizona Daily Star*, July 13, 2020; Curt Prendergast, "Builder of Border Wall in So. AZ Accused of Poor Work in Texas," *Arizona Daily Star*, July 19, 2020 ("PowerPoint" quote from this article).

Earlier wall corruption: Margery Beck, "1st Border Wall Contractor's Past Includes Lawsuits, Government Audit," *Arizona Daily Star*, Mar. 3, 2018; Scott Horsley, "Border Fence Firm Snared for Hiring Illegal Workers," All Things Considered, NPR, Dec. 14, 2006.

Call for investigation: Prendergast, "Legislators Want Review of AZ Border Wall Contract with ND Firm."

Court rulings on wall funding: Curt Prendergast, "High Court Ruling Opens Door for $1B Ariz. Border Wall Project," *Arizona Daily Star*, July 28, 2019; Katelyn Burns, "Trump Is Diverting Another $7.2 Billion in Military Funds to Build His Border Wall," Vox.com, Jan. 14, 2020; Howard Fischer, "Appeals Court: $2.5B for Wall Illegally Diverted by Trump," *Arizona Daily Star*, June 27, 2020; David Savage, "High Court: Trump Can Divert Military Funds for Border Wall," *Arizona Daily Star*, Aug. 1, 2020.

Democratic letter, COVID-19 on border: Curt Prendergast, "Dems Seeking to Reallocate Funds Meant for Border Wall," *Arizona Daily Star*, Apr. 27, 2020; Simon Romero, "Arizona Finds Coronavirus Among Border Wall

Workers," *New York Times*, June 12, 2020; Innes, "The Number of Patients Hospitalized for Covid-19 Has Tripled in Yuma"; and Weber, "'We Are No Less American': Virus Deaths Piling Up in Poor Border Region of Texas."

Trump wall visits: Astrid Galvan, "Trump Set for Ariz. Trip to Celebrate 200 Miles of Border Wall," *Arizona Daily Star*, June 23, 2020; and Jill Colvin, Zeke Miller, and Deb Riechmann, "In Latest Yuma Visit, Trump Blasts Biden on Immigration," *Arizona Daily Star*, Aug. 19, 2020.

Wall impacts, ponds drying: Prendergast, "Builder of Border Wall in So. AZ Accused of Poor Work in Texas" ("slapdash" quote from this article); Curt Prendergast, "Future of Border Wall About to be Handed Over to Voters," *Arizona Daily Star*, Oct. 18, 2020 ("monstrous" quote from this article); Curt Prendergast, "Rare Watering Hole Is Drying Up near Border Wall in SW Arizona," *Arizona Daily Star*, July 4, 2020; Curt Prendergast, "'Dire Emergency' at Wildlife Refuge Created by Border Wall," *Arizona Daily Star*, Aug. 17, 2020; Curt Prendergast, "Border Cameras Show Wildlife Facing 'Unprecedented' Barrier," *Arizona Daily Star*, Aug. 30, 2020 ("unprecedented" and "struggling fruitlessly" quotes from this article); Curt Prendergast, "Rancher Sues, Citing Damage from Border-Wall Blasting," *Arizona Daily Star*, Dec. 6, 2020; and Tim Steller, "Biden's Border-Wall Duty: Repair Damage to S. Arizona," *Arizona Daily Star*, Dec. 27, 2020 ("emergency measures" quote from this article).

Indigenous Peoples Day protest: Paul Ingram, "Native Demonstration at Border Patrol Checkpoint Ended with DPS Tear Gas," TucsonSentinel.com, Oct 13, 2020; Curt Prendergast, "2 O'odham Women Arrested by Rangers After Protest Halts Wall Construction on Ancestral Land," *Arizona Daily Star*, Sept. 13, 2020; Henry Brean, "Tribes from US, Mexico Meet Where Wall Will Soon Be Built," *Arizona Daily Star*, Sept. 28, 2020; Claire Chandler, "Feds Cite Safety for Quitobaquito Closing; Border Wall Critics Indicate Other Motives," *Arizona Daily Star*, Oct. 1, 2020; "Grijalva Seeks Probe into Response at Wall Protest," *Arizona Daily Star*, Oct. 15, 2020.

Trump's post-riot wall visit: Jill Colvin and Zeke Miller, "Trump Takes No Responsibility for Riot, Visits Texas Wall Site," *Arizona Daily Star*, Jan. 13, 2021. Biden wall plans: Ben Fox and Elliot Spagat, "Some Big, Early Shifts on Immigration Expected Under Biden," *Arizona Daily Star*, Nov. 11, 2020; and Nomaan Merchant and John L. Mone, "High Hopes, Tough Choices on Horizon when Biden Tackles Border Wall Issues," *Arizona Daily Star*, Dec. 5, 2020. Border conservation corps: Steller, "Biden's Border-Wall Duty: Repair Damage to S. Arizona."

Water and wastewater: Bryce Newberry, "Transborder Sewer System Repaired, but Metals, Aging Are Problems," *Arizona Daily Star*, Oct. 6, 2018; Chloe Jones, "A Different Border Crisis: It's Not Security or Immigration, It's Sewage," *Arizona Daily Star*, May 27, 2019; Nick Esquer, "Binational Pipeline Legislation Passed in House, Moves On to Senate," chamberbusinessnews.com, July 18, 2019; Victoria Harker, "Nogales Sewer Project to Aid Economy in the Region," chamberbusinessnews.com, July 21, 2020; Manuel Coppola, "Publisher's Note: IOI Hot Potato Belongs Squarely to the IBWC," *Nogales International*, Jul. 31, 2020; "Cochise Declares Sewage Emergency," *Arizona Daily Star*, Sept. 19, 2018; "Immunizations Offered After Naco Sewage Spill," *Arizona Daily Star*, Oct. 21, 2019; Joshua Emerson Smith, "San Diego-Area Cities Fight US to Keep Mexico Sewage from Beaches," *Arizona Daily Star*, Aug. 15, 2018.

Ports of entry and staffing: Russ Wiles and Daniel González, "Sunday Scans of Trucks at Border Halted; Could It Cause Trade Issues?," *Arizona Daily Star*, Apr. 4, 2019; "Douglas Border Crossing Inspection Booths to Be Replaced in Revamp Starting Monday," *Arizona Daily Star*, Dec. 14, 2019; Shaq Davis, "$134M Project in Nogales Aims to Ease Truck Traffic," *Arizona Daily Star*, Mar. 9, 2020; Nate Airulla, "New Cross-Border Cargo Inspection Cuts Wait Time," *Arizona Daily Star*, Apr. 4, 2017 (this article mentions USC study); Cedar Attanasio, "750 Inspectors to Be Reassigned to Cope with Migrant Processing," *Arizona Daily Star*, Mar. 28, 2019; Philip Athey, "Temporary Rotations Being Used to Staff Nogales Ports of Entry," *Arizona Daily Star*, Feb. 6, 2018.

Aid to Central America: Carmen Monico, "Figure Out Which Aid Programs Work, and Fewer Migrants May Come North," *Arizona Daily Star*, June 27, 2019 (history of intervention and amount of foreign aid since 1946 from this article). Also, Schlesinger, Kinzer, and Coatsworth, *Bitter Fruit*, and many other books.

Marshall Plan, food aid: Robert Valencia, "Does Central America Need a Marshall Plan?" *World Policy*, July 28, 2014; Conor Walsh, "Central America Climate Change Helps Drive Migration," *Arizona Daily Star*, Mar. 19, 2019;

William Lambers, "Marshall Plan for Central America Would Restore Hope, End Migrant Border Crisis," *USA Today*, July 15, 2019 (George Marshall quote from this article); Tom Gallagher, "The US Needs a Marshall Plan for Central America," Common Dreams, July 23, 2019; "UN to Boost Food Aid for Four Countries," *Arizona Daily Star*, Aug. 10, 2019; and Claudio Escalon and María Verza, "Hurricanes Likely to Spur More Central American Migration," *Arizona Daily Star*, Nov. 25, 2020.

Projects in Central America: GUAMAP website, www.guamap.net, and newsletters; Perla Trevizo, "Tucsonans Help Raise Money, Awareness for Guatemala Volcano Victims," *Arizona Daily Star*, June 15, 2018 (Xajab and Melrood quotes from this article); APRODE website, www.aprode.net; Eugene Medina, "Getting Clean Water to Guatemala," *Arizona Daily Star*, Mar. 11, 2019 (quotes from this letter and author phone interview with Medina, Aug. 13, 2020).

Selected Bibliography

Andersson, Ruben. *Illegality, Inc.: Clandestine Migration and the Business of Bordering Europe*. California Series in Public Anthropology. Oakland: University of California Press, 2014.

Annerino, John. *Dead in Their Tracks: Crossing America's Desert Borderlands*. New York: Four Walls Eight Windows, 1999.

Annerino, John. *Dead in Their Tracks: Crossing America's Desert Borderlands in the New Era*. Tucson: University of Arizona Press, 2009.

Bacon, David. *The Right to Stay Home: How U.S. Policy Drives Mexican Migration*. Boston: Beacon, 2013.

Brown, David. *Borderland Jaguars: Tigres de la Frontera*. Salt Lake City: University of Utah Press, 2001.

Cantú, Francisco. *The Line Becomes a River: Dispatches from the Border*. New York: Riverhead, 2018.

Corbett, Jim. *Goatwalking*. New York: Viking, 1991.

Corbett, Jim. *Sanctuary for All Life: The Cowbalah of Jim Corbett*. Berthoud, CO: Howling Dog, 2005.

Corchado, Alfredo. *Midnight in Mexico: A Reporter's Journey Through a Country's Descent into Darkness*. New York: Penguin, 2013.

Davidson, Miriam. *Convictions of the Heart: Jim Corbett and the Sanctuary Movement*. Tucson: University of Arizona Press, 1988.

Davidson, Miriam. *Lives on the Line: Dispatches from the U.S.-Mexico Border*. Tucson: University of Arizona Press, 2000.

Ferguson, Kathryn, Norma Price, and Ted Parks. *Crossing with the Virgin: Stories from the Migrant Trail*. Tucson: University of Arizona Press, 2010.

Fernandes, Deepa. *Targeted: Homeland Security and the Business of Immigration.* New York: Seven Stories, 2007.

García Hernández, César Cuauhtémoc. *Migrating to Prison: America's Obsession with Locking Up Immigrants.* New York: New Press, 2020.

Gipe, Lawrence. *Operation Streamline: An Illustrated Reader.* Tucson: University of Arizona Confluence Center, 2014.

Holmes, Seth M. *Fresh Fruit, Broken Bodies: Migrant Farmworkers in the United States.* Oakland: University of California Press, 2013.

Martínez, Oscar. *Border People: Life and Society in the U.S.-Mexico Borderlands.* Tucson: University of Arizona Press, 1994.

Martínez, Oscar. *Troublesome Border.* Tucson: University of Arizona Press, 1988.

Mehta, Suketu. *This Land Is Our Land: An Immigrant's Manifesto.* New York: Farrar, Straus and Giroux, 2019.

Miller, Todd. *Border Patrol Nation: Dispatches from the Front Lines of Homeland Security.* San Francisco: City Lights, 2014.

Miller, Todd. *Empire of Borders: The Expansion of the U.S. Border Around the World.* London: Verso, 2019.

Miller, Todd. *Storming the Wall: Climate Change, Migration and Homeland Security.* San Francisco: City Lights, 2017.

Nabhan, Gary. *Food from the Radial Center.* Washington, D.C.: Island, 2018.

Quinones, Sam. *Dreamland: The True Tale of America's Opioid Epidemic.* New York: Bloomsbury, 2015.

Regan, Margaret. *The Death of Josseline: Immigration Stories from the Arizona Borderlands.* Boston: Beacon, 2010.

Regan, Margaret. *Detained and Deported, Stories of Immigrant Families Under Fire.* Boston: Beacon, 2015.

Rubio-Goldsmith, Raquel, Celestino Fernández, Jessie K. Finch, and Araceli Masterson-Algar, eds. *Migrant Deaths in the Arizona Desert: La Vida No Vale Nada.* Tucson: University of Arizona Press, 2016.

Schlesinger, Stephen, Stephen Kinzer, and John Coatsworth. *Bitter Fruit: The Story of the American Coup in Guatemala.* 2nd ed. New York: David Rockefeller Center for Latin American Studies, 2005.

Slack, Jeremy. *Deported to Death: How Drug Violence Is Changing Migration on the U.S.-Mexico Border.* Oakland: University of California Press, 2019.

Taylor, Richard Cachor. *Birds of Southeastern Arizona.* Olympia, Wash.: R. W. Morse, 2010.

Urrea, Luis Alberto. *The Devil's Highway: A True Story.* Boston: Little, Brown, 2004.

Woodard, Colin. *American Nations: A History of the Eleven Rival Regional Cultures of North America.* New York: Penguin, 2011.

Index

About the Author

Miriam Davidson is a Tucson-based writer whose work focuses on border issues. Her award-winning journalism has appeared in the *New York Times*, the *AARP Bulletin*, the *Arizona Republic*, *The Nation*, *The Progressive*, and many other outlets. She attended Yale College and the University of Southern California's Annenberg School for Communication and Journalism. She is author of two previous University of Arizona Press books, *Convictions of the Heart* and *Lives on the Line*.